Pressing Forward
with the Book of Mormon

The FARMS Updates of the 1990s

Related FARMS Books
on the Book of Mormon

An Ancient American Setting for the Book of Mormon
Warfare in the Book of Mormon
Rediscovering the Book of Mormon
Reexploring the Book of Mormon
The Allegory of the Olive Tree
Feasting on the Word: The Literary Testimony of the Book of
     Mormon
Book of Mormon Authorship Revisited: The Evidence for Ancient
     Origins
Images of Ancient America: Visualizing Book of Mormon Life
Isaiah in the Book of Mormon
King Benjamin's Speech: "That Ye May Learn Wisdom"
King Benjamin's Speech Made Simple
Charting the Book of Mormon

Pressing Forward with the Book of Mormon

The FARMS Updates of the 1990s

**edited by John W. Welch
and Melvin J. Thorne**

The Foundation for Ancient Research
and Mormon Studies
Provo, Utah

Cover image: "Nephi Leads His Followers into the Wilderness," by Minerva Teichert

John W. Welch (J.D., Duke University) is Robert K. Thomas Professor of Law at Brigham Young University. As the founder of FARMS, Welch originated the idea of the FARMS Updates, now enjoyed monthly by thousands of readers.

Melvin J. Thorne (Ph.D., University of Kansas) is Director of Publications for the Foundation for Ancient Research and Mormon Studies at BYU. For the last decade he has been responsible for soliciting and editing the FARMS Updates.

The Foundation for Ancient Research and Mormon Studies (FARMS)
at Brigham Young University
P.O. Box 7113
University Station
Provo, Utah 84602

Library of Congress Cataloging-in-Publication Data

Pressing forward with the Book of Mormon : the FARMS updates of the
    1990s / edited by John W. Welch and Melvin J. Thorne.
      p.   cm.
    Includes bibliographical references and index.
    ISBN 0–934893–42–X (pbk. : alk. paper)
    1. Book of Mormon—Criticism, interpretation, etc. I. Welch,
John W. (John Woodland) II. Thorne, Melvin J. III. Foundation for
Ancient Research and Mormon Studies.
BX8627.P72   1999
289.3'22—dc21   99–36849
                                                        CIP

CONTENTS

Introduction

In December 1984, the Foundation for Ancient Research and Mormon Studies (FARMS), based in Provo, Utah, issued its first monthly Update. Since that time, researchers have written and circulated a steady stream of innovative findings and insights. The results of the first decade of that research were collected in 1992 and published as *Reexploring the Book of Mormon.* The present volume is a continuation of that project, comprising Updates from 1992 through 1999, together with similar short studies published during that same period of time in the *Journal of Book of Mormon Studies,* all edited for current inclusion. Encapsulated here is nearly a decade of ongoing exploration about the Book of Mormon, pressing forward with further research on the words and messages of the Book of Mormon.

As was explained in the introduction to the 1992 volume, the Updates are brief, easy-to-read reports of new research on the Book of Mormon, aimed at a general audience. They set forth the essence of a research topic and new discoveries that bear on it. They represent ongoing studies from a variety of fields. They report intriguing ideas and developments that emerged while reexploring the Book of Mormon from many perspectives.

Most Updates shed new light on a particular passage or concept in the Book of Mormon. As before, this book arranges these short studies in the order that those key passages or concepts appear in the Book of Mormon.

Many of these Updates have emerged from collaborative research efforts, and no Update has been released without close scrutiny by several scholars. In many cases, the Updates were the leading edge of new discoveries that were subsequently developed, expanded, debated further, and published in scholarly articles or books. And in a few cases, Updates have corrected previously published information when new data have made obsolete old assumptions. For example, John Gee's 1997 article revealing the Egyptian shawabti-figurines found in El Salvador as forgeries corrected the tentative information put forth in a 1984 Update.[1]

At first, FARMS wanted to communicate research developments to a small audience of donors and researchers. However, the Updates proved so popular that they were soon distributed in annual packets. Eventually the demand became so great that they became and have remained a regular part of the FARMS newsletter.[2]

The sixty-nine chapters in this book chronicle much of the ongoing Book of Mormon research of the 1990s. Not all Book of Mormon research projects lend themselves to short Update treatment, of course, but in many cases a topic can be opened up to the public by such a report. Often they remain the most useful, concise statements available on the topic or issue.

In many ways the Updates have changed the face of Book of Mormon research. No longer are new scholarly insights into the Book of Mormon held in remote corners of cluttered file cabinets. Approaches taken and discoveries made by Hugh Nibley and others a generation ago[3] have expanded in type and number. Respect for the Book of Mormon has grown because of FARMS research and publications like the Updates. President Gordon B. Hinckley has praised these efforts. "FARMS represents the efforts of sincere and dedicated scholars. It has grown to provide strong support and defense of the Church on a professional basis," he said. "I wish to express my strong congratulations and appreciation for those who started this effort and who have shepherded it to this point. I see a bright future for this effort."[4] Even scholars who are critics of the LDS church, such as the evangelicals Carl Mosser and Paul Owen, consider FARMS "the primary producer of academic defenses of Mormonism."[5]

These Updates will interest all people who want to know what's new in Book of Mormon research. They will be informative to inquisitive minds—old and young—who want to know the questions that many scholars are asking, researching, and answering. They will appeal to minds that enjoy thinking about novel approaches and prospecting for new information. They will appeal to all who enjoy learning more about the Book of Mormon—its messages, language, and setting; its astonishing details, miraculous existence, and incomparable mission.

Believers of the Book of Mormon as ancient scripture, however, realize that human ingenuity will never be enough to answer all questions about its origin and contents. But people can separate the questions that cannot be answered (either in whole or part) from those that can. Then they can work on the viable ones, gather relevant information, and propose and evaluate possible answers as far as current knowledge will allow.

Thinking this way about Book of Mormon issues has been a part of Latter-day Saint intellectual history since the days of Joseph Smith. After reading an extract from Stephen's *Incidents of Travel in Central America,* the Prophet commented: "We can not but think the Lord has a hand in bringing to pass his strange act, and proving the Book of Mormon true in the eyes of all the people. . . . The world will prove Joseph Smith a true prophet by circumstantial evidence, in experiments, as they did Moses and Elijah."[6] Thus, to probe and ponder the circumstantial evidences of the scripture's truthfulness is one of the purposes of Book of Mormon research.

Circumstantial evidence, however, is not the primary source of knowledge that the Book of Mormon is true. Perhaps still the clearest statement to this effect was published by B. H. Roberts in 1909. His classic comments embrace both the primary evidence that comes from the Holy Ghost and all other forms of evidence, which, although secondary, may still be of first-rate importance:

> It is frequently the case that a proper setting forth of a subject makes its truth self-evident; and all other evidence becomes merely collateral, and all argument becomes of secondary importance. Especially is this the case when setting forth the Book of Mormon for the world's acceptance . . . that its truth shall be attested to individuals by the operations of the Holy Spirit upon the human mind. . . .
>
> This must ever be the chief source of evidence for the truth of the Book of Mormon. All other evidence is secondary to this, the primary and infallible. No arrangement of evidence, however skilfully ordered; no argument, however adroitly made, can ever take its place; for this witness of the Holy Spirit to the soul of man for the truth of the Nephite volume of scripture, is God's evidence to the truth. . . .
>
> To be known, the truth must be stated and the clearer and more complete the statement is, the better opportunity will the Holy Spirit have for testifying to the souls of men that the work is true. . . . [However,] I would not have it thought that the evidence and argument presented in [here] are unimportant, much less unnecessary. Secondary evidence in support of truth, like secondary causes in natural phenomena, may be of firstrate importance, and mighty factors in the achievement of God's purposes.[7]

All who have given their time and talents to the continuing task of researching and writing these Updates, as well as those who have helped produce and distribute them, echo these convictions and perspectives of Elder Roberts.

John W. Welch

Notes

1. See John Gee, "New and Old Light on Shawabtis from Mesoamerica," *Journal of Book of Mormon Studies* 6/1 (1997): 64–69.

2. Anyone interested in receiving the newsletter, now issued twelve times a year, is invited to contact FARMS at P. O. Box 7113, University Station, Provo, UT 84602, or at 1–800–327–6715.

3. See especially volumes 5–8 on the Book of Mormon in *The Collected Works of Hugh Nibley* (Salt Lake City: Deseret Book and FARMS, 1987–88).

4. "FARMS Joins BYU Community," *Brigham Young Magazine,* spring 1998, p. 8; see also reports in the *Deseret News* (4 November 1997) and in *Insights* (October 1997).

5. Carl Mosser and Paul Owen, "Mormon Scholarship, Apologetics, and Evangelical Neglect," *Trinity Journal* 19 (1998): 182 n. 7.

6. Joseph Fielding Smith, ed. and comp., *Teachings of the Prophet Joseph Smith* (Salt Lake City: Deseret Book, 1976), 267.

7. B. H. Roberts, *New Witnesses for God* (Salt Lake City: Deseret Book, 1909), 2:vi–viii.

1

FOUR SUGGESTIONS ON THE
ORIGIN OF THE NAME *NEPHI*

*"I, Nephi . . . make a record of my
proceedings in my days." (1 Nephi 1:1)*

The opening words of the Book of Mormon, "I, Nephi" (1 Nephi 1:1), raise an interesting issue: Was this name or others like it in use around Jerusalem in Lehi's day? In general one may ask: Are the "personal names contained in the story . . . satisfactory for that period and region"?[1] While an answer to that issue for all names in the Book of Mormon still awaits investigation, several suggestions have been made for the name *Nephi*.

Early in the Book of Mormon (1 Nephi 1:2), Nephi notes the connections between Egypt and Israel at his time. Three of the four etymologies proposed for the name *Nephi* are Egyptian; these are the Egyptian names *Nfr* "good,"[2] *Nfw* "captain," and *Nfy* "wind."[3] We can rule out *Nfy* as a possibility since so far it has not been attested as a name in Egypt at any time period.[4] Similar considerations also rule out the fourth proposed etymology deriving from Akkadian *napāḫu* "to be kindled,"[5] such as *napḫu* "kindled,"[6] *nipḫu* "rising,"[7] and *nappāḫu* "smith,"[8] none of which are used as personal names.[9] This leaves us with two suggestions: *Nfr* and *Nfw*. While it might appear that *Nfr* is disqualified for ending in an

-r, by the time of Lehi (end of the seventh century B.C.), the final *r* had long since fallen out of pronunciation.[10] Although the consonants look different between the two names, in Lehi's day the only difference in pronunciation would have been in the vowels.

Unfortunately, neither Egyptians nor Hebrews wrote vowels in Lehi's day. But we can still get some ideas of how *Nfr* and *Nfw* were vocalized from foreign transcriptions of Egyptian names and from later versions of these words from times when Egyptians did write vowels (i.e., Coptic).

Transcriptions of the Coptic forms of *Nfr* and *Nfw* are *noufi* and *neef* respectively.[11] In the fifth century B.C., the Egyptian name ꜥ*nḫ-ḥr-nfr*[12] is transcribed in Aramaic ꜥ*ḤRNPY*,[13] while Aramaic transcriptions of the Egyptian name *K3-nfr.w*[14] are *KNPY*,[15] *QNPY, KNWPꜣ*,[16] and *KNWPY*.[17] The transcriptions indicate that the vowel might be *o* or *u*, matching the initial vowel of the later Coptic word *noufi*. The problem with this proposed etymology, however, is that *K3-nfr.w* is a stative verb form. In Egyptian, as in Semitic languages, different verbal forms are indicated by a change in vowels. *K3-nfr.w* is a stative, whereas *Nfr* is probably a participle, and the vowel in the participle from Greek transcriptions seems to be an *e*, as opposed to the stative case vowels *o* or *u*.[18] On the other hand, Assyrian scribes transcribed the name *B3k-n-nfw*[19] as *Bu-uk-ku-na-an-ni-iꜣ-pi* or *Bu-uk-ku-na-an-ne-eꜣ-pi*.[20] These transcriptions indicate that the vowel in *Nfw* was an *e* or *i*, matching the vowel in later Coptic. So the vowel matches better with *Nfw* than with *Nfr*.

The advantage that *Nfr* has over *Nfw* is that *Nfr* is actually attested at the right time,[21] whereas *Nfw* is attested but not at the right time.[22] As previously noted, neither *Nfy* nor forms of *napāḫu* are attested as names at any time. Thus, one may confidently conclude, whether from *Nfr* or *Nfw*, the name *Nephi* is an attested Egyptian name.

Research by John Gee, 1999; an earlier article on this topic was published in the Journal of Book of Mormon Studies 1/1 *(1992): 189–91.*

NOTES

1. Hugh W. Nibley, *Lehi in the Desert; The World of the Jaredites; There Were Jaredites* (Salt Lake City: Deseret Book and FARMS, 1988), 3, citing criteria put forward by William F. Albright. Interestingly, the name *Nephi* is also found as a place name in the King James translation Apocrypha in 2 Maccabees. Although the Apocrypha was part of the Smith family Bible, and it is possible that Joseph Smith may have been acquainted with the name from that source, Joseph Smith apparently did not personally own a Bible when he translated the Book of Mormon and had not read it much when he was growing up; see John Gee, "La Trahison des Clercs: On the Language and Translation of the Book of Mormon," review of *New Approaches to the Book of Mormon: Explorations in Critical Methodology*, ed. Brent L. Metcalfe, *Review of Books on the Book of Mormon* 6/1 (1994): 100–101. Furthermore, that Joseph Smith may have been completely ignorant of the Apocrypha and its contents is indicated by the fact that he had to ask the Lord about them and in response received D&C 91. The issue is not whether Joseph Smith could have known the name, but whether it is suitable for the time and place from which it claims to derive. The answer to the former is perhaps; the answer to the latter is decidedly yes.

2. John Gee, "A Note on the Name *Nephi*," *Journal of Book of Mormon Studies* 1/1 (1992): 189–91; see also Gee, "A Note on the Name *Nephi*," FARMS Update, *Insights* (November 1992): 2.

3. John A. Tvedtnes, review of *New Approaches to the Book of Mormon: Explorations in Critical Methodology*, ed. Brent L. Metcalfe, *Review of Books on the Book of Mormon* 6/1 (1994): 39. Tvedtnes conflates *Nfw* and *Nfy*, but they are distinct words in Egyptian.

4. The name *Nfw-iw* "the wind is come" is attested from the 22nd Dynasty (Georges Legrain, "Deux stèles trouvées à Karnak en février 1897," *Zeitschrift für ägyptische Sprache und Alterthumskunde* 35 [1897]: 15, line 14, though this perhaps should be read *T3w-iw*) as well as other names compounded with *nfy* (see Hermann Ranke, *Die Ägyptischen Personennamen* [Glückstadt: Augustin, 1935], 1:193.

5. *The Assyrian Dictionary of the Oriental Institute of the University of Chicago,* ed. John A. Brinkman et al. (Chicago: Oriental Institute, 1980), N1:263–70; see Wolfram von Soden, *Akkadisches Handwörterbuch* (Wiesbaden: Harrassowitz, 1972), 2:732–33.

6. *Chicago Assyrian Dictionary,* N1:295–96; see von Soden, *Akkadisches Handwörterbuch,* 2:737–38.

7. *Chicago Assyrian Dictionary,* N2:242–45; see von Soden, *Akkadisches Handwörterbuch,* 2:791.

8. *Chicago Assyrian Dictionary,* N1:307–10; see von Soden, *Akkadisches Handwörterbuch,* 2:739.

9. Although *nappāḫu* is used as an epithet of the god Ea; see *Chicago Assyrian Dictionary,* N1:307–10.

10. See William F. Edgerton, "Stress, Vowel Quantity, and Syllable Division in Egyptian," *Journal of Near Eastern Studies* 6/1 (1947): 5–6, 10–17; see Günther Vittmann, "Zu den in den phönikischen Inschriften enthaltenen ägyptischen Personennamen," *Göttinger Miszellen* 113 (1989): 93; Elmar Edel, *Altägyptische Grammatik,* Analecta Orientalia, vol. 34 (Rome: Pontificium Institutum Biblicum, 1955), 1:56 §§127–28; and Walter C. Till, *Koptische Grammatik* (Leipzig: VEB, 1970), 48 §39.

11. See Walter E. Crum, *A Coptic Dictionary* (Oxford: Clarendon, 1939), 240 and 238 respectively; see Jaroslav Černý, comp., *Coptic Etymological Dictionary* (Cambridge: Cambridge University Press, 1976), 116 and 115 respectively. *Nfy* "wind" becomes Coptic *nife* (ibid., 116).

12. Not in Ranke, *Ägyptische Personennamen,* but see Vittmann in next note.

13. See Vittmann, "Zu den in den phönikischen Inschriften enthaltenen ägyptischen Personennamen," 94; Arthur E. Cowley,

ed. and trans., *Aramaic Papyri of the Fifth Century B.C.* (Oxford: Clarendon, 1923), 183, inscription 72:23.

14. See Ranke, *Ägyptischen Personennamen*, 1:338; Erich Lüddeckens et al., *Demotisches Namenbuch* 15 Leiferungen to date (Wiesbaden: Reichert, 1980–97), 1.13:1004.

15. See M. Lidzbarski, *Phönizische und aramäische Krugaufschriften aus Elephantine* (Berlin: Verlag der königlichen Akademie der Wissenschaften, 1912), 24; Frank L. Benz, *Personal Names in the Phonician and Punic Inscriptions* (Rome: Biblical Institute Press, 1972), 192; Vittmann, "Zu den in den phönikischen Inschriften enthaltenen ägyptischen Personennamen," 95.

16. See Vittmann, "Zu den in den phönikischen Inschriften enthaltenen ägyptischen Personennamen," 95.

17. See Cowley, *Aramaic Papyri*, 89–90, 155, inscriptions 26:9, 21, and 50:7.

18. See Lüddeckens et al., *Demotisches Namenbuch*, 1.9:640–41; Wolja Erichsen, *Auswahl frühdemotischer Texte* (Copenhagen: Munksgaard, 1950), 2:71; Heinz J. Thissen, "Ägyptologische Beiträge zu den griechischen magischen Papyri," in *Religion und Philosophie im alten Ägypten*, ed. Ursula Verhoeven and Erhart Graefe (Leuven: Peeters, 1991), 295. It should be noted that transcriptions of *nfr* that have an *e* vowel also tend to retain the *r* because of suffixes.

19. See Ranke, *Ägyptischen Personennamen*, 1:91.

20. See Assurbanipal prism A, col. 1, line 94, conveniently in Rykle Borger, *Babylonisch-Assyrische Lesestücke*, 2nd ed., Analecta Orientalia, vol. 54 (Rome: Pontificium Institutum Biblicum, 1979), 1:90, 2:337.

21. Ranke, *Ägyptischen Personennamen*, 1:194.

22. Ranke, *Ägyptischen Personennamen*, 1:193.

2

SARIAH IN THE ELEPHANTINE PAPYRI

"He did travel . . . with . . . my mother, Sariah,
and my elder brothers." (1 Nephi 2:5)

The Book of Mormon introduces Sariah, the faithful wife of the prophet Lehi and mother of Nephi and his brothers (see 1 Nephi 2:5). What can be said about her distinctive name?

The conjectural Hebrew spelling of *Sariah* would be שריה (*śryh*) and would be pronounced something like *Saryah*. The skeptic might suggest that this name was an invention of Joseph Smith, since *Sariah* does not appear in the Bible as a female personal name. However, in a significant historical parallel to the Book of Mormon, the Hebrew name *Sariah*, spelled שריה (*śryh*), has been identified in a reconstructed form as the name of a Jewish woman living at Elephantine in Upper Egypt during the fifth century B.C.

The reference to Sariah of Elephantine is found in Aramaic Papyrus #22 (also called Cowley #22 or C–22) and appears in *Aramaic Papyri of the Fifth Century B.C.* Although the language of the documents is Aramaic, A. E. Cowley specifies that the names are in fact Hebrew.[1] Line 4 of C–22 lists the personal name שרי]ה בר[ת הושע בר חרמנ, transliterated *śry[h br]t hwśᶜ br ḥrmn*. The probable vocalization is *Sariah barat Hosheaᵃ bar Ḥarman*, and the text means "Sariah daughter of Hoshea son of Ḥarman." Cowley had to reconstruct part of the text, supplying the final *h* of *Sariah* and the initial *b-r* of *barat*, but the spacing is adequate, and the comparative context of the papyrus leaves little doubt that the reconstruction is accurate. The extant final *t* of *barat* assures us that the person was a daughter, not a son; and, after the letters *b-r* are supplied, there is only room for one additional letter—the final *h* of *Sariah*.

A more recent and exhaustive work on the Elephantine Papyri, *Archives from Elephantine*, published in 1968 by Bezalel Porten, concurs with Cowley's reconstruction and translation. The Porten volume includes significant research concerning the Jewish military colony on Elephantine Island and also contains a black-and-white photo of C–22, including Line 4.[2]

Although *śryh* is not found as a female name in the Bible, it is well documented as a male name in ancient Israel, appearing nineteen times in the Hebrew Old Testament, representing eleven different men. The male name *śryh* is thought to be the short form of *śryhw*, whose full form is probably pronounced *Saryahu*, featuring the common theophoric element *Yahu* from the divine name *Yahuweh*, or *Jehovah*.[3] The longer form *śryhw* is found only once in the Hebrew Old Testament (see Jeremiah 36:26), but it is also known from several instances on Iron Age seals and clay bullae found in Israel.[4] In the King James Version of the Bible, the nineteen instances of the male name *śryh* and the single appearance of *śryhw* are all rendered in English as *Seraiah*. (The English equivalents of many biblical *Yahu* names omit the final syllable, such as Isaiah [*Yeshayahu*], Jeremiah [*Yirmyahu*], Zedekiah [*Zidkiyahu*], etc.) Cowley follows the KJV in using the *S-e-r-a-i-a-h* spelling to render *śry[h br]t hwśᶜ* as "Seraiah daughter of Hoshea."[5] The English *Seraiah* spelling is an effort to represent a Hebrew pronunciation of *Sera-yah* or *Sra-yah*, which would essentially mean "Yah has struggled" (the first element of *śryh* and *śryhw* is usually interpreted as deriving from the *śrh* root, meaning to "struggle" or "strive"). But in light of evidence from Iron Age seals and clay bullae, Nahman Avigad suggests that *śryhw* may be read *Saryahu*, meaning "Yahuweh is prince *(śr)."* By extension, the shorter name *śryh* would be read *Sar-yah*, both in the case of the eleven biblically noted men and in the case of the female from Elephantine. And by the same extension, rather than Cowley's *Seraiah* spelling, the Book of Mormon *Sariah* spelling would more correctly represent the name of our lady of Elephantine.

But what had she done, this Sariah of Elephantine, to merit mention in Papyrus C–22? Line 1 indicates a contribution to *Yahu Elaha*, "the Lord God." And while the purpose of the monetary offering is not explained, Cowley believes that it was for the expenses of the Jewish temple on Elephantine Island.[6] He also dates the donation and the writing to the year 419 B.C. The complete text of Line 4 indicates that Sariah had donated two sheqels of silver *(ksf)*, a generous subscription given the generally high value of silver in ancient Egypt.

It is of particular note here that there was a Jewish (i.e., Israelite) temple at Elephantine, since this would parallel the existence of the temple "like unto the temple of Solomon" that Nephi built in the New World (2 Nephi 5:16). The Elephantine temple was built and used by the military colony of Jewish mercenaries and their families who lived on the island, which was known to them as *Yeb*, a name meaning ivory. (Elephantine was the Greek name of the island.) This colony had probably been established at a time when Judah was a subservient ally of Egypt, perhaps as early as the reign of Manasseh (c. 650 B.C.) or possibly at the outset of the reign of Jehoiakim (c. 609 B.C.). At the time of Sariah's donation to the temple (419 B.C.), the Jewish military garrison (known by the Hebrew word *degel*, meaning "banner") protected the interests of the Persian Empire in the southern part of Egypt.

The Elephantine Papyri were discovered at the beginning of the twentieth century (prior to 1903), far too late for Joseph Smith to have known of the female name *Sariah* in Papyrus C–22. For Latter-day Saint students today, however, the historical parallels between Sariah of Elephantine and Sariah the wife of Lehi are interesting, even if coincidental. Aside from sharing the same Hebrew name and the same Judahite-Israelite background, both women lived a great distance from Jerusalem. One's location would indicate that she probably used Egyptian as a language in addition to Aramaic, whereas the other's husband and at least one son were schooled in "the language of the Egyptians" as well as their native Hebrew tongue (1 Nephi 1:2). Both women reverenced "the Lord God" (Aramaic *Yahu Elaha*; compare 2 Nephi 5:30). Both women lived among Judahite-Israelite colonies that built their own temples outside the sphere of the temple at Jerusalem (see 2 Nephi 5:16), a practice which we are beginning to understand was not uncommon among Israelites both in the land of the Bible and of the Book of Mormon.[7]

Of course, this is not the first time that a Book of Mormon proper name which appeared to defy the normal rules of gender has been vindicated by the archaeological discovery of an ancient Jewish document. In 1973 Hugh Nibley pointed out that those who maintained that *Alma* was a Latin female personal name out of place in the Book of Mormon would have to rethink their positions.[8] The reason for this was Yigael Yadin's discovery of the Hebrew male personal name *Alma ben Yehuda* (Alma son of Yehuda) in a land deed among the Bar Kokhba Letters from the wilderness of Judea.[9] As with the *Alma* episode, Latter-day Saint students may now be assured that the appearance of the female Hebrew name *Sariah* in the Book of Mormon stands vindicated—vindicated by the single line in Papyrus C–22 that mentions the donation of *Sariah barat Hoshea*, Sariah daughter of Hoshea.

Research by Jeffrey R. Chadwick, originally published in the Journal of Book of Mormon Studies *2/2 (1993): 196–200.*

NOTES

1. See Arthur E. Cowley, ed. and trans., *Aramaic Papyri of the Fifth Century B.C.* (Oxford: Clarendon, 1923), xv, 67, inscription 22:4.

2. See Bezalel Porten, *Archives from Elephantine* (Berkeley and Los Angeles: University of California Press, 1968), 320 and plate 11.

3. The divine name *Yahu* is present in Line 1 of Papyrus Cowley #22 (See Cowley, *Aramaic Papyri,* 66). Cowley believed it not to be a short form of YHWH but rather an "earlier form." In any case, both forms of the name represent the same Israelite Deity.

4. See Nahman Avigad, *Hebrew Bullae from the Time of Jeremiah: Remnants of a Burnt Archive* (Jerusalem: Israel Exploration Society, 1986), 46, 103–4.

5. Cowley, *Aramaic Papyri,* 71.

6. See Ibid., 65.

7. In addition to the temple built by Nephi in the New World, small shrines built at Arad and Beersheba in ancient Judah also qualify as temples "like unto the temple of Solomon" in their tripartite form and function.

8. See Hugh W. Nibley, *The Prophetic Book of Mormon* (Salt Lake City: Deseret Book and FARMS, 1989), 281–82.

9. Ibid., 282; Yigael Yadin, *Bar Kokhba* (Jerusalem: Steimatzky, 1971), 176–77; see Paul Y. Hoskisson, "Alma as a Hebrew Name," What's in a Name, *Journal of Book of Mormon Studies* 7/1 (1998): 72–73; and Terrence L. Szink, "Further Evidence of a Semitic Alma," New Light, *Journal of Book of Mormon Studies* 8/1 (1999): 70.

3

NEPHI'S JERUSALEM
AND LABAN'S SWORD

*"And I beheld his sword, and I drew it forth
from the sheath thereof." (1 Nephi 4:9)*

When Nephi returns to obtain the plates of Laban, he finds Laban unconscious in the streets of Jerusalem. One of Laban's personal possessions that greatly fascinates Nephi is Laban's sword. As a matter of fact, Nephi is so intrigued that he describes the sword explicitly in 1 Nephi 4:9 as having a blade of the most expensive steel and a hilt of well-worked gold.

What were swords of Nephi's time like? Archaeology has unfortunately found few swords, mainly because swords are made of iron, which can quickly rust away. But one exciting find was excavated by Avraham Eitan at a site three miles south of Jericho called Vered Jericho.[1]

The sword found at Vered Jericho is three feet long, about three inches wide, is made of iron, and has a bronze haft with a wooden grip. Even the tip of the sword remains intact. The strata from which the sword was excavated dates to the late seventh century or about 620 B.C. Most swords from the Middle East, as portrayed in pictures and reliefs, were short and seem to have been used like daggers. Thus, this three-foot sword from Vered Jericho seems to be unique in its large size.

Something else makes the Vered Jericho sword unique, and that is the fact that Israelite men of this time seem to have been only about five feet tall.[2] Thus, a sword three feet long and three inches wide would be quite a large hand weapon and brings the image of the medieval broadsword to mind. Perhaps the Israelite warriors used this sword in a similar manner.

Finally, 1 Nephi 4:18 indicates that Nephi took Laban by the hair and with the other hand he swung the sword of Laban in such a way as to decapitate him. I do not believe that a short, almost dagger-sized sword would decapitate Laban, but I can imagine that a longer, three-foot sword would have the weight and momentum to do what is described in 1 Nephi 4:18.

Now, with these comments in mind, let us compare the sword found at Vered Jericho with the sword of Laban as described in 1 Nephi 4:9:

	Vered Jericho Sword	Laban's Sword
Handle	Bronze, with wooden grip	Gold, well worked
Blade	Iron, three feet long	Expensive steel, in a sheath, heavy enough to decapitate

Today, we would refer to the Vered Jericho sword as a "factory" product, whereas Laban's sword would be considered an expensive, "customized" product.

The discovery of the seventh-century B.C. sword found at Vered Jericho gives us a tangible artifact with which we can gain a more vivid picture of Nephi and his times.

Research by William J. Adams Jr., originally published in the Journal of Book of Mormon Studies 2/2 (1993): 194–95.

Notes

1. See Avraham Eitan, "BAR Interviews Avraham Eitan: Antiquities Director Confronts Problems and Controversies," interview by Hershel Shanks, *Biblical Archaeology Review* 12/4 (1986): 30–38.

2. See Joseph A. Callaway to Patrick A. Parnell, "The Height of Ancient Israelites," *Biblical Archaeological Review* 10/1 (1984): 20.

4

THE WORKMANSHIP THEREOF WAS EXCEEDINGLY FINE

"And I beheld his sword . . . and the workmanship thereof was exceedingly fine." (1 Nephi 4:9)

So much has been written about the sword of Laban that it sometimes seems that there is nothing more to be said.[1] But no one appears to have drawn a parallel between the description of the sword of Laban and a similar sword description in one of the Dead Sea Scrolls. Hence this brief note.

Let's begin by reviewing what Nephi wrote about the sword of Laban, which he examined with care and evident awe:

> And I beheld his sword, and I drew it forth from the *sheath* thereof; and the *hilt* thereof was of *pure gold*, and the *workmanship* thereof was *exceedingly fine*, and I saw that the *blade* thereof was of the *most precious steel*. (1 Nephi 4:9)

Compare this with the description given in the *War Scroll* of the swords to be used by the Israelites during the final battle between the forces of good and evil:

> The swords shall be of *purified iron,* refined in a crucible and *whitened like a mirror,* work of a *skilful craftsman*; and it will have shapes of an ear of wheat, of *pure gold,* encrusted in it on both sides. And it will have two straight channels right to the tip, two on each side.

14

Length of the sword: one cubit and a half. And its width: four fingers. The *scabbard* will be four thumbs; it will have four palms up to the scabbard and diagonally, the scabbard from one part to the other (will be) five palms. The *hilt* of the sword will be of select horn, *craftwork,* with a pattern in many colours: *gold, silver and precious stones.*[2]

The fact that both texts mention the hilt and the sheath or scabbard of the sword is relatively insignificant. More important is the composition of the hilt and the blade. Laban's sword blade is made of "the most precious steel," while the future swords of the Israelite army will have blades "of purified iron . . . whitened like a mirror." Nephi describes the hilt as being made "of pure gold." The future Israelite swords will have a hilt "of select horn . . . with a pattern in many colours: gold, silver and precious stones," though designs in "pure gold" are also mentioned. Both the Nephite and the Qumran descriptions refer to the "workmanship" or "craftwork" of the swords, saying it was "exceedingly fine" or "of a skilful craftsman." The *War Scroll* is particularly detailed when it describes the sword's ornamentation and size.

Interestingly, the sword described in the Qumran document measures a cubit and a half in total length with a blade four fingers wide (i.e., its width is three inches, while the length depends on which cubit was meant). Using a cubit measure of 17.5 inches, it would have been 26.25 inches long (just over two feet), while a cubit of 20.4 inches would give a length of 30.6 inches or 2.5 feet. This reminds us that the seventh-century B.C. iron Israelite sword found at Vered Jericho measured three feet in length with a three-inch-wide blade. We do not know the size of Laban's sword, but William J. Adams, in his discussion of the unusually long Vered Jericho sword, noted that Nephi would have had an easier time decapitating Laban with his sword (see 1 Nephi 4:18) if it were longer than the usual short swords known from the ancient Near East.[3]

I am not suggesting a direct connection between the account in 1 Nephi and the one in the *War Scroll*. But it may be that the idealized Israelite sword described in the latter reflects the concept of precious swords carried by earlier Israelite leaders such as Laban.

Research by John A. Tvedtnes, originally published in the Journal of Book of Mormon Studies *6/1 (1997): 73–75.*

NOTES

1. In the *Journal of Book of Mormon Studies* alone, the following articles have discussed the subject: Todd R. Kerr, "Ancient Aspects of Nephite Kingship in the Book of Mormon," *Journal of Book of Mormon Studies* 1/1 (1992): 85–118; Brett L. Holbrook, "The Sword of Laban as a Symbol of Divine Authority and Kingship," *Journal of Book of Mormon Studies* 2/1 (1993): 39–72; Daniel N. Rolph, "Prophets, Kings, and Swords: The Sword of Laban and Its Possible Pre-Laban Origin," *Journal of Book of Mormon Studies* 2/1 (1993): 73–79; William J. Adams Jr., "Nephi's Jerusalem and Laban's Sword," *Journal of Book of Mormon Studies* 2/2 (1993): 194–95; and John A. Tvedtnes, "The *Iliad* and the Book of Mormon," *Journal of Book of Mormon Studies* 5/1 (1996): 147.

2. *1QM*, col. 5, lines 11–14, in Florentino García Martínez, *The Dead Sea Scrolls Translated* (Leiden: Brill, 1994), 99; italics added.

3. For details, see Adams, "Nephi's Jerusalem."

5

Better That One Man Perish

"It is better that one man should perish
than that a nation should dwindle and
perish in unbelief." (1 Nephi 4:13)

When constraining Nephi to slay Laban, the Spirit gave the sober justification that "it is better that one man should perish than that a nation should dwindle and perish in unbelief" (1 Nephi 4:13). Alma invoked this same justification when reluctantly subjecting Korihor to divine punishment (see Alma 30:47). This principle runs sharply contrary to modern liberal jurisprudence, but a different view prevailed in certain cases under biblical law.

A pivotal example is found in 2 Samuel 20. King David sought the life of Sheba, a rebel guilty of treason. When Sheba took refuge in the city of Abel, Joab, the leader of David's army, demanded that Sheba be released to him. The people of Abel beheaded Sheba instead, and Joab retreated. This episode became an important legal precedent justifying the killing of one person in order to preserve an entire group.

Another Old Testament case, preserved more fully in the Jewish oral tradition, involved Jehoiakim, the king of Judah, who rebelled against Nebuchadnezzar. Nebuchadnezzar went to Antioch and demanded that the great Jewish council surrender Jehoiakim or the nation would be destroyed. Jehoiakim protested, "Can ye sacrifice one life for another?" Unmoved, the council replied, "Thus did your ancestors do to Sheba the son of Bichri."[1] Jehoiakim was released to Nebuchadnezzar, who took him to Babylon (see 2 Chronicles 36:6), where presumably he was executed. Because Zedekiah became king less than four months later (see verses 9–10), at the time the Book of Mormon account begins (see 1 Nephi 1:4), Nephi was probably keenly aware of how the "one for many" principle was used to justify Jehoiakim's death. Clearly, the cases of Laban and Korihor fit within this tradition.

Over the years, the proper balance between the rights of the individual and the needs of the community was debated in Jewish law. On one extreme, the Pharisees held that no individual was ever to be surrendered for the good of the community. On the other extreme, the Sadducees, who often cooperated with the Romans, argued that so long as the authorities named a specific victim, that was all that was necessary. This ruling, known as the Hadrianic Resolve, is found in the Jerusalem Talmud.[2]

Taking a middle position, most rabbinical scholars have accepted the "one for many" principle, but they limit it to cases like Sheba's in which (1) the demand was made by a recognized leader, (2) the person requested was already guilty, (3) the person was identified by name, (4) the people in the group were innocent, and (5) the group faced certain destruction if they refused.

Of course, the "one for many" principle was also invoked, ironically, by Caiaphas (a Sadducee) when he argued for Jesus' death (see John 11:49–50).[3] While the audience evidently knew this familiar principle, as Sadducees and Pharisees they were probably divided on its application.

Based on the New Testament alone, the "one for many" principle in the Book of Mormon might have appeared anachronistic. Yet the fuller picture shows that this principle operated much earlier in Israelite culture, notably in Nephi's own day. This was something that Joseph Smith would have had no way of knowing, and it is a point that few legal historians are aware of even today.

Research by John W. Welch and Heidi Harkness Parker, originally published as a FARMS Update in Insights *(June 1998): 2.*

NOTES

1. *Genesis Rabbah* 94:9, vol. 2 of *Midrash Rabbah,* ed. and trans. H. Freedman and Maurice Simon (London: Soncino, 1939), 879.

2. See *Terumot* 8:10, 46b.

3. See Roger David Aus, "The Death of One for All in John 11:45–54 in Light of Judaic Traditions," in *Barabbas and Esther and Other Studies in the Judaic Illumination of Earliest Christianity,* South Florida Studies in the History of Judaism, no. 54 (Atlanta: Scholars, 1992), 29–63.

6

METAL PLATES AND THE BOOK OF MORMON

*"The law was engraven upon the
plates of brass." (1 Nephi 4:16)*

In the past, critics of the Book of Mormon have attacked the alleged absurdity of the Book of Mormon having been written on golden plates and its claim of the existence of an early sixth-century-B.C. version of the Hebrew Bible written on brass plates.[1] Today, however, critics almost universally admit that there are numerous examples of ancient writing on metal plates. Ironically, some critics now claim instead that knowledge of such plates was readily available in Joseph Smith's day. Hugh Nibley's 1952 observation seems quite prescient: "It will not be long before men forget that in Joseph Smith's day the prophet was mocked and derided for his description of the plates more than anything else."[2]

Recent reevaluation of the evidence now points to the fact that the Book of Mormon's description of sacred records written on bronze plates fits quite nicely in the cultural milieu of the ancient eastern Mediterranean.

One of the earliest known surviving examples of writing on "copper plates" are the Byblos Syllabic inscriptions (eighteenth century B.C.), from the city of Byblos on the Phoenician coast. The script is described as a "syllabary [that] is clearly inspired by the Egyptian hieroglyphic system, and in fact is the most important link known between the hieroglyphs and the Canaanite alphabet."[3] It would not be unreasonable to describe the Byblos Syllabic texts as eighteenth-century-B.C. Semitic "bronze plates" written in "reformed Egyptian characters."[4]

Walter Burkert, in his recent study of the cultural dependence of Greek civilization on the ancient Near East, refers to the transmission of the practice of writing on bronze plates (Semitic root *dlt*) from the Phoenicians to the Greeks. "The reference to 'bronze *deltoi* [plates, from *dlt*]' as a term [among the Greeks] for ancient sacral laws should point back to the seventh or sixth century [B.C.]" as the period in which the terminology and the practice of writing on bronze plates was transmitted from the Phoenicians to the Greeks.[5] Students of the Book of Mormon will note that this is precisely the time and place in which the Book of Mormon claims that there existed similar bronze plates which contained the "ancient sacred laws" of the Hebrews, the close cultural cousins of the Phoenicians.

Burkert also maintains that "the practice of the *subscriptio* in particular . . . connects the layout of later Greek books with cuneiform practice, the indication of the name of the writer/author and the title of the book right at the end, after the last line of the text; this is a detailed and exclusive correspondence which proves that Greek literary practice is ultimately dependent upon Mesopotamia. It is necessary to postulate that Aramaic leather scrolls formed the connecting link."[6] Joseph Smith wrote that "the title-page of the Book of Mormon is a literal translation, taken from *the very last* leaf, on the left-hand side of the collection or book of plates, which contained the record which has been translated."[7] This idea would have been counterintuitive in the early nineteenth century when title pages appeared at the beginning, not the end, of books.

Why, then, did Joseph claim the Book of Mormon practiced *subscriptio*—writing the name of the author and title at the end of the book? If the existence of the practice of *subscriptio* among the Greeks represents "a detailed and exclusive correspondence which proves that Greek literary practice is ultimately dependent upon Mesopotamia [via Syria]," as Burkert claims, cannot the same thing be said of the Book of Mormon—that the practice of *subscriptio* represents "a detailed and exclusive correspondence" which offers proof that the Book of Mormon is "ultimately dependent" on the ancient Near East?

Research by William J. Hamblin, originally published as a FARMS Update in Insights *(July 1994): 2.*

NOTES

1. See, for example, John Hyde Jr., *Mormonism: Its Leaders and Designs* (New York: Fetridge, 1857), 217–18; M. T. Lamb, *The Golden Bible* (New York: Ward and Drummond, 1887), 11; and Stuart Martin, *The Mystery of Mormonism* (New York: Dutton, 1920), 27; see also William J. Hamblin, "Sacred Writing on Bronze Plates in the Ancient Mediterranean," (FARMS, 1994) for full references and analysis of the issues raised in this article.

2. Hugh W. Nibley, *Lehi in the Desert; World of the Jaredites; There Were Jaredites* (Salt Lake City: Deseret Book and FARMS, 1988), 107.

3. See Stephen A. Kaufman, "Languages (Aramaic)," Anchor Bible Dictionary, ed. David N. Freedman (New York: Doubleday, 1992), 4:178; see 4:178–80. Byblos is only about 170 miles north of Jerusalem.

4. Nibley, *Lehi in the Desert*, 105–6, mentions these plates, which were not deciphered until 1985.

5. Walter Burkert, *The Orientalizing Revolution: Near Eastern Influence on Greek Culture in the Early Archaic Age* (Cambridge, Mass: Harvard University Press, 1992), 30.

6. Ibid., 32.

7. *History of the Church*, 1:71, emphasis added; see 6:366.

7

LEHI'S JERUSALEM AND WRITING ON SILVER PLATES

"The law was engraven upon the plates of brass." (1 Nephi 4:16)

Lehi sent his sons back to Jerusalem to obtain scriptures engraved on "brass plates" (see 1 Nephi 3 and 4). Later we read that Lehi and his son Nephi kept records on metal "plates" (see 1 Nephi 6 and 9). These incidents raise the question: Did others in Lehi's Jerusalem inscribe records on metal plates?

The use of metal plates upon which records are inscribed is fairly well attested throughout the Middle and Far East from many centuries before to many centuries after Lehi, but none so far appear to be from Lehi's seventh-century B.C. Judea.[1]

This lack of metal inscriptions from Judea could be interpreted to mean that (1) Judeans did not write on metal plates, or (2) archaeology has not found artifacts which would support the practice of writing on metal plates in seventh-century B.C. Jerusalem. Alternative 2 seems to have been the problem, for inscribed silver plates have been excavated only recently.

Dr. Gabriel Barkay of the Institute of Archaeology, Tel Aviv University, directed an excavation on a ridge behind modern Jerusalem's railroad station and next to the

Scottish Presbyterian Church of St. Andrew. The dig was begun in 1979, and in 1980 the team opened a tomb that dates to the end of the seventh century and the beginning of the sixth (or about 600 B.C.). Dr. Barkay notes that "Among the rich finds in the repository were two small, rolled-up strips of silver. Similar artifacts are completely unknown elsewhere in the archaeology of this period."[2]

It took three years to unroll the strips of silver, which were about one inch by four inches. One of the exciting facts is that the strips of silver had been inscribed. In 1983 only the Divine Name could be read. This consists of the four Hebrew letters *yod-hey-vav-hey*, YHWH, which are translated as *Jehovah* or *Lord*.

"The scribe who wrote on the strips in antiquity scratched them without much pressure, so the inscriptions sit only on the surface. It will take a long time before we are able to decipher these two texts. We can now say only that the texts are prayer-like, or amuletic, in nature."[3]

Since then Dr. Barkay has published tentative translations of the two silver plates.[4] Here is his suggested translation for Plate I:

1.	JEHOV[AH]
2.	. . .
3.	love
4.	the covenant
5.	and the mercy
6.	for Aaron and for my obedience
7.	. . .
8.	eternity that . . .
9.	. . . from the grave
10.	and what (is) evil
11.	for . . . save
12.	will smite JEHOVAH
13.	that they be weary
14.	. . .

15.   may bless
16.   you JEHOVAH and
17.   watch over you May cause
18.   to shine JEHOVAH
19.   His face upon you and favor you.

The suggested translation for Plate II is as follows:

1.   the blessing
2.   JEHOV[AH]
3.   . . . JE[HOVAH]
4.   evil
5.   that may bless you
6.   JEHOVAH and
7.   watch over you.
8.   May cause to shine JEHO-
9.   VAH His face
10.   upon you and
11.   give you pe
12.   ace.
13–18.   unreadable

Plate I, lines 14–19 and Plate II, lines 5–12 are quotations from Numbers 6:24–26 and thus are quite readable on the plates. In fact, this text preserves an astonishingly early copy of this famous priestly blessing from the Pentateuch. The other parts of the plates are not quotations and are more difficult to read.

The conclusion for Book of Mormon studies is that the gap has been filled, and we can be certain that religious texts were written on precious metal plates in Lehi's Jerusalem.

Research by William J. Adams Jr., originally published in the Journal of Book of Mormon Studies *3/1 (1994): 204–6.*

NOTES

1. See, for example, Franklin S. Harris Jr., *The Book of Mormon: Message and Evidences,* 2nd ed. (Salt Lake City: Deseret News, 1961), 98–108.

2. Gabriel Barkay, "News from the Field: The Divine Name Found in Jerusalem," *Biblical Archaeology Review* 9/2 (1983): 17.

3. Ibid., 19.

4. See Gabriel Barkay, "Priestly Blessings on Silver Plates" (in Hebrew), *Cathedra* 52 (1989): 46–59.

8

MORE ON THE SILVER PLATES FROM LEHI'S JERUSALEM

"The law was engraven upon the
plates of brass." (1 Nephi 4:16)

In the spring 1994 issue of the *Journal of Book of Mormon Studies*, I described the discovery, unwrapping, and translation of silver plates found in a Jerusalem burial site that dates just before the Babylonian captivity.[1] This time frame is that of Lehi and his family. The importance of this find for Book of Mormon studies is that sacred texts were written on precious metal plates, and thus Lehi's search for the plates of Laban and his writing on precious metal plates are real possibilities.

A recent issue of *Biblical Archaeology Review* gives additional importance to these plates in the article "Ten Great Finds," by Michael D. Coogan.[2] Dr. Coogan was asked to sift through all the archaeological finds in Palestine and determine the ten most significant for biblical archaeology. In doing so he tried to list finds that are representative of whole areas of endeavors. For example, one of his choices was the Gibeon water system. Not only is it a marvel by itself, but it also represents other engineering feats of the Israelites.

Coogan selected these plates as one of his ten great finds because, in the overall picture of biblical archaeology, they "are the earliest inscriptions containing a text also found in the Bible."[3] These texts represent the work of scribes, such as those of the Dead Sea Scrolls, who preserved

27

the Bible for us. He concludes that the significance of the texts "is inversely proportionate to their size, for they are our earliest witnesses to the text of the Bible."[4]

This discovery is every bit as important for the Book of Mormon. Nephi reported in the sixth century B.C. that the plates of brass from Jerusalem contained "the five books of Moses" (1 Nephi 5:11). Now, from the same time and place comes another "plate," inscribed in a very small script, that preserves words not only from a biblical text, but even more so from the Mosaic book of Numbers.

Research by William J. Adams Jr., originally published in the Journal of Book of Mormon Studies 4/2 (1995): 136–37.

NOTES

1. See William J. Adams Jr., "Lehi's Jerusalem and Writing on Metal Plates," *Journal of Book of Mormon Studies* 3/1 (1994): 204–6.

2. See Michael D. Coogan, "Ten Great Finds," *Biblical Archaeology Review* 21/3 (1995): 36–47.

3. Ibid., 45.

4. Ibid.

9

A VISIONARY MAN

*"I know that I am a visionary man; for if I had not
seen the things of God in a vision I should not have
known the goodness of God." (1 Nephi 5:4)*

In the Book of Mormon, Lehi is three times referred to as
"a visionary man" (1 Nephi 2:11; 5:2, 4). The term does
not appear in the King James Version of the Bible, but is
nonetheless authentic. It is the Hebrew word *ḥôzeh*, the
active participle of the root from which derive *ḥāzôn* and
ḥizzāyôn, "vision" (see 2 Samuel 24:11; 1 Chronicles 21:9;
25:5; 2 Chronicles 9:29; 12:15; 19:2; 29:25, 30; 35:15; Amos
7:12). In each case, the King James Version translates the
term as "seer," which is the same as the KJV rendering for
rô'eh (from the verb *to see*), used of the prophet Samuel in
1 Samuel 9:9, 11, 19; 1 Chronicles 9:22; 26:28; 29:29, of the
priest Zadok in 2 Samuel 15:27, and of the prophet Hanani
in 2 Chronicles 16:7, 10 (Hanani is termed a *ḥôzeh* in
2 Chronicles 19:2).

Both Hebrew roots have the verbal meaning of "to see,"
but it is likely that *ḥôzeh* is behind the Book of Mormon
term *visionary man*, while *rô'eh* is probably the word behind
seer in 2 Nephi 3:6–7, 11, 14 and Mosiah 8:13–17. The latter
passage, along with Mosiah 28:13–16 and Joseph Smith—
History 1:35, indicates that the term *seer* was used by the
Nephites to designate one who had power to use the

interpreters, which have come to be known to us as the Urim and Thummim.

In the Book of Mormon, both Lehi's wife and his elder sons derisively call him "a visionary man." In response to Sariah, Lehi said, "I know that I am a visionary man; for if I had not seen the things of God in a vision I should not have known the goodness of God" (1 Nephi 5:4). In Amos 7:12, Amaziah, priest of the apostate shrine erected at Bethel by King Jeroboam, uses the term when addressing the prophet Amos, telling him, "O thou seer, go, flee thee away into the land of Judah." Amos's response is similar to that of Lehi: "I was no prophet, neither was I a prophet's son; but I was an herdman, and a gatherer of sycomore fruit: and the Lord took me as I followed the flock, and the Lord said unto me, Go, prophesy unto my people Israel" (Amos 7:14–15).

Lehi's visionary powers were again manifest when he told his family, "Behold, I have dreamed a dream; or, in other words, I have seen a vision" (1 Nephi 8:2; compare 8:36).[1] The idiom "dreamed a dream" is clearly an example of the cognate accusative, known from Hebrew[2] and other ancient languages, in which the verb is followed by a noun (here used as direct object or accusative) deriving from the same root. From this, it also seems likely that the words "seen a vision" represent another cognate accusative. We can illustrate this by rendering the English as "seen a scene," "vised a vision," or "envisioned a vision." It is likely that the original read *ḥāzîtî ḥāzôn*, using a verb and noun deriving from the same root as *ḥôzeh*, "visionary."[3] The fact that this Hebrew root is found in cognate constructions in both Isaiah 1:1 and Ezekiel 12:27; 13:7, 16 adds strength to this suggestion.

Research by John A. Tvedtnes, originally published in the Journal of Book of Mormon Studies *6/2 (1997): 260–61.*

NOTES

1. For a tie between dreams and visions, see Job 33:15; Isaiah 29:7; Daniel 1:17.

2. The Hebrew idiom is found in Genesis 37:5, 9; 40:5, 8; 41:11; Deuteronomy 13:3; Judges 7:13; Daniel 2:3.

3. I realize that this view is at variance with Nibley's suggestion that the term *visionary* used in reference to Lehi was the same as *ha-piqqeah* found in one of the Lachish letters; see Hugh W. Nibley, *The Prophetic Book of Mormon*, ed. John W. Welch (Salt Lake City: Deseret Book and FARMS, 1989), 393–94. But *ha-piqqeah* really refers to one whose eyes are open. In my opinion, the fact that *hôzeh* derives from the same root as the word for *vision* makes it a better candidate.

10

ROD AND SWORD AS THE WORD OF GOD

"And I beheld a rod of iron, and it extended along the bank of the river, and led to the tree by which I stood. And I also beheld a strait and narrow path, which came along by the rod of iron, even to the tree by which I stood; and it also led by the head of the fountain, unto a large and spacious field, as if it had been a world." (1 Nephi 8:19–20)

Thus Lehi described the rod and the path seen in his vision of the tree of life. Those who "caught hold of the end of the rod of iron" and clung to it through the "mist of darkness" were able to "come forth and partake of the fruit of the tree" (1 Nephi 8:24; compare 8:30).

The term *rod of iron* is found in Psalm 2:9 and in three passages in the book of Revelation. The first of these (Revelation 2:27) paraphrases the psalm, while the others (Revelation 12:5; 19:15) build on it. All of them imply that the rod is a symbol of ruling power.

In the Old Testament, the rod is typically used to chastise children and wrongdoers (see 2 Samuel 7:14; Proverbs 13:24; 29:15). Even the Lord is said to wield a rod in punishing the wicked (see Job 9:34; 21:9; Psalm 89:32; Lamentations 3:1). Nephi, referring to the serpent Moses placed on the pole, wrote that the Lord "did straiten [Israel] . . . with his rod" (1 Nephi 17:41). Isaiah indicated that the Lord used the power of other nations like a rod to punish the Israelites when they had gone astray (see Isaiah 10:5, 15, 24, 26; 14:29; 30:31; Micah 5:1). Similarly, the Lord used the Lamanites as a scourge (whip or flail) to punish the Nephites in times of wickedness (see 1 Nephi 2:24; 2 Nephi 5:25; Jacob 3:3) and scourged the people for their wickedness (see D&C 84:96; 97:22–24). In Isaiah 10:26 (also in 2 Nephi 20:26), the Lord declares that other nations would be a scourge to Israel and speaks also of the rod. "What will ye?" Paul asked the Corinthians, "Shall I come unto you with a rod, or in love, and in the spirit of meekness?" (1 Corinthians 4:21).

Anciently, the rod was used both for correction and for gentle guidance. This dual role came from the world of the shepherd as pastor and defender of the flock. Most familiar to us is the description of the Lord as a shepherd, in which David wrote, "Yea, though I walk through the valley of the shadow of death, I will fear no evil: for thou art with me; thy rod and thy staff they comfort me" (Psalm 23:4; compare 80:1).[1] Micah used the same imagery when he wrote, "Feed thy people with thy rod, the flock of thine heritage" (Micah 7:14; see also Isaiah 40:11; Jeremiah 31:10; Ezekiel 34:6, 8, 10–17, 19, 22–24, 31; Hebrews 13:20; 1 Peter 2:25; 5:4).

The shepherd's rod was a weapon, normally a piece of wood with a knob at one end. With it, he could defend the flock from predators. It was also used to count the sheep at the day's end (see Leviticus 27:32; Ezekiel 20:37). The staff was a long walking stick, sometimes with a crook at the top. It could also be used for handling sheep, including separating sheep and goats.

The Rod as Scepter

The use of the rod and staff for care of the flock and for inflicting injury on predators was carried over in the ancient Near East to rulers. Israel's rulers are termed shepherds in Ezekiel 34:2, 23 and Jeremiah 2:8. The kings of Egypt are frequently depicted with a flail in one hand and a small shepherd's crook in the other. The staff or crook, which ultimately became the scepter used by royalty (and by bishops in various Christian churches), represented the king's responsibility to care for his people, while the flail or whip symbolized his role as punisher of criminals.

The use of the rod or staff as a symbol of rule is mentioned in a number of Bible passages (see Psalm 110:2; Isaiah 14:5; Jeremiah 48:17; Ezekiel 19:11–12, 14; compare D&C 85:7). The Israelite crown prince Jonathan, son of King Saul, carried a rod (see 1 Samuel 14:27, 43). Ezekiel 19:11 equates rods with scepters. In Numbers 24:17, the scepter of the Messiah is symbolically used to smite Israel's enemies. Later Jewish tradition indicates that possession of the rod denotes rule over the world (Midrash *Ba-Midbar Rabbah* 13:14).

It is interesting that when Laman and Lemuel were stopped from beating their younger brothers Sam and Nephi with a rod, the angel said to them, "Why do ye smite your younger brother with a *rod*? Know ye not that the Lord hath chosen him to be a *ruler* over you, and this because of your iniquities?" (1 Nephi 3:29; compare 1 Nephi 2:22; 2 Nephi 5:19). It is possible that the elder brothers deliberately selected the rod to punish their brother to symbolize their claim to ruling authority in the family. Compare the story in Numbers 17:2–10, where Aaron's authority as high priest in Israel was established by the miraculous blossoming of his rod.

The Royal Sword

Another symbol of power in the ancient world was the sword, still used by monarchs for conferring knighthood. As we shall see later, the sword, like the rod, symbolizes the word of God in the scriptures.

Because of the scarcity of iron in the early kingdom of Israel, in Saul's day only he and his son Jonathan had a sword (see 1 Samuel 13:19–22).[2] Jonathan, acknowledging David as the rightful king (see 1 Samuel 23:16–17), gives him his royal garments, his sword, and his bow (see 1 Samuel 18:4).

The messianic hymn in Psalm 45:3 speaks of the royal sword, and there are a fair number of passages in which the "sword of the Lord" is mentioned (Judges 7:18, 20; 1 Chronicles 21:12; see Isaiah 27:1; 34:5–6; 66:16; Jeremiah 12:12; 47:6; Ezekiel 21:3–5; 30:24–25; 32:10; 3 Nephi 29:4; compare Numbers 22:23, 31; D&C 1:13; 35:14). It is perhaps in this light that we should understand the comparison of the sword with famine or pestilence as the means of punishing wicked nations. Jesus declared, "Think not that I am come to send peace on earth: I came not to send peace, but a sword" (Matthew 10:34).

Among the Nephites, the sword of Laban, taken by Nephi and used as a pattern for other swords (see 1 Nephi 4:9, 18–19; 2 Nephi 5:14), was wielded only by the rulers (see Jacob 1:10; Words of Mormon 1:13; compare Alma 2:29, 31). Considered to be one of the Nephites' most precious possessions, it was kept with the plates of brass and the plates of Nephi, along with the Liahona (see Mosiah 1:16), and was later shown to Joseph Smith and the Three Witnesses (see D&C 17:1).

Significantly, the sword and the rod appear together in some Bible passages (see Ezekiel 21:9–10, 13; Revelation 19:15). In Jeremiah 51:19–20, the rod is paralleled by weapons of war.

The Word of God

Nephi explained "that the rod of iron, which my father had seen, was the word of God, which led to the fountain of living waters, or to the tree of life; which waters are a representation of the love of God; and I also beheld that the tree of life was a representation of the love of God" (1 Nephi

11:25). When his brothers asked about the meaning of the rod, he explained that "it was the word of God; and whoso would . . . hold fast unto it, they would never perish; neither could the temptations and the fiery darts of the adversary overpower them unto blindness, to lead them away to destruction" (1 Nephi 15:24).[3]

This makes the rod both a source of support (as the word of God) and a weapon of defense against the devil's "fiery darts," which, in Ephesians 6:16, are warded off by the shield of faith. As such, the rod reminds us of the admonition to don the "armour of God," including the "sword of the Spirit, which is the word of God" (Ephesians 6:13, 17; compare Romans 13:12; 2 Corinthians 6:7; 1 Thessalonians 5:8; 2 Nephi 1:23). The passage is paraphrased in Doctrine and Covenants 27:15–17.

The use of a rod to represent words or speech is found in Proverbs 10:13 and 14:3. In other passages, it refers specifically to the word of God. In Isaiah 30:31, "the voice of the Lord" is contrasted with the rod of the Assyrians. In a few passages, the rod is compared to a covenant with God which, like a rod, can be broken (see Ezekiel 20:37; Zechariah 11:10, 14). Micah wrote, "The Lord's voice crieth unto the city, and the man of wisdom shall see thy name: hear ye the rod, and who hath appointed it" (Micah 6:9). Isaiah wrote of the Messiah, "But with righteousness shall he judge the poor, and reprove with equity for the meek of the earth: and he shall smite the earth with the rod of his mouth, and with the breath of his lips shall he slay the wicked" (Isaiah 11:4).[4] A similar thought, obviously based on the Isaiah passage, is expressed in a modern revelation in which the Lord threatens to punish the unrepentant with "the rod of my mouth" (D&C 19:15).

In his revelation to the apostle John, the Lord also drew upon the imagery in Isaiah 11:4, placing a sword in the mouth of God, while noting that Christ is to rule "with a rod of iron" (Revelation 2:27; 12:5). In this, he follows Old Testament precedent, where the mouth, words, tongue, and even teeth are frequently compared to a sword.[5] "And out of his mouth goeth a sharp sword, that with it he should smite the nations: and he shall rule them with a rod of iron: and he treadeth the winepress of the fierceness and wrath of Almighty God" (Revelation 19:15; compare 19:21). In Hosea 6:5, the Lord declares, "Therefore have I hewed them by the prophets; I have slain them by the words of my mouth." The prophets, as God's spokesmen, utter his words.

The sword has two edges, reminding us that the word of the Lord can bring either salvation or destruction, depending on whether we wield it or are judged by it (see Revelation 1:16; 2:12, 16). This is explained in Hebrews 4:12, which is one of the most frequently quoted biblical passages in the early revelations given to Joseph Smith (see D&C 6:2; 11:2; 12:2; 14:2; 33:1):

> For the word of God is quick, and powerful, and sharper than any two-edged sword, piercing even to the dividing asunder of soul and spirit, and of the joints and marrow, and is a discerner of the thoughts and intents of the heart.

The epistle to the Hebrews probably quoted a more ancient source, which was also borrowed in Helaman 3:29–30:

> Whosoever will may lay hold upon the word of God, which is quick and powerful, which shall divide asunder all the cunning and the snares and the wiles of the devil, and lead the man of Christ in a strait and narrow course across that everlasting gulf of misery which is prepared to engulf the wicked—And land their souls, yea, their immortal souls, at the right hand of God in the kingdom of heaven.

The inclusion of the "strait and narrow course" and the "gulf of misery," along with the "snares and the wiles of the devil," clearly ties this passage to Lehi's vision, where it is the rod or the word of God that brings people safely past Satan's obstacles (the mist of darkness, the gulf, the fiery darts of the adversary, and the forbidden paths) to the tree of life (see 1 Nephi 8:19–24, 28; 12:17–18; 15:24, 28). In the Helaman passage, however, the word of God seems to be compared to a sword.

The power of the word of God was emphasized by Alma; he noted that "it had had more powerful effect upon the minds of the people than the sword, or anything else, which had happened unto them" (Alma 31:5; compare 61:14; Ecclesiastes 9:18). This reminds us that Nephi and other Book of Mormon prophets spoke with "the sharpness of the power of the word of God" (2 Nephi 1:26; see Words of Mormon 1:17; Moroni 9:4; compare Alma 1:7).

By comparing the word of God with a sword and a rod, the prophets have shown us that there is both strength and love in obedience to the Lord. With the word of the Lord, we can fight off sin and temptation as with a sword and nurture our families and ourselves as did ancient shepherds with the rod. In the end, the word of God will also serve to judge us, meting out justice to those who disobey and justifying those who follow its precepts. In this, too, it is like both the sword and the rod.

Research by John A. Tvedtnes, originally published in the Journal of Book of Mormon Studies *5/2 (1996): 148–55.*

NOTES

1. It seems natural that David, who was a shepherd before he became king, should call the Lord his shepherd. (The comparison of David, the shepherd, with David, the king, is made in Psalm 151, which, while not in our current Bible, was on a Psalms scroll found at Qumran and is known from other ancient sources as well.)

2. The sword of Goliath was so revered that it was kept by the priests in the Tabernacle until David asked for it when fleeing Saul (1 Samuel 21:8–10; 22:13).

3. According to William P. Smith in an 1890 interview (William Smith, interview by J. W. Peterson and W. S. Pender, in *Early Mormon Documents*, ed. and comp. Dan Vogel [Salt Lake City: Signature Books, 1996], 1: 508–9), the Urim and Thummim used by Joseph Smith to translate the Book of Mormon was held by a rod attached to the breastplate given to Joseph Smith. In the original wording of D&C 8:6–9 (*Book of Commandments* 7:3), Oliver Cowdery, when authorized to attempt a translation of the plates, was to have the "gift of working with the rod." The wording was later changed to "gift of Aaron," in line with the rod of Aaron mentioned in Exodus 7:9–10, 19–20; 8:5, 16–17; Numbers 17:6–10.

4. The passage is cited in 2 Nephi 30:9 and is paraphrased in one of the Dead Sea Scrolls, *1Q28b (1QSb 5)*, col. 5, lines 24–25. In another of the Dead Sea Scrolls, the *Isaiah Pesher* known as 4Q161, col. 3, line 22, the passage is explained by saying, "his sword will judge all the peoples" (Florentino Martínez and Eibert J. C. Tigchelaar, *The Dead Sea Scrolls Study Edition* [Leiden: Brill, 1997], 317). One of the Nag Hammadi texts, *The Apocalypse of Paul* V, 2 22:2–10, depicts an angel with an iron rod in his hand herding souls to judgment.

5. See Job 5:15; Psalms 42:10; 55:21; 57:4; 59:7; 64:3; 149:6; Proverbs 12:18; 25:18; 30:14; Isaiah 1:20; 49:2 (see 1 Nephi 21:2); compare the longer version of Isaiah 50:8 in 2 Nephi 7:8, "I will smite him with the strength of my mouth." In connection with the flail mentioned earlier, note that, in Job 5:20–21, "the power of the sword" parallels "the scourge of the tongue." One of the Dead Sea Scrolls *(1QH[a])* speaks of lion cubs with teeth like a sword or a spear (col. 13, lines 9–10, 13, 14–15), while another compares the mouth to a sharpened sword and the tongue to words of holiness (4Q436, col. 1, line 7). *Mandaean Prayerbook* 24 speaks of being delivered "from the sword of enemies and from the third tongue which is softer than fat and sharper than a sword" (E. S. Drower, trans., *The Canonical Prayerbook of the Mandaeans* [Leiden: Brill, 1959], 20). According to *Pirqê de Rabbi Eliezer* 48, when Moses saw the Egyptian striking the Hebrew, he rebuked him "with the sword of his lips." Compare Psalm 59:7; Isaiah 11:4. Clement of Alexandria, regarding the passage, says, "the mystics say that he slew the Egyptian by a word only."

11

"THE LAMB OF GOD" IN PRE-CHRISTIAN TEXTS

*"Behold the Lamb of God, yea, even the Son
of the Eternal Father." (1 Nephi 11:21)*

One of Nephi's favorite titles for Jesus Christ was "the Lamb of God." Forty-four references to "the Lamb" appear in Nephi's vision in 1 Nephi 11–14 alone. Aside from the Latter-day Saint understanding of a similar reference in Moses 7:47 and perhaps Isaiah 53:7, what evidence supports the Old World origins of this terminology?

In a 1979 article, recently selected as one of the most illuminating studies on the background of the New Testament, J. C. O'Neill contends that the phrase *Lamb of God* was not a Christian invention, as some scholars have supposed, but was rooted in earlier Jewish language and imagery.[1] His main evidence comes from the *Testament of Joseph*, a Jewish text probably from the second century B.C.

O'Neill reasons, for example, that no Christian editor would have added the references to the Lamb of God to the Jewish *Testament of Joseph* 19, because doing so would presuppose two Messiahs (the lion and the lamb figures), a non-Christian tradition that would detract from Christ's preeminence in the work of salvation.

The ancient roots of *Testament of Joseph* 19 are further evident when that text is compared with the visions in 1 Nephi and related passages in the Book of Mormon:

1. The author of *Testament of Joseph* 19 learned of the coming Lamb in a dream. Lehi saw in a dream the same vision that Nephi saw, a vision featuring the Lamb of God (see 1 Nephi 11:1, 20–21, 24, 27–36).

2. *Testament of Joseph* 19 describes the scattering of the twelve tribes (compare 1 Nephi 10:12–13; 11:35–12:1).

3. Nephi and the author of *Testament of Joseph* 19 behold a virgin, mother of the Lamb (see 1 Nephi 11:13–21).

4. The "robe of fine linen" in *Testament of Joseph* 19 recalls the virgin's description in 1 Nephi 11:15 as "beautiful and fair" and the white robe in 1 Nephi 8:5 and 14:19.

5. The beautiful mother gives birth to a "spotless lamb" in *Testament of Joseph* 19 and to "the Son of God" in 1 Nephi 11:18.

6. In *Testament of Joseph* 19 the Lion (Judah?) was found on the Lamb's left hand and proved ineffective, leaving the Lamb to destroy the beast alone (compare 1 Nephi 11:31, 33; 14:13, 15).

7. Both texts prophesy that evil will be destroyed in the last days (see 1 Nephi 11:36; 13:37; 14:14–17).

8. In *Testament of Joseph* 19 the faithful rejoice and are exhorted by their father to keep the commandments of God, common themes in the Book of Mormon (see 1 Nephi 8:38; 2 Nephi 1:16; 2:30).

9. In *Testament of Joseph* 19 Joseph's posterity is to honor Judah and Levi, the Jews in Jerusalem (compare 1 Nephi 14:8; 2 Nephi 3:12; 29:4–6).

10. Both texts recognize that salvation through the Lamb will come "by grace" (2 Nephi 25:23), saving Gentiles and Israelites (see 1 Nephi 13:42–14:2) by taking away the "sin of the world" (*Testament of Joseph* 19; compare 1 Nephi 11:33).

When John the Baptist announced Christ's approach with the words "Behold the Lamb of God, which taketh away the sin of the world" (John 1:29), he was no doubt using a distinctive messianic title already familiar to the Jews of his day. Although modern Christian readers may consider Nephi's use of the phrase *Lamb of God* centuries before the Christian era to be anachronistic, the parallels between the Book of Mormon and *Testament of Joseph* 19 confirm O'Neill's position on the pre-Christian antiquity of the phrase. Thus John was not the first to use it in reference to Christ; and John and Nephi, as well as Isaiah, may have been drawing on earlier common sources.

Research by John W. Welch, originally published as a FARMS Update in Insights *(August 1998): 2.*

NOTE

1. See J. C. O'Neill, "The Lamb of God in the Testaments of the Twelve Patriarchs," *Journal for the Study of the New Testament* 2 (1979): 2–30. Reprinted in Craig A. Evans and Stanley E. Porter, eds., *New Testament Backgrounds* (Sheffield: Sheffield Academic Press, 1997), part of a series that collects the best articles from the first fifty issues (1978–93) of the *Journal for the Study of the New Testament*.

12

FURTHER LIGHT
ON ENALLAGE

"Thou rememberest the twelve apostles of the Lamb?
Behold they are they who shall judge the twelve
tribes of Israel; wherefore, the twelve ministers
of thy seed shall be judged of them; for ye are
of the house of Israel." (1 Nephi 12:9)

Recent experience suggests this brief addendum to my essay on *enallage* in the Book of Mormon.[1] As I have discussed in detail in that 1994 article, *enallage*, which is Greek for "interchange," refers to a syntactic device that is fairly common in the Old Testament, where an author intentionally shifts from the singular to the plural (or vice versa) for rhetorical effect. In that article I show that while there are difficulties involved in demonstrating the presence of enallage in the Book of Mormon, a careful reading of contextual and verbal clues reveals that enallage does indeed appear to exist in some passages.

One evening, I happened to be reading Genesis 17,[2] when I became intrigued by what I found in verses 9 through 13:

> [9] And God said unto Abraham, Thou shalt keep [*wᵉʾattāh . . . tišmōr*] my covenant therefore, thou, and thy seed after thee [*ʾattāh wᵉzarʿăḵā ʾăchăreyḵā*] in their generations. [10] This is my covenant, which ye shall keep [*tišmᵉrû*], between me and you [*ûḇênêḵem*] and thy seed after thee [*zarʿăḵā ʾăchăreyḵā*]; Every man child

among you *[lāḵem]* shall be circumcised. [11] And ye shall circumcise *[ûnᶜmaltem]* the flesh of your foreskin *[ᶜarlaṯᶜḵem]*; and it shall be a token of the covenant betwixt me and you *[ûḇênêḵem]*. [12] And he that is eight days old shall be circumcised among you *[lāḵem]*, every man child in your generations *[lᵉḏōrōṯêḵem]*, he that is born in the house, or bought with money of any stranger, which is not of thy seed *[mizzārᶜāḵā]*. [13] He that is born in thy house *[bêṯᶜḵā]*, and he that is bought with thy money *[kaśpᶜḵā]*, must needs be circumcised: and my covenant shall be in your flesh *[biḇsarᶜḵem]* for an everlasting covenant.

The distribution of the singular and plural forms in this passage is illustrated by the following table:

Verse	Singular Forms	Plural Forms
9	5	0
10	2	3
11	0	3
12	1	2
13	2	1

A trip to the library revealed that, while most commentators completely fail to mention this numerical variation, those who do mention it account for it in one of two ways. Some claim that the verses are in disarray, and that an earlier stratum of a more general nature has been swelled by a subsequent stratum of more explicit directives. Others, without actually using the term, see the numerical variation in these verses as an instance of enallage. Whether we see the passage as a unified composition or whether we see the priestly writer as incorporating into the passage a legal specification based on its "utterly impersonal legal style,"[3] the meaning of the finished version should be clear to us today. Although God was speaking to Abraham alone, when he describes the requirements of his covenant he changes to a plural form of address, so as vividly and directly to address not only Abraham, but also his posterity, as if they were actually present.

I must have read this passage at least a dozen times in English in the past, but I never before noticed the numerical variation in the English pronouns between the singular *th*-forms (as in "*thou* shalt keep my covenant") and the plural *y*-forms (as in "which *ye* shall keep"). Because in modern English *y*-forms have become invariable as to number, enallage is generally lost by modern English translations. Although it is discernible in the King James Version due to that version's use of archaic pronouns, my experience has been that most people simply do not see it in English (due to either a lack of familiarity with archaic pronouns or the invariability of modern *y*-forms as mentioned above). I personally find enallage to be more easily discernible in Hebrew, partly because the pronominal suffixes and other forms that indicate number in Hebrew fairly obviously differ from one another, but mostly because reading in Hebrew forces me to concentrate on even the smallest textual details.

While working on my article concerning enallage, I was actively searching for examples (working mostly in English and merely spot-checking items in Hebrew for the sake of efficiency); this was the first time that I happened to stumble across a biblical example of enallage in the original language, and I must say that I found the effect quite striking. So much so, in fact, that I thought it likely that over the course of time there would have been scribal pressure to singularize some of the unexpected plural forms. A quick look at the critical apparatus at the bottom of the page confirmed my suspicion, as the Septuagint in verse 10 suggests "*thou* shalt keep" [*tišmor*] rather than the plural "*ye* shall keep" [*tišmᵉrû*], so as to conform to the singular in verse 9.

The main thing I noticed about this passage was a pattern in verses 9 and 10 that particularly struck me because I had seen the same pattern in several verses of the Book of Mormon. In the first eight verses of Genesis 17, God is speaking to Abraham and establishing his covenant with him. The verbs in this section are for the most part first-person singulars (such as "I will make," "have I made thee," "I will make thee," "I will establish my covenant," "I will give unto thee," and "I will be their God"). In verse 9, the subject of the verbs shifts from a first-person singular "I" (referring to God) to a second-person singular "thou" (referring to Abraham) in "*thou* shalt keep my covenant." This shift is emphatic,[4] both because the Hebrew actually uses the second-person singular pronoun ʾattāh (which is not necessary here, because the person and number of the subject are defined in the form of the verb itself), and because the pronoun is repeated a second time following the verb. God then refers to Abraham's posterity in the third person, "and thy seed after thee in their generations." At this point Abraham's seed is associated with the verbal idea, but the verb is not repeated (if it had been, the form would have been third person). Finally, God addresses both Abraham and his seed together in the second-person plural: "which ye shall keep." Thus the pattern is as follows:

1. A divine being or a prophet directly addresses an individual.

2. He addresses the individual in the second-person singular, "thou."

3. He makes a third-person reference to that individual's posterity, "thy seed."

4. Finally, he directly addresses the individual and his posterity together in the second-person plural, "ye."

In my original article I listed a number of possible Book of Mormon examples of enallage.[5] As I studied this passage in Genesis 17, I realized that three of those Book of Mormon examples, 1 Nephi 12:9, 2 Nephi 1:31–32, and 2 Nephi

3:1–2, each follow this same pattern precisely. This may be illustrated by 1 Nephi 12:9:

> And he said unto me: *Thou* rememberest the twelve apostles of the Lamb? Behold they are they who shall judge the twelve tribes of Israel; wherefore, the twelve ministers of *thy seed* shall be judged of them; for *ye* are of the house of Israel.

In this passage, an angel is addressing Nephi in vision. He addresses Nephi in the second-person singular, "thou"; he makes a third-person reference to Nephi's posterity, "thy seed"; and then he directly addresses both Nephi and his posterity together in the second-person plural, "ye are of the house of Israel."[6]

This pattern may be represented by the following formula: thou + thy seed = ye. On the strength of the parallel usage in Genesis 17:9–10, I would suggest that those three Book of Mormon passages should be upgraded from possible to probable examples of enallage, and that (1) in 1 Nephi 12:9 the word *ye* is a plural referring not just to Nephi, but to Nephi and his posterity; (2) in 2 Nephi 1:31–32, the word *ye* is a plural referring not just to Zoram, but to Zoram, Nephi, and their respective posterities; and (3) in 2 Nephi 3:1–2, the word *ye* is a plural referring not just to Joseph, but to Joseph, his brethren, and their respective posterities.

Research by Kevin L. Barney, originally published in the Journal of Book of Mormon Studies *6/2 (1997): 229–34.*

NOTES

1. See Kevin L. Barney, "Enallage in the Book of Mormon," *Journal of Book of Mormon Studies* 3/1 (1994): 113–47.

2. My selection of Genesis 17 was not quite random. I had been researching Joseph Smith's experience in learning Hebrew,

and we know from his Ohio journal that Genesis 17 is one of the chapters the Prophet actually read in Hebrew. See Dean C. Jessee, ed., *The Papers of Joseph Smith* (Salt Lake City: Deseret Book, 1992), 2:186.

3. Claus Westermann, *Genesis 12–36: A Commentary* (Minneapolis: Augsburg, 1985), 264.

4. Such an emphasis is to be expected in covenantal language, which emphasizes the promises of the parties to each other. The sense may perhaps be captured by rendering "I, for my part" and "thou, for thy part."

5. See Barney, "Enallage," 142–43.

6. It is possible that the plural ye is meant to refer only to the twelve ministers, but logically the statement "ye are of the house of Israel" would apply not only to Nephi and the twelve ministers, but also to all Nephi's descendants. The point of these verses seems to be that, because Nephi's seed is of the house of Israel, his descendants shall be judged by the twelve apostles (directly, in the case of the twelve ministers, and indirectly, through the twelve ministers, in the case of the remainder of Nephi's seed). Monte S. Nyman writes about this in "The Judgment Seat of Christ," in *The Book of Mormon: Fourth Nephi through Moroni, from Zion to Destruction,* ed. Monte S. Nyman and Charles D. Tate Jr. (Provo, Utah: BYU Religious Studies Center, 1995), 202–4.

13

CONNECTIONS BETWEEN THE VISIONS OF LEHI AND NEPHI

"And I bear record that I saw the things which my father saw, and the angel of the Lord did make them known unto me." (1 Nephi 14:29)

Although a simple book in several respects, the Book of Mormon is also marvelously complex, as in the interconnections between several of its texts. No example of this phenomenon is more instructive than the case of Lehi's and Nephi's visions.

As reported in 1 Nephi 8, Lehi saw the tree of life, an iron rod, a great and spacious building, and various people reaching the tree or falling away. In 1 Nephi 11–14, Nephi beheld the condescension of God, the twelve apostles of the Lamb, wars between his posterity and the seed of his brothers, a great and abominable coalition of evil, and the eventual victory of God's people.

The two visions are very different in character. Lehi's dream is intimate, symbolic, and salvific; Nephi's vision is collective, historic, and eschatological. Yet both visions embrace the same prophetic elements, only from different angles. Consider the following:

Lehi's dream began in a dark and dreary wilderness (see 8:4) and Nephi's on a remote high mountain (see 11:1), and they both saw first a man who guided them into their visions. Lehi saw a man dressed in a white robe (see 8:5), and Nephi saw a Spirit who asked him introductory questions (see 11:2).

Next, the man in white left Lehi alone (see 8:7, original manuscript), and the Spirit likewise departed from Nephi (see 11:12).

Lehi next beheld a dark and dreary waste, causing him personally to pray for mercy (see 8:8). Nephi was historically more explicit: it was Jerusalem that he beheld (11:13), in need of mercy.

Lehi's vision quickly opened onto a large and spacious field (see 8:9), and then onto the symbolically rich tree of life (see 8:10). Nephi too focused next on the tree, giving its meaning in terms of Jesus Christ (see 11:7, 13–18, 20–25). Lehi saw that its fruit was "desirable to make one happy" (8:10), sweet and white above all (see 8:11); and Nephi similarly recognized the tree and its fruit as the love of God, "most desirable" (11:22), "most beautiful and fair" (11:15).

As Lehi's soul filled with joy (see 8:12), and Nephi was "carried away in the Spirit" (11:19); Lehi's attention was drawn to the head of a river near the tree (see 8:14), while Nephi spoke of a "fountain of living waters" (11:25).

Lehi's intimate attention was on his family, to whom he called with a "loud voice" (8:15). At the same place in the sequence, Nephi's focus was on the broader human family and the preaching of Jesus Christ, John, and the apostles (see 11:24–31). While Lehi saw that some came and partook of the fruit, Laman and Lemuel did not (see 8:17–18), just as Nephi saw that people would reject the Christ (see 11:32–33).

Both then mentioned the "rod of iron" (8:19; 11:25). For Lehi it extended along the straight and narrow path (see 8:20), which for Nephi was "the word of God" (15:24) and seems to correspond intentionally with the apostles' preaching (see 11:34).

A "large and spacious field" (8:20) next correlates

with a great and spacious building (see 11:35), making Lehi's numberless concourses (see 8:21) the same as Nephi's multitudes as numerous as sand (see 12:1). Lehi and Nephi both continued by mentioning the mist or mists of darkness (see 8:23; 12:17) that cause these people to lose their way and become lost on broad roads (see 8:23; 12:17).

In both cases, however, others came to the tree and partook of its fruit (see 8:24). Lehi left these people unidentified, but at the same place in the vision Nephi mentioned the four generations that lived in righteousness after the coming of Christ to the Nephites at Bountiful (see 12:10–12).

A river divided the righteous from the wicked in Lehi's vision (see 8:26). In more ominous detail, Nephi detailed the great gulf that divides them (see 12:18). And on the other side, both prophets saw a "great and spacious" building (8:26; see also 12:18). Lehi noted the fine dress and mocking attitude of its inhabitants (see 8:27); Nephi, their pride and vain imaginations (see 12:18). Lehi concluded this segment with the fact that these people fell away (see 8:28); Nephi told how the good were overpowered (see 12:19).

At this point in Lehi's vision the record is interrupted; we do not know what was omitted here (see 8:29). But at this place in Nephi's vision we learn of the painful prospect of war between the seed of Lehi (see 12:20–23).

Lehi's vision continued on the happier prospect that other multitudes would partake of the tree (see 8:30), just as Nephi turned his attention to the coming of the gospel among the Gentiles (see 13:1–3).

Soon, however, Lehi saw multitudes going to the great and spacious building (see 8:31), and Nephi charted the rise of the great and abominable church (see 13:4–9). This all suggests that the great and spacious building was the same as the great and abominable church.

Adding a unique historical section to this revelation, Nephi then spoke at length about the restoration of Lehi's seed through a great and marvelous work (see 13:10–14:7), in contradistinction to the great and abominable.

Finally, both visions ended with the vanquishing of evil. Lehi spoke generally of the wicked being drowned in the depths of the river or becoming lost in strange roads (see 8:32), and Nephi expressed it eschatologically as the whore upon the waters (see 14:11) rising in wars and chaos (see 14:16) and ultimately being defeated by God.

If this comparison is sound, it leads to several intriguing conclusions. Obviously, Nephi meant what he said when he testified that he had seen the same things his father saw (see 14:29). When we set these two visions side by side, they are indeed significantly the same, element for element. Although the casual reader might not see any connection between these two texts at first, the correlation between them is extensive and precise. It is unlikely that this occurred accidentally. Nephi was well aware of his father's vision, so much so that he desired "to behold the things which [his] father saw" (11:3). As different as these two visions may appear at first glance, Nephi clearly and correctly bore record "that I saw the things which my father saw" (14:29). Thus Nephi spoke from personal experience when he subsequently interpreted the meanings of the tree, the iron rod, and the river of water in his father's vision (see 15:21–29).

At the same time, Nephi's vision is not a mere rerun of Lehi's. The second clearly develops each element of the first, from different perspectives and for different purposes. Nevertheless, it is hard to imagine that Joseph Smith or others at first were aware of the nature or extent of this development, because the styles of the two texts are so different.

Further analysis will shed additional light on these texts, but for now it is evident that the interrelatedness of 1 Nephi 8 and 1 Nephi 11–14 is very meaningful, subtle, and true as life.

Research by John W. Welch, originally published as a FARMS Update in Insights *(July 1993): 2. For a chart comparing Lehi's dream with Nephi's vision, see John W. Welch and J. Gregory Welch,* Charting the Book of Mormon: Visual Aids for Personal Study and Teaching *(Provo, Utah: FARMS, 1999), chart 89.*

14

THE EXODUS OF LEHI REVISITED

"Do ye suppose that they would have been led out of
bondage, if the Lord had not commanded Moses that
he should lead them out of bondage? . . . Wherefore,
the Lord commanded my father that he should depart
into the wilderness." (1 Nephi 17:24, 44)

In the past decade, there have been many reports on what
has been called the "Exodus Pattern" in the Book of
Mormon.[1] Although these reports have been fairly comprehensive, I feel a few points have been missed. To the numerous comparisons that have been made between the exodus
of the children of Israel out of Egypt and the exodus made
by the Lehites from Jerusalem, such as the divine call of the
leader accompanied by fire, the deliverance of the people on
the other side of a water barrier, the extended wandering,
and the complaints and rebellion, I would like to add two
additional parallels. The first deals with death in the desert
and the second with transfiguration.

The Burial of Ishmael

In 1952, Hugh Nibley first pointed out the significance
of the name *Nahom* in relationship to the death of Ishmael.[2]
He also mentioned the importance of Ishmael's daughters
mourning his loss. What also becomes apparent is that, by
the way Ishmael is buried in the desert, they (the Lehites)
are following in the footsteps of their fathers (the children

of Israel under Moses). Let us examine, side by side, two accounts of death and burial in the desert:

And it came to pass that Ishmael died, and was buried in the place which was called Nahom. (1 Nephi 16:34)

And the bones of Joseph, which the children of Israel brought up out of Egypt, buried they in Shechem, in a parcel of ground which Jacob bought. (Joshua 24:32)

I feel that it is most likely that Ishmael died well before (possibly weeks or even months) the Lehites arrived at Nahom. Dr. Nibley points out it is not uncommon for desert people to carry their dead many miles to locate the proper place of burial.[3] Just as Joseph was buried in a special parcel of land, it seems only natural that the Lehites would wait until they found a proper place to bury Ishmael.

In their report to FARMS, Warren and Michaela Aston show that the place of Nahom is a few miles off the main trail that the Lehites took.[4] It is unlikely that they would go out of their way unless it was rather important. Surely, one thing that would make them go out of their way would be the death of a loved one. It is important to note, as do the Astons, that Nahom already existed and was already a place of burial.[5] The chances seem slim that Ishmael would die as the party arrived at Nahom. The logical conclusion is that Ishmael died along the way and was carried to Nahom.

We cannot conclude whether the Lehites were aware of the parallels to the Exodus as they were reenacting them, although it appears that Nephi did at least thirty years later.[6] We can be sure that, like the children of Israel, they honored their patriarchs and also were following ancient ritual in burying their dead.

The Transfiguration of Nephi

Bruce R. McConkie defines transfiguration as "a special change in appearance and nature which is wrought upon a person . . . by the power of God."[7] Let us examine two accounts of transfiguration in the desert.

And it came to pass that I, Nephi, said many things unto *my brethren,* insomuch that they were confounded and could not contend against me; neither durst *they lay their hands upon me nor touch me with their fingers,* even for the space of many days. Now they durst not do this lest they should wither before me, *so powerful was the Spirit of God;* and thus it had wrought upon them. (1 Nephi 17:52)	And when *Aaron* and all the children of Israel saw Moses, behold, the *skin of his face shone;* and *they were afraid to come nigh him.* (Exodus 34:30)

It is interesting to note that in both instances the literal brothers of Moses and Nephi witnessed the transfiguration. Both sets of brethren weren't quite sure what to make out of the situation. Aaron was afraid to go to Moses while Nephi's brothers were shocked by the power of the Lord which was in him (see 1 Nephi 17:54).

In both accounts, the effect of the power of God upon mortal flesh is detailed. Moses's skin shone while Nephi mentions that he was "filled with the power of God, even to the consuming of my flesh" (1 Nephi 17:48). Nephi was indeed transfigured by the Lord and therefore was able to better understand Moses's situation. In fact, Nephi gives a powerful sermon on the symbolism of the exodus of the children of Israel just prior to his state of transfiguration.

We find that the parallels between the exodus of Israel from Egypt and the departure of Lehi from Jerusalem are numerous. Through these parallels we are able to understand the mentality of the Lehites as they emulated the children of Israel. We also can better recognize the hand of the Lord in guiding his covenant people.

Research by Mark J. Johnson, originally published in the Journal of Book of Mormon Studies *3/2 (1994): 123–26. For a chart comparing the exodus of the children of Israel from Egypt with the exodus of Lehi, see John W. Welch and J. Gregory Welch,* Charting the Book of Mormon: Visual Aids for Personal Study and Teaching *(Provo, Utah: FARMS, 1999), chart 91.*

NOTES

1. The exodus from Egypt is a "type" of God's deliverance. The comparison between Lehi's deliverance from the Babylonian captivity and the Israelites' deliverance from Egypt is specifically mentioned in 1 Nephi 17:23–43 and Alma 36:28–29. On the exodus motif in the Book of Mormon generally, see George S. Tate, "The Typology of the Exodus Pattern in the Book of Mormon," in *Literature of Belief,* ed. Neal E. Lambert (Provo: Religious Studies Center Monograph Series, 1978); Terrence L. Szink, "Nephi and the Exodus," in *Rediscovering the Book of Mormon,* ed. John L. Sorenson and Melvin J. Thorne (Salt Lake City: Deseret Book and FARMS, 1991), 38–51; S. Kent Brown, "The Exodus: Seeing It as a Test, a Testimony, and a Type," *Ensign* (February 1990): 54–57; S. Kent Brown, "The Exodus Pattern in the Book of Mormon," *BYU Studies* 30/3 (1990): 111–26; and "Nephi and the Exodus," *Ensign* (April 1987): 64–65.

2. See Hugh W. Nibley, *Lehi in the Desert; World of the Jaredites; There Were Jaredites* (Salt Lake City: Deseret Book and FARMS, 1988), 79.

3. See Ibid.

4. See Warren P. Aston and Michaela Knoth Aston, "The Place Which Was Called Nahom: The Validation of an Ancient Reference to Southern Arabia" (FARMS, 1991); see Aston and Aston, *In the Footsteps of Lehi: New Evidence for Lehi's Journey across Arabia to Bountiful* (Salt Lake City: Deseret Book, 1994); and Noel B. Reynolds, "Lehi's Arabian Journey Updated," in *Book of Mormon Authorship Revisited*, ed. Noel B. Reynolds (Provo, Utah: FARMS, 1997), 379–89.

5. See Ibid., 10.

6. For further discussion, see Bruce J. Boehm, "Wanderers in the Promised Land: A Study of the Exodus Motif in the Book of Mormon and Holy Bible," *Journal of Book of Mormon Studies* 3/1 (1994): 189–90.

7. Bruce R. McConkie, *Mormon Doctrine* (Salt Lake City: Bookcraft, 1994), 803.

15

THE BOOK OF LEHI AND THE PLATES OF LEHI

"And upon the plates which I made I did engraven the record of my father." (1 Nephi 19:1)

In the preface to the 1830 edition of the Book of Mormon, Joseph Smith wrote that the lost 116 pages included his translation of "the Book of Lehi, which was an account abridged from the plates of Lehi, by the hand of Mormon." However, in Doctrine and Covenants 10:44, the Lord told Joseph that the lost pages contained "an abridgment of the account of Nephi." Some critics have argued that these statements are contradictory and therefore somehow provide evidence that Joseph Smith was not a prophet. However, a more careful reading of the Book of Mormon demonstrates that this criticism is invalid.

The description of the lost pages as "an abridgment of the account of Nephi" is clearly accurate. Nephi wrote that he made his large plates so that he could "engraven upon them the record of [his] people" (1 Nephi 19:1). The phrase *account of Nephi* acknowledges Nephi as the principal author and copyist of this portion of the large plates, as well as the maker of those plates. This account of Nephi was later abridged by Mormon, whose abridgment was translated by Joseph Smith; the translation was ultimately lost.

At first, the reference to "the plates of Lehi" appears to be in error. However, although he may not have personally engraved his record upon Nephi's large plates, Lehi was in a very real sense the first author of those plates. Nephi gave the following description of the contents of the large plates: "And upon the plates which I made I did engraven the record of my father, and also our journeyings in the wilderness, and the prophecies of my father; and also many of mine own prophecies have I engraven upon them" (1 Nephi 19:1). First on Nephi's list is the record of his father. In contrast to the small plates, on which Nephi made an abridgment of the record of his father (see 1 Nephi 1:17), the large plates apparently contained the full record of Lehi.[1] Nephi probably copied his father's record onto the large plates of Nephi in the same way that he later copied the Isaiah chapters from the brass plates onto the small plates of Nephi.[2]

If the large plates of Nephi began with Lehi's record, this portion of the large plates could accurately be called the plates of Lehi. In fact, Lehi's son Jacob confirmed such a practice when he wrote: "These plates are called the plates of Jacob, and they were made by the hand of Nephi" (Jacob 3:14). In other words, although Nephi made the small plates of Nephi, the portion of the small plates that contained the record of Jacob was referred to as the "plates of Jacob." In the same way, although Nephi made the large plates of Nephi and wrote on them, the portion of the large plates upon which he copied the record of Lehi was referred to as the "plates of Lehi." Therefore, Mormon's abridgment of Lehi's record found on the large plates could accurately be described as an account abridged from the plates of Lehi, by the hand of Mormon.

According to the preface to the 1830 edition of the Book of Mormon, Mormon gave the title "the Book of Lehi" to his abridgment of the plates of Lehi. This action is consistent with Mormon's practice throughout his abridgment of the large plates, in which he frequently grouped multiple authors together in a single book and then named the book after the first author. For example, although the death of Helaman is recorded near the beginning of the book of Helaman (see 3:37), and Helaman's sons Nephi and Lehi were therefore the source of the majority of Mormon's abridgment,[3] the book still bears Helaman's name. Similarly, because Nephi's large plates began with his father Lehi's record, it should not surprise us that Mormon entitled his abridgment of this portion of the large plates "the Book of Lehi."[4]

In conclusion, the terms *Book of Lehi, plates of Lehi,* and *account of Nephi* are distinct phrases with distinct meanings.[5] As usual, both Joseph Smith and the Book of Mormon demonstrate complete internal consistency in their use of these different terms.

Research by David E. Sloan, originally published in the Journal of Book of Mormon Studies *6/2 (1997): 269–72.*

NOTES

1. See S. Kent Brown, "Nephi's Use of Lehi's Record," in *Rediscovering the Book of Mormon,* ed. John L. Sorenson and Melvin J. Thorne (Salt Lake City: Deseret Book and FARMS, 1991), 3–5. Either way, Lehi's record would have come to us in abridged form. The translation of the small plates includes Nephi's abridgment of Lehi's record. The lost pages contained Mormon's abridgment of that record.

2. The fact that Nephi copied his father's record onto metal plates suggests that Lehi's record was written on perishable material rather than on more durable plates. See Brown, "Nephi's Use of Lehi's Record," 5. Nephi's brother Jacob wrote:

"Whatsoever things we write upon anything save it be upon plates must perish and vanish away" (Jacob 4:2).

3. Although Helaman's eldest son, Nephi, was probably the custodian of the Nephite records (see Helaman 3:37), ultimately passing them on to his own son Nephi (see 3 Nephi 1:2), Helaman's son Lehi also apparently participated in the writing of the records. The preface to the book of Helaman records that the abridgment is an account which is "according to the records of Helaman" and is "also according to the records of his sons" (see also Helaman 16:25).

4. Another example of this practice is found in the book of Omni, in which Omni's son Amaron wrote: "And now I, Amaron, write the things whatsoever I write, which are few, in the book of my father" (Omni 1:4).

5. In addition to Lehi's record, the book of Lehi may have included some or all of Mormon's abridgment of Nephi's writings on the large plates. At the same time, in addition to the personal record of Nephi, the term *account of Nephi* may include Lehi's record that Nephi copied onto the large plates.

16

FIRSTBORN IN THE WILDERNESS

"Thou art my first-born in the days of my
tribulation in the wilderness." (2 Nephi 2:1)

In their book, *Fathers and Sons in the Book of Mormon,*
E. Douglas Clark and Robert S. Clark maintain that Lehi
named his sons Jacob and Joseph after their distant ancestors, in much the same manner that Helaman the Younger
named his sons Lehi and Nephi (see Helaman 5:5–7).[1] The
fact that Lehi referred to the patriarchal founder of his tribe
when blessing his own son Joseph lends credence to this
idea (see 2 Nephi 3). But there seems to be more to the story.

Lehi called Jacob "my first-born in the days of my
tribulation in the wilderness" (2 Nephi 2:1–2). The tribu-
lations Lehi suffered in the wilderness were brought on
principally by the disobedience of Laman and Lemuel
(see 1 Nephi 2:11–13, 18, 21; 3:5, 28; 7:6–7, 16–19; 15:2–5;
16:20, 22, 35–39; 17:17–22, 45; 18:17–18). The use of the
term *firstborn* implies that Lehi may have considered
Jacob to be a replacement for his eldest son, Laman, with
his younger son Joseph being a replacement for the second son, Lemuel.

We have a parallel to this situation in Genesis 48:5, 16,
where Jacob adopted Joseph's sons Manasseh and Ephraim
in place of Reuben and Simeon, who had sinned (see Genesis

34:30; 35:22; 49:3–5). In consequence of Reuben's sins, he was replaced as firstborn by Joseph (see 1 Chronicles 5:1–2).

Another parallel is found in Genesis 4:25, where we read, "And Adam knew his wife again; and she bare a son, and called his name Seth [Hebrew *shet*]: For God, said she, hath appointed [Hebrew *shat*] me another seed instead of Abel, whom Cain slew." In this case, we should perhaps understand Seth to mean "replacement." (Similarly, Abel [Hebrew *habel*] may derive from the Semitic root reflected in Arabic as *hbl*, referring to a woman bereft of a son.)

The name Jacob is explained as "supplanter" in the King James Bible of Genesis 27:36 (compare 25:23–26), but could just as easily be read "successor" or "replacement," since Jacob replaced Esau as firstborn and received the birthright and the blessing (see Genesis 25:29–34; 27:22–40). Esau was unfit to serve as firstborn. In Hebrews 12:16, he is called a "fornicator" and a "profane person." He sought Jacob's life, waiting only for the death of his father to proceed with his plan (see Genesis 27:41). Similarly, after the death of Lehi, Laman and Lemuel sought the life of their brother Nephi, who fled with Jacob, Joseph, and others (see 2 Nephi 5:1–6). It was because of their "rudeness" that Laman and Lemuel were unfit to succeed their father as head of the family. Though "rude" has come to mean "impolite" in twentieth-century English, at the time Joseph Smith translated the Book of Mormon it meant "wild" or "savage."[2] Lehi made a point of mentioning the effect of the rudeness of Laman and Lemuel on Jacob (see 2 Nephi 2:1), as did Nephi, who referred to the "afflictions" caused by his elder brothers (1 Nephi 18:9, 19).

Lehi termed Joseph "my last-born . . . born in the wilderness of mine afflictions" and spoke to him of his inheritance in the New World, calling it "a most precious land" (2 Nephi 3:1–2). He then went on to speak of their common ancestor, Joseph, who had been sold into Egypt (see 2 Nephi 3:4). The original Joseph was the last-born son of the patriarch Jacob (Israel) before he returned to the land promised to him (see Genesis 28:13–15). It is significant, therefore, that Lehi's son Joseph was born in the wilderness, then went, as his ancestor Joseph, with his father to a land of promise.

While Lehi may have considered Jacob and Joseph to be replacements for the fallen Laman and Lemuel, he did not give the right of the firstborn to Jacob. That blessing fell to Nephi, to whom Jacob and Joseph were to look for leadership (see 1 Nephi 2:21–22; 3:29; 2 Nephi 2:3; 3:25; 5:19–20).

Research by John A. Tvedtnes, originally published in the Journal of Book of Mormon Studies *3/1 (1994): 207–9.*

NOTES

1. E. Douglas Clark and Robert S. Clark, *Fathers and Sons in the Book of Mormon* (Salt Lake City: Deseret Book, 1991), 32–35, 181–82.

2. See the description of Laman and Lemuel's "rudeness" and its effects on Jacob and Joseph in 1 Nephi 18:9–19.

17

SAM: A JUST AND HOLY MAN

"[Lehi] spake unto Sam, saying: Blessed art
thou, and thy seed; for thou shalt inherit the
land like unto thy brother Nephi." (2 Nephi 4:11)

Some of the most notable people in the Book of Mormon are the prophets and men of God: Lehi, Nephi, Jacob, Alma, Mormon, and Moroni. But many others are mentioned in the Book of Mormon of whom we know little. Some of these are witnesses to great events; however, because they are not main characters in the event, they are only mentioned in passing. One of these lesser-known individuals is Nephi's older brother Sam.

Though Sam is mentioned quite often in the first two books of Nephi, we have only the barest sketch of him as a person. This would not seem out of the ordinary except when we realize that Sam was witness to early Nephite history. Almost every hardship and adventure that Lehi's family went through—leaving Jerusalem, obtaining the brass plates, voyaging across the ocean, settling the new land—were probably also experienced by Sam. Yet how much do we know of him? Let's explore the few verses that mention him specifically and those that imply his presence, and from these come to a better understanding of the man called "just and holy" (Alma 3:6) in the book of Alma.

We know nothing of Sam's childhood, nor do we know how old he was when the events in 1 Nephi began.[1] It has been conjectured that Nephi was in his midteens when his family left Jerusalem.[2] If so, then Sam must have been in his late teens (or early twenties).[3] We can safely assume Sam was given the same parental care and training as Nephi. Sam was probably also taught "somewhat in all the learning of [his] father" (1 Nephi 1:1): languages, customs (see v. 2), vocational and survival skills, and spiritual training.

Sam would also have known, as Nephi did, of the prophets who came "prophesying unto the people that they must repent, or the great city Jerusalem must be destroyed" (1 Nephi 1:4; compare v. 13). As Lehi taught his family, Sam would have learned of the "many things which [Lehi] saw in visions and in dreams" and the "many things which [Lehi] prophesied and spake"—particularly since Nephi writes that Lehi "spake unto his children" of these things (1 Nephi 1:16). Most difficult of all, Sam would have known that the "Jews did mock" his father and sought his father's life (1 Nephi 1:19–20). Sam was also no doubt an important part of the preparation for Lehi's exodus into the desert (a familiarity gained, perhaps, from previous desert journeys)[4] and was part of the caravan that plodded across the desert for eight years. As the division between Nephi and his two oldest brothers widened, it is interesting to consider what influence the two older brothers, Laman and Lemuel, might have tried to exert over Sam. Imagine how Laman and Lemuel must have constantly urged Sam to follow them and their ways, not to listen to their younger brother, and to remember that the oldest is the rightful heir of all the father has. One of Sam's greatest trials must have been resisting the example and enticements of Laman and Lemuel and, instead, finding the faith and courage to follow Nephi.

Though the journey had barely begun in 1 Nephi 2:8–10, already we find Lehi cautioning Laman and Lemuel because of their "stiffneckedness" (1 Nephi 2:11). Yet no mention is made of a word of warning to Sam; it appears that Sam had made righteous decisions early in life. This is further confirmed in 1 Nephi 2:16–17, where we read of Nephi's cry: "I did cry unto the Lord; and behold he did visit me." Significantly, Nephi first shares this experience with his brother Sam. From this, one can deduce a special relationship of trust between these two brothers.

In 1 Nephi 3:1–4, we read of Lehi's dream commanding Nephi and his brethren to return to Jerusalem to get Laban's records. Sam is obviously one of the "brethren," but is he also among the "brothers" who murmur in 1 Nephi 3:5? We do not know, but it would not be extraordinary if he did so—Lehi and Sariah murmured (see 1 Nephi 16:20; 5:2–3). However, if Sam murmured, it doesn't appear to be for long, for in 1 Nephi 3:28, Nephi writes that "Laman and Lemuel did speak many hard words unto *us*, their younger brothers, and they did smite *us* even with a rod." Sam is verbally and physically abused along with his younger brother Nephi. Yet, oddly enough, the angel who stops Laman and Lemuel mentions only the abuse of Nephi (see 1 Nephi 3:29). We do not know if this is an intentional omission in the record or not.

In 1 Nephi 7:1–3, Nephi and his brothers again return to Jerusalem to get Ishmael and his family. All goes well on the trip to Jerusalem, but on the journey back into the desert, Laman, Lemuel, and others rebel against Nephi, Sam, Ishmael, his wife, and three of Ishmael's daughters. Two things in this rebellion are noteworthy. First, Sam is mentioned as being on Nephi's side (see 1 Nephi 7:6). Sam is spiritually strong enough that he can stand with Nephi during the rebellion. The second item is a bit more enigmatic.

In verse 16, after the rebels have been called to repentance, Nephi's brothers "did bind [Nephi] with cords, for they sought to take away [his] life." One cannot help but wonder where Sam is during this event. Is it simply a matter of being outnumbered? Is Sam restrained in some way? The record does not mention what Sam does, only that the problem is ultimately diffused by pleading from Ishmael's family.

The next mention of Sam is from Lehi, who says, "I have reason to rejoice in the Lord because of Nephi and *also of Sam*; for I have reason to suppose that they, and also many of their seed, will be saved" (1 Nephi 8:3). And in verse 14 of the same chapter, Lehi reports that he "beheld . . . Sariah, and Sam, and Nephi"; he beckons to them, and they come and "partake of the fruit also" (1 Nephi 8:16). Sam has made and will continue to make right choices, and his efforts will bring him salvation.

The next few recorded episodes are unfortunately silent about Sam and his role:

- In 1 Nephi 15:2, is Sam part of the "brethren" who are "disputing one with another concerning the things which [their] father had spoke unto them"? Is he one of those who later "humble themselves before the Lord" (1 Nephi 16:5)?

- In 1 Nephi 16:20, has Sam learned his lessons well enough not to murmur? He is not mentioned as being among those who complain because of Nephi's broken bow.

- In 1 Nephi 17:17–18, Nephi is silent about Sam's part in this ship-building incident. Did he have other duties to attend to? Was he just not around for this?

- In 1 Nephi 18:9, is Sam part of this group that "began to make themselves merry"? Where is he when Nephi is tied up? Does he try to help Nephi but is stopped?

The next reference to Sam is found in 2 Nephi 1:28: Lehi admonishes him, along with Laman and Lemuel and the sons of Ishmael to "hearken unto the voice of Nephi." As we find in Lehi's final patriarchal blessing of Sam's family, Sam takes Lehi's exhortation to heart. In 2 Nephi 4:11, Lehi blesses Sam, and though the blessing is short, it is very powerful. Sam is told that he and his posterity shall "inherit the land like unto thy brother Nephi"—implying that all Nephi's blessings can be Sam's. This blessing also implies that Nephi is receiving a double portion of inheritance— just as his ancestor Joseph did through Ephraim and Manasseh[5]—and that Sam and his descendants are to be the second half of that double portion. Sam is told his "seed shall be numbered with [Nephi's] seed"[6] and he is to "be even like unto thy brother [Nephi], . . . and thou shalt be blessed in all thy days" (2 Nephi 4:11). Sam must have rejoiced at this great blessing.

The last we read of Sam in the plates of Nephi is found during the time that the Lord warns Nephi that he should flee from his murderous brothers. Second Nephi 5:6 declares that "Sam, [Nephi's] elder brother and his family," are part of those who have chosen to go with Nephi. Nephi's feelings would have been bittersweet: heartbroken over the wickedness of Laman and Lemuel but joyful over Sam's righteousness. We last see Sam as he embarks on his journey into the wilderness with Nephi. From then on, Sam and his descendants are literally, as prophesied by Lehi, numbered with Nephi's seed.

One further reference to Sam in the Book of Mormon is found in Alma 3:6. Mormon, in writing of the Lamanites' wickedness, says they were cursed because of their transgression and rebellion against Nephi, Jacob, Joseph, and Sam, "who were just and holy men." These four of the original six brothers in Lehi's family are described as holy and just men—men who are fair and treat others with consideration and who follow God and are sanctified by their efforts. This is the Sam that we should come to appreciate and remember.

Research by Ken Haubrock, originally published in the Journal of Book of Mormon Studies *5/2 (1996): 164–68.*

NOTES

1. See Hugh W. Nibley, *An Approach to the Book of Mormon,* 3rd ed. (Salt Lake City: Deseret Book and FARMS, 1988), 76, indicates that Sam's name has Egyptian roots and that Sam was probably "born in the days of [Lehi's] prosperity" (p. 77).

2. See Rodney Turner, "The Prophet Nephi," in *The Book of Mormon: First Nephi, the Doctrinal Foundation,* ed. Monte S. Nyman and Charles D. Tate Jr. (Provo, Utah: BYU Religious Studies Center, 1988), 81–82.

3. See John L. Sorenson, "The Composition of Lehi's Family," in *By Study and Also by Faith: Essays in Honor of Hugh W. Nibley,* ed. John M. Lundquist and Stephen D. Ricks (Salt Lake City: Deseret Book and FARMS, 1990), 2:193.

4. For further information about Lehi's familiarity with the desert, see Nibley, *An Approach to the Book of Mormon,* 76–82.

5. See Genesis 48:5–6 and Deuteronomy 21:17. Using the latter verse, we can infer that Lehi, in his blessing, has purposefully supplanted Laman with Nephi by giving Nephi a double portion of inheritance as is the firstborn's (Laman) right.

6. John Welch comments on this verse that "Sam would not have a separate tribal interest. . . . Consequently, there are . . . never any Samites [in the Book of Mormon]." John W. Welch, "Lehi's Last Will and Testament: A Legal Approach," in *The Book of Mormon: Second Nephi, the Doctrinal Structure,* ed. Monte S. Nyman and Charles D. Tate Jr. (Provo, Utah: BYU Religious Studies Center, 1989), 72.

18

THE PSALM OF NEPHI
AS A POST-LEHI DOCUMENT

"And it came to pass after my father, Lehi, had spoken unto all his household, according to the feelings of his heart and the Spirit of the Lord which was in him, he waxed old. And it came to pass that he died, and was buried." (2 Nephi 4:12)

Nephi's masterful meditation in 2 Nephi 4:16–35, known today as the Psalm of Nephi, stands in 2 Nephi immediately after the death and burial of Lehi. Nephi's words have universal import, but they become even more poignant and vivid if we recognize that this psalm was written while Nephi was feeling painfully vulnerable after losing his father.

Shortly after blessing his posterity, Lehi died in the land of first inheritance (2 Nephi 4:12). "Not many days" later, Laman, Lemuel, and the sons of Ishmael became extremely angry with Nephi (2 Nephi 4:13; 5:1–2). Nephi's lament that he was "angry because of mine enemy" (2 Nephi 4:27, 29) refers most directly to his rebellious brothers, his only known "enemies," who, as the psalm recalls, had once been "confounded" and made "to quake before" Nephi (2 Nephi 4:22; see 1 Nephi 17:52–54). As tensions between the brothers mounted again at this time, Nephi hoped for deliverance once more.

In his psalm, Nephi rejoiced that God had preserved him "upon the waters of the great deep" (2 Nephi 4:20).

These words recall the group's safe voyage as well as Nephi's personal deliverance from his brothers' evil designs toward him. In previous conflicts with his brothers, Nephi could count on Lehi's emotional support; but after Lehi's death, Nephi had to muster courage on his own, and thus his psalm speaks strongly in the first person: "My God hath been my support; he hath led me. . . . He hath heard my cry by day, and he hath given me knowledge by visions in the nighttime" (2 Nephi 4:20, 23).

With Lehi dead, every report in the small plates account that likens Nephi to Lehi (e.g., 1 Nephi 14:29; 17:44) takes on new significance. Every prophecy that Nephi would become a ruler over his brothers, every comment about his brothers' wickedness, and every prediction of the downfall of his brothers' posterity helps position Nephi as Lehi's rightful and righteous successor. Accordingly, Nephi's psalm reinforces several links between Nephi and his deceased father. Just as Lehi had seen visions, so had Nephi (1 Nephi 1:8; 2 Nephi 4:23). Just as angels had appeared to Lehi, so they had ministered to Nephi (1 Nephi 1:11; 2 Nephi 4:24). And just as Lehi had praised God's mercy, so had Nephi (1 Nephi 1:14; 2 Nephi 4:26).

Most of all, Nephi's heartfelt psalm reflects the deep sorrow he felt at the time he composed it (2 Nephi 4:17, 19). While he redirected this grief by speaking of his own "iniquities" (2 Nephi 4:17), it would have been the death of his father that would have made him feel his own mortality and inadequacies so keenly.

Knowing that Lehi's soul slumbered, Nephi included several powerful couplets emphasizing the reawakening atonement of the Lord. He exclaims, "Awake, my soul!" (2 Nephi 4:28). He praises God, "the rock of my salvation," and pleads, "O Lord, wilt thou redeem my soul?" (2 Nephi 4:30, 31).

Nephi ended his psalm with strong assurances that God would also deliver him from his enemies (2 Nephi 4:31, 33). After his father's death, Nephi knew he would have to rely on God alone as he confronted the challenges of securing peace and prosperity for his people (2 Nephi 4:34).

It is a great tribute to the spirituality of Nephi that he could deal with such hardships and mourning by marshaling increased faith in God. The small plates were written to fill many needs that arose after Lehi's death. Nephi's psalm is particularly at home in that post-Lehi context.

Research by John W. Welch, originally published as a FARMS Update in Insights *(June 1999): 2.*

19

WHEN DID NEPHI WRITE THE SMALL PLATES?

"And it came to pass that the Lord God said unto me: Make other plates." (2 Nephi 5:30)

In reading 1 and 2 Nephi, few people stop to think when Nephi actually wrote the account of his family's flight from Jerusalem and journey across the sea to a land of promise. Knowing when Nephi began to write the small plates (beginning with the account we now have in 1 Nephi) clarifies the purposes that stand behind that record and influenced its final form and content.

Nephi's first set of plates were his large plates, fashioned after his arrival in the New World (1 Nephi 19:1–2). On these plates he recorded the book of Lehi and the secular affairs of his people.

Nephi made the small plates even later, after he had left the land of first inheritance and moved to the land of Nephi. The Lord instructed Nephi to make these plates so he could "engraven many things . . . which are good in my sight, for the profit of thy people" (2 Nephi 5:30). Thus the small plates should be understood as having been written after the death of Lehi, after the separation of Nephi from his brothers Laman and Lemuel, after the small Nephite party knew of the life-threatening animosity of the Lamanites against them, after Nephi knew that he would eventually accept the role of king, and after the temple of Nephi had been constructed.

We tend to read 1 Nephi as if it were a daily journal, but it is a reminiscent, retrospective account and a purposeful revision of the earlier book of Lehi and the other words previously recorded on the large plates. This matter of timing was important enough to Nephi that he stated three times in 1 Nephi that he was writing the small plates somewhat late in his life.

As early as in 1 Nephi 6:1, Nephi openly acknowledged that the small plates were being written after he knew what the book of Lehi contained. The book of Lehi would have been finished after Lehi and Nephi arrived in the New World.

In 1 Nephi 9, Nephi distinguished his small plates from the large plates, "upon which I make a full account of the history of my people" (verse 2), and explained that he had already been commanded to make the small plates so they might contain "an account engraven of the ministry of my people" (verse 3). From this we can confirm that Nephi began writing the small plates after the large plates were well under way—after the reign of kings was established, after Nephi received the Lord's commandment mentioned in 2 Nephi 5:30, and after he had a distinct group of people whom he could call (five times in this short chapter) "my people."

In 1 Nephi 19, Nephi was again self-conscious of the difference between his large plates and his small plates. Immediately after Lehi's party arrived in the New World, the group found ore out of which Nephi was able to make the large plates (1 Nephi 18:25–19:1). Once again he explained on his small plates that the large plates already contained material that was reported "more particularly" (1 Nephi 19:1–2). Again he affirmed that the small plates were being written by way of commandment, specifically "for the instruction of my people" and also for other purposes known to the Lord (verse 3).

These overt disclosures invite us to ask how the timing of Nephi's writing influenced the final form of the first parts of the Book of Mormon. How happy biblical scholars would be to know the time and place when the book of Exodus or the Gospel of Matthew took their final forms, for then they could probe the nature of those texts more certainly. In the case of Nephi's writings, because we know when, where, and why he wrote what he did, we can confidently turn our attention to pursue intriguing interpretive questions and to extract meaning from the lessons he left behind.

Research by John W. Welch, originally published as a FARMS Update in Insights *(March 1999): 2.*

20

WHY NEPHI WROTE THE SMALL PLATES: SERVING PRACTICAL NEEDS

*"And thou shalt engraven many things upon
them which are good in my sight." (2 Nephi 5:30)*

Nephi wrote his small plates soon after important events such as Lehi's death, Nephi's separation from his rebellious brothers, and the establishment of the reign of kings (see chapter 11). Recognizing when he wrote, we can better appreciate not only Nephi's stated reasons for writing the small plates but also subtle underlying motivations behind his inspired selection and treatment of this material.

We can assume that Nephi wrote his second account (the small plates) for many good reasons and from a particular vantage point. Although the large plates contained the prophecies of Lehi and Nephi (see 1 Nephi 19:1), that earlier record nevertheless must have been insufficient in certain respects, thus warranting the construction of an entirely new set of plates and the rewriting of the basic story. What was missing with the large plates? Why did the Lord direct Nephi to make the small plates, and what additional purposes guided Nephi in that undertaking?

We can begin to answer these questions by noting several characteristics of the small plates. Six practical features yield important clues about the new contributions added by the small plates.

1. Stated purposes. The small plates of Nephi feature several overt statements of purpose. The Lord may have needed Nephi to state his purposes more directly than before. Nephi says the small plates were written for the "instruction" and "profit" of his people (1 Nephi 19:3; 2 Nephi 5:30). The record thus served two purposes: to record Nephi's ministry among his people and to help others (such as Jacob and Joseph) to teach the people faith in God (see 1 Nephi 1:20; 6:4).

2. A small, manageable document. Nephi may have wanted to secure a record smaller than the presumably cumbersome large plates. A smaller record could be hidden more readily and carried more easily by a priest. If the large plates contained longer text that rambled, Nephi may have seen a need to make the small plates version concise and thus more manageable and useful.

3. A clear, plain text. Compared with the large plates, the small plates contained words that were "plain and precious" (1 Nephi 19:3). With hindsight, Nephi could see the end from the beginning, so his account could be clearer, plainer, and focused on information deemed more precious than the earlier material.

4. A polished, organized presentation. The writing on the small plates was carefully crafted. Several people have suggested various ways in which Nephi employed chiastic and other literary features in presenting his story. It would seem that these literary refinements were introduced into the text as the materials on the large plates were revised.

5. A specific audience. The small plates are directed explicitly to a specific audience: Nephi's own people (see 1 Nephi 19:3; 2 Nephi 5:30). While modern readers are the beneficiaries of Nephi's attentions, his immediate concern was chiefly with the survival of his own small group as they precariously forged their way into yet another wilderness, hoping to withstand the attacks of their enemies that were sure to follow.

6. *A second witness.* The small plates comprised a second witness to the information contained in the large plates. It was common practice in the ancient world for important documents to be prepared in duplicate to safeguard against loss or alteration and to satisfy the spirit of the Mosaic law of witnesses.

These and several other characteristics shed light on our understanding of the precious small plates. Their characteristics mesh thoroughly with the known circumstances in which they were written.

Research by John W. Welch, originally published as a FARMS Update in Insights *(April 1999): 2.*

21

WHY NEPHI WROTE THE SMALL PLATES: THE POLITICAL DIMENSION

"For the profit of thy people." (2 Nephi 5:30)

To conclude our reflections on when, where, and why Nephi wrote his final small plates account, we can now turn attention to three political dimensions of those plates. Once again, the real-life situations of Nephi and his people supply important contexts that bring interesting things to light.

1. A post-fallout document. The small plates were clearly written after Nephi's group left the land of first inheritance to escape the antagonisms of Laman and Lemuel and their sympathizers. The large plates probably contained expressions of great feelings of gratitude for the party's deliverance from perils. Accordingly, because the large plates had been started immediately after the group's arrival in the New World, that record may have been overly optimistic and conciliatory if not euphoric. There, in a spirit of hope and joy, Nephi may have given Laman and Lemuel credit at least for working on board ship (as all hands must have done) and for staying with the party (despite their desire to return to Jerusalem). Writing during something of a honeymoon period, Nephi may have expressed himself cautiously, uncritically, even hesitantly. The bold declarations

81

of Nephi's preeminence and Laman and Lemuel's stiff-neckedness later found in the small plates, however, would have offended Laman and Lemuel implacably and ruined any small chance of family harmony that existed upon the group's arrival in the New World.

2. A selective, thematic presentation. As Noel B. Reynolds has shown, Nephi's small plates served important political purposes for several centuries.[1] Knowing that this account was written shortly after, if not as part of, Nephi's coronation strengthens the thesis that this record was influenced by political needs from its inception. For example, the following incidents in 1 Nephi have clear political overtones: Nephi's obtaining the plates of brass, being designated a ruler and a teacher over his brethren (1 Nephi 2:22), possessing the only usable bow in camp (leadership implications), supplanting "elder brethren" (1 Nephi 16:37), succeeding in building the ship when the others could not, refusing to be worshipped (1 Nephi 17:55), and being rejected as ruler (1 Nephi 18:10).

3. A separator of religious and political power. Finally, at the time he began writing the small plates, Nephi knew that a division of power should exist in his new city. Kings would rule in the palace, but priests would control the temple (2 Nephi 5:18, 26). If the kings held the only copy of the law, they could prevent the priests from carrying out their functions. So Nephi gave the large plates to the kings, for that record would contain "an account of the reign of the kings, and the wars and contentions" of the people; whereas the small plates, devoted to "the more part of the ministry" and for other divine purposes, were given to the priestly lineage of Jacob (1 Nephi 9:4). In addition, Nephi assured a balance between the royal and priestly leaders in his city by entrusting to the kings the brass plates (containing the temple laws of sacrifice that the priests would need) and entrusting to the priests the small plates (containing the narratives that were necessary to legitimize the kings).

Once again and from yet another dimension, we can appreciate the depth and value of the precious small plates of Nephi. In the end, Mormon included them in his final compilation of the Nephite records for a reason yet unknown to him (Words of Mormon 1:7), but in their own day these plates served many choice and crucial purposes for the immediate "profit" of the "people" of Nephi (2 Nephi 5:30).

Research by John W. Welch, originally published as a FARMS Update in Insights *(May 1999): 2.*

NOTE

1. See Noel B. Reynolds, "The Political Dimension in Nephi's Small Plates," *BYU Studies* 27/4 (1987): 15–37.

22

SHEREM'S ACCUSATIONS AGAINST JACOB

"I, Sherem, declare unto you that this is blasphemy;
for no man knoweth of such things; for he cannot
tell of things to come." (Jacob 7:7)

An interesting encounter is reported in Jacob 7 between Sherem and Jacob. In light of the ancient Israelite criminal law that was in force among the Nephites at this time and at least up to the time of the reforms of Mosiah (see 2 Nephi 5:10; Jarom 1:5; Mosiah 17:7–8; Alma 1:17), it is evident that Sherem's accusations were serious allegations. On three accounts, he accused Jacob of offenses punishable by death:

> Ye have [1] led away much of this people that they pervert the right way of God, and keep not the law of Moses which is the right way; and convert the law of Moses into the worship of a being which ye say shall come many hundred years hence. And now behold, I, Sherem, declare unto you that this is [2] blasphemy; for no man knoweth of such things; for he [3] cannot tell of things to come. (Jacob 7:7)

Each of Sherem's accusations can be traced to specific provisions in pre-exilic Israelite law:

1. Causing public apostasy. Leading other people or a city into apostasy was recognized as a serious infraction under the law of Moses and the Talmud. Deuteronomy 13:1–18 condemns to death any person, whether a prophet, or brother, or son, or wife, who says to the inhabitants of their city, "Let us go and serve other gods, which ye have not known" (Deuteronomy 13:13; see 13:2, 6). "Thou shalt not consent unto him, nor hearken unto him; . . . but thou shalt surely kill him" (Deuteronomy 13:8–9).

In essence Sherem first claimed that Jacob had led the people away, i.e., into a state of apostasy from the way of God. Sherem claimed that Jacob had caused the people to pervert the right way of God, to keep not the law, and to convert the law into the worship of an unknown god. Indeed, the law of Moses defines the crime of causing apostasy as trying to thrust the people "out of the way which the Lord [their] God commanded [them] to walk in" (Deuteronomy 13:5).

Moreover, Sherem's point that Jacob had converted the observance of the law of Moses into the worship of an unknown future being seems to have been based on the Deuteronomic prohibition against turning to serve new gods "which ye have not known" (Deuteronomy 13:2, 6, 13).

2. Blasphemy. Sherem's second accusation also raised a capital charge. It was a felony under the law of Moses to blaspheme (see Exodus 20:7; Leviticus 24:10–16). Leviticus 24 established that any person who blasphemed, even in a brawl, was to be stoned to death. Sherem raised the charge of blasphemy against Jacob when he formally accused him, saying, "I, Sherem, declare unto you that this is blasphemy" (Jacob 7:7).

While the ancient history of the crime of blasphemy is obscure, this offense apparently embraced many forms of insolent or seditious speech, whether against God, against the king (see 1 Kings 21:10), against another man, or against holy places or things, including the law (compare Acts 6:13).

3. False Prophecy. Sherem's words also advanced a claim of false prophecy. The test for whether a prophet had

spoken truly or falsely was usually to see "if the thing follow not, nor come to pass" (Deuteronomy 18:22).
Apparently Sherem tried to preclude this defense when he
objected that Jacob had spoken of things too far distant in
the future. When Sherem asserted categorically that "no
man knoweth of such things" (Jacob 7:7), he seems to be
arguing that prophecies of that nature should not be easily
tolerated under the law. With shorter-term prophecies, one
has the chance to test them within a reasonable time.

Deuteronomy 18:20 requires that a man shall be put to
death if he speaks "in the name of other gods." One can
understand how Jacob's "preaching . . . the doctrine of
Christ" (Jacob 7:6) could have been deviously characterized by Sherem as a form of speaking "in the name of"
another god, for the Nephites had begun worshipping God
in the name of Christ (see 2 Nephi 25:13–19; Jacob 4:5).
Perhaps Book of Mormon prophets insisted so emphatically
that God and his Son were but "one God" (2 Nephi 31:21;
Alma 11:28–29, 35), partly to affirm that speaking in the
name of one was not to be construed legally as speaking in
the name of any other god.

Thus Sherem's allegations were not merely vague
rhetorical criticisms; they were well-formulated accusations, logically derived from specific provisions of the
ancient law. Sherem's words put Jacob's life in jeopardy. If
allowed to stand, these accusations would have justified
Jacob's execution.

At the same time, Sherem also put his own life on the
line. The ancient punishment for a false accuser was to suffer that which "he had thought to have done unto his
brother" (Deuteronomy 19:19). Not only does this show
that Sherem was deeply committed to his views and dead
serious about the charges he raised against his "brother
Jacob" (Jacob 7:6), it also explains the sense of legal justice

that exists in the fact that, in the end, Sherem was smitten by God and he himself soon died.

Research by John W. Welch, originally published as a FARMS Update in Insights *(January 1991): 2.*

23

THE HEBREW ORIGIN OF THREE
BOOK OF MORMON PLACE-NAMES

*"They came down into the land which is called
the land of Zarahemla." (Omni 1:13)*

Anumber of scholars have discussed the possible
Hebrew meaning of some of the place-names in the
Book of Mormon. Three that have drawn particular atten-
tion are the names *Zarahemla, Jershon,* and *Cumorah.*

Zarahemla

Zarahemla was the Nephite capital for longer than any
other city, yet it was actually named from Zarahemla, a
descendant of Mulek (see Omni 1:12–15; Mosiah 25:2).
Mulek, the son of Zedekiah, the last king of Judah, had come
to the New World with other immigrants not long after
Lehi's departure from Jerusalem (see Helaman 6:10; 8:21).

The name *Zarahemla* probably derives from the Hebrew
zeraḥemlāh, which has been variously translated as "seed
of compassion"[1] or "child of grace, pity, or compassion."[2]
It may be that the Mulekite leader was given that name
because his ancestor had been rescued when the other sons
of King Zedekiah were slain during the Babylonian conquest of Jerusalem. To subsequent Nephite generations, it
may even have suggested the deliverance of their own
ancestors from Jerusalem prior to its destruction or the
anticipation of Christ's coming.

Jershon

When the Lamanites converted by the sons of Mosiah fled their homeland to escape persecution, the Nephites allowed them to settle in the land of Jershon. The name, though not found in the Bible, has an authentic Hebrew origin, the root *YRŠ, meaning "to inherit," with the suffix -ôn that denotes place-names. Wilhelm Borée, in his outstanding study, *Die alten Ortsnamen Palästinas (The Ancient Place Names of Palestine)*, cites fully eighty-four ancient Canaanite place names with the ending -ôn in biblical and extrabiblical sources (Egyptian and Mesopotamian writings, the El-Amarna letters, ostraca), including Ayyalon (Elon) (see Joshua 19:42, 43), Eltekon (see Joshua 15:59), Askelon (see Judges 1:18), Gibeon (see Joshua 9:3), Gibbethon (see Joshua 19:44), Dishon (see Genesis 36:21), Ziphron (see Numbers 34:9), Helbon (see Ezekiel 27:18), Holon (see Joshua 21:15), Hammon (see Joshua 19:28), Hebron (see Joshua 10:36), Hannathon (see Joshua 19:14), Dibon (see Numbers 21:30), and Heshbon (see Numbers 21:30).[3]

It is in this light that we should understand the words in Alma 27:22 ("and this land Jershon is the land which we will give unto our brethren for an inheritance"), Alma 27:24 ("that they may inherit the land Jershon"), and Alma 35:14 ("they have lands for their inheritance in the land of Jershon").

Cumorah

Cumorah is the name of the hill in which Mormon buried the Nephite records before turning his abridgment of it over to his son Moroni (see Mormon 6:6). Suggested etymologies range from a corruption of the biblical Gomorrah to a comparison with Qumran, the name of the site near the caves where the Dead Sea Scrolls were found. An early suggestion linked Cumorah to the Hebrew words found in Isaiah 60:1, *qûmî ʾûrî*, "arise, shine." Related to this is David Palmer's suggestion that Cumorah means "Arise, O Light," on a reconstructed form of *qûm°ôrāh*.[4] But there are two problems with this. One is that the Hebrew word for light, though feminine in gender, does not usually take the feminine suffix *-āh* and is simply *°ôr*. This objection is lessened by the fact that the Bible uses the form *°ôrāh* twice, in Psalm 139:12 and Esther 8:16. But the second problem is more serious: because the Hebrew word for "light" is feminine, the word would take the feminine form *qûmî* for the imperative, not the masculine *qûm*. For a meaning of "arise, O light," one would expect the Hebrew form *qûmî °ôr*, though *qûmî °ôrāh* would not be impossible. The suggested etymology *kûm °ôrāh*, "mound of light/revelation," is a better explanation.

Both proposals seem to be based on the idea of truth coming to light or being revealed out of the hill in the form of the Book of Mormon, and one must acknowledge that Hebrew *°ôr* is occasionally used in the sense of "revelation" (see Numbers 27:21; 1 Samuel 28:6; Isaiah 2:5; 49:6; 51:4; Proverbs 6:23). But the coming forth of the Book of Mormon in the last days hardly explains why the place where Mormon hid the plates should have such a name in the late fourth century A.D.[5]

A more plausible etymology for Cumorah is Hebrew *kəmôrāh*, "priesthood," an abstract noun based on the word *kômer*, "priest." This form is based on the Hebrew noun pattern *(mišqal) pe°ullāh*,[6] with the vowel of the second consonant of the root, "m," lengthened "compensatorially" from "u" to "ō/ô" because the third consonant of the root, "r," cannot be doubled.[7] *Kōmer/kômer* and *kəmôrāh* may be compared in both form and meaning with the Hebrew nouns *kōhēn*, "priest," and *kəhunnāh*, "priesthood."[8]

Some have privately objected that this explanation is unlikely because the term *kômer* is always used in the Old

Testament in reference to false priests (see 2 Kings 23:5; Hosea 10:5; Zephaniah 1:4), while the word *kôhēn* is used to denote Israelite priests.[9] But this objection fails to note that both terms are used together in the Zephaniah passage. It seems more likely to us that the term *kômer* was simply used to denote a priest who was not of the tribe of Levi, while *kôhēn* in all cases refers to a Levitical priest. Since Lehi's party did not include descendants of Levi, they probably used *kômer* wherever the Book of Mormon speaks of priests.

Research by Stephen D. Ricks and John A. Tvedtnes, originally published in the Journal of Book of Mormon Studies *6/2 (1997): 255–59.*

NOTES

1. John A. Tvedtnes, "Since the Book of Mormon is largely the record of a Hebrew people, is the writing characteristic of the Hebrew language?" I Have a Question, *Ensign* (October 1986): 65; Tvedtnes, "What's in a Name? A Look at the Book of Mormon Onomasticon," review of *I Know Thee By Name: Hebrew Roots of Lehi-ite Non-Biblical Names in the Book of Mormon,* by Joseph R. and Norrene V. Salonimer, *FARMS Review of Books* 8/2 (1996): 41.

2. Joseph R. and Norrene V. Salonimer, *I Know Thee by Name: Hebrew Roots of Lehi-ite Non-Biblical Names in the Book of Mormon* (Independence, Mo.: Salonimer, 1995).

3. See Wilhelm Borée, *Die alten Ortsnamen Palästinas,* 2nd ed. (Hildesheim: Olms, 1968), 57–62; Anson F. Rainey, "The Toponymics of Eretz-Israel," *Bulletin of the American Schools of Oriental Research* 231 (1978): 5, calls *-ôn* an "appellative" suffix that describes "some feature or aspect of the site."

4. David A. Palmer, *In Search of Cumorah: New Evidences for the Book of Mormon from Ancient Mexico* (Bountiful, Utah: Horizon, 1981), 21.

5. The Book of Mormon never tells us that Moroni hid the plates in the same hill in which his father hid the bulk of the

Nephite records, and a number of scholars have argued that the hill in New York State from which Joseph Smith removed the abridged record is not the one mentioned in the Book of Mormon, which, from internal evidence, could not have been far from the "narrow neck of land."

6. See James L. Sagarin, *Hebrew Noun Patterns (Mishqalim): Morphology, Semantics, and Lexicon* (Atlanta: Scholars, 1987), 33–34.

7. See P. Paul Joüon, *Grammaire de l'hébreu biblique* (Rome: Institut biblique pontifical, 1923), 54.

8. Francis Brown, S. R. Driver, and Charles Briggs, *A Hebrew and English Lexicon of the Old Testament* (Oxford: Clarendon, 1974), 464; compare also Ernest Klein, *A Comprehensive Etymological Dictionary of the Hebrew Language for Readers of English* (New York: Macmillan, 1987), 279, who defines the neologism *kəmôrāh* as "Christian clergy, priesthood," but also notes the Hebrew noun pattern *peˤullāh* upon which it is based.

9. One suggestion was that this would give a meaning of "priestcraft," rather than "priesthood" to the name Cumorah were it to derive from *kômer*. But note that 2 Nephi 10:5 indicates that it would be "because of priestcrafts . . . at Jerusalem" that Christ would be rejected. The "chief priests" who opposed Christ were descendants of Levi and were designated by the term *kōhēn*. See the definition of "priestcraft" in 2 Nephi 26:29.

24

SWORD OF LABAN AS A SYMBOL OF DIVINE AUTHORITY

"But behold, king Benjamin gathered together his armies
. . . and he did fight with the strength of his own arm,
with the sword of Laban." (Words of Mormon 1:13)

The sword that Nephi took from Laban played an important role in Nephite history, not only as the model after which the Nephites later made swords to defend themselves, but also and perhaps more importantly as a symbol of the legitimate authority of the Nephite rulers, beginning with Nephi himself.

Many histories and traditions have used weapons as symbols of royalty and authority. Swords in particular have had cultic importance in almost every culture. Gordon Thomasson has pointed out that the sword of Laban as a symbol of rule among the Nephites fits a long tradition, often portrayed in royal and relgous art.[1] Most of these symbolic swords can be categorized as either kingly or heroic swords.

In the kingly pattern, the sword helped to establish the possessor as the ruler, the one on whom divine kingship was conferred. It symbolized his responsibility to protect the society and to mete out justice. It originated with a deity and ratified the king's office. The sword was passed on to the heir as a transfer of authority, and the giving of the sword to the new king was a widespread feature of coronation ceremonies.

The heroic pattern, found mainly in literature and mythology, established the possessor as one invested with divine authority for some holy quest or heroic deed. The sword was more than a weapon, giving the hero extra power and the blessing of the gods. For example, Beowulf used magical swords to overcome the monster Grendel.

In some tales, elements from both the kingly and the heroic combine to symbolize complete divine kingship and authority. For example, King Arthur drew Excalibur from the stone, which symbolized his divine right to kingship and gave him power to defeat the Saxons. David is another example, as he took Goliath's sword and cut off the Philistine's head. That sword was preserved and revered as it was kept with the ephod and priestly garments. David later obtained the sword again and heroically led the Israelites against the Philistines and later became king.

Like David, Nephi used the sword of Laban to cut off the head of its owner. This act led to his obtaining the records and helping to lead his people to a promised land, where he was made ruler. He apparently passed the sword to his successors, for it was used later by King Benjamin when he "did fight with the strength of his own arm, with the sword of Laban," to defend his people against the Lamanites (Words of Mormon 1:13). King Benjamin passed the sword to his son Mosiah along with other sacred objects when he transferred "charge concerning all the affairs of the kingdom" (Mosiah 1:15; see also v. 16).

Even after the reign of kings came to an end and judges began to rule, the "sacred things," which apparently included the sword, were passed on amongst the judges or the prophets as a symbol of divine authority. Even though the sword is not mentioned, textual clues show that it was probably still part of the sacred implements of authority.

When Alma passed the sacred treasures to his son Helaman, he explained:

> And now remember, my son, that God has entrusted you with these things, which are sacred, which he has kept sacred, and also which he will keep and preserve for a wise purpose in him, that he may show forth his power unto future generations. (Alma 37:14)

Clearly the records were intended for a future generation, but was the sword intended to have some purpose at a later time?

In the restoration of the Church of Jesus Christ to the earth through Joseph Smith, the sword of Laban appears to have provided an additional witness to the Prophet's divine authority. There is no direct evidence as to whether Joseph Smith ever possessed the sword of Laban, but it was part of the sacred relics along with the plates revealed by Moroni. Some of Joseph's contemporaries thought that he did possess and even use the sword, which belief clearly lent legitimacy to his authority in their minds. This is also shown in connection with the famous "cave story" by Brigham Young and authenticated by others, where the sword of Laban was seen in a cave along with piles of plates.

In Nauvoo Joseph was prophet, mayor, and lieutenant governor of the Nauvoo Legion and held the three kingly roles of priest, civil administrator, and military leader. In the view of the Saints, Joseph was their leader and held the implements of divine authority, including the sword of Laban. As it had been with the Nephites, the sword of Laban was a symbol of the Lord's authority and kingship in the latter days and showed "forth his power unto future generations."

Research by Brett L. Holbrook, originally published as a FARMS Update in Insights *(May 1993): 2. For further information, see*

Brett L. Holbrook, "The Sword of Laban as a Symbol of Divine Authority and Kingship," Journal of Book of Mormon Studies *2/1 (1993):39–72.*

NOTE

1. See Gordon C. Thomasson, "Mosiah: The Complex Symbolism and Symbolic Complex of Kingship in the Book of Mormon," *Journal of Book of Mormon Studies* 2/1 (1993): 25–32.

25

UPON THE TOWER OF BENJAMIN

*"He caused a tower to be erected, that thereby
his people might hear the words which he should
speak unto them." (Mosiah 2:7)*

When King Benjamin crowned his son Mosiah, all the
people in Zarahemla sat in tents around the temple
while Benjamin addressed them. Because he "could not
teach them all within the walls of the temple, therefore he
caused a tower to be erected, that thereby his people might
hear the words which he should speak unto them" (Mosiah
2:7). Was the need to improve the acoustics the only reason
for the construction of this tower? Recent research has discovered ancient precedents for the use of such "towers" in
royal convocations and coronation ceremonies. These biblical and Jewish precedents are not obvious to the casual
reader and may well shed light on Benjamin's tower.

In the King James translation of 2 Kings 11:14, we read
that King Joash, at the time of his coronation, "stood *by a
pillar*, as the manner was" (emphasis added). After Joash
was made king (see 2 Kings 11:12), the priest Jehoiada conducted two covenant ceremonies, one "between the Lord
and the king and the people," and the other "between the
king also and the people" (2 Kings 11:17).

Likewise, when King Josiah rededicated the temple of
Solomon, he stood *"by a pillar"* to read the book of the
covenant and to put the people under covenant to keep its

commandments (2 Kings 23:3; emphasis added. See also v. 2). The Hebrew text in both these instances is ʿal-haʿammud. The preposition ʿal can be translated "by," but it is much more often rendered "on" or "upon."[1] The Greek Septuagint version of these passages uses the comparable preposition *epi*, which on occasion can also mean "near," "by," or "at," but more generally means "upon" or "on." One manuscript of the Jewish historian Josephus, accordingly, placed King Joash "upon the stage" *(epi tēs skēnēs)* at the time of his coronation.[2] Consistent with this technical textual detail, the Book of Mormon is on strong ancient ground when it reports that King Benjamin spoke, not while standing *beside* a pillar or post, but "from the tower," presumably while positioned *on top* of his tower (Mosiah 2:8; compare also Nephi's speech in Helaman 7:10, from *upon* his tower).

The pillar *(ʿammud)* mentioned in connection with the coronation of Joash and Josiah can also be associated with the "brasen scaffold" that Solomon built (2 Chronicles 6:13), *upon* which he stood and knelt "before all the congregation of Israel," and from which he offered the dedicatory prayer for the temple in Jerusalem (2 Chronicles 6:13; see also vv. 14–42).

Another such structure is mentioned in Nehemiah 8:4, when Ezra "stood *upon* a pulpit of wood" to read the law to the people as they sat in booths for seven days following their return to Jerusalem from Babylon (emphasis added; see also vv. 5–18). Ezra's platform is clearly related to the platform that was used by the king during the Feast of Tabernacles according to the Mishnah:

> After the close of the first Festival-day of the Feast of Tabernacles, in the eighth year, after the going forth of the Seventh Year, they used to prepare for him in the Temple Court a wooden platform on *which he* sat, for it

98

is written, "At the end of every seven years in the set time" (Deuteronomy 31:10).[3]

As has been discussed elsewhere, the Feast of Tabernacles and ancient coronation ceremonies have many points in common with King Benjamin's speech.[4] One of the clearest yet subtlest points of comparison is the tower that Benjamin stood upon when addressing his people.

Research by John W. Welch, Terry L. Szink, and others, originally published as a FARMS Update in Insights *(August 1995): 2.*

NOTES

1. Francis Brown, Samuel R. Driver, and Charles A. Briggs, *Hebrew and English Lexicon of the Old Testament* (Oxford: Clarendon, 1980), 752.

2. Josephus, *Antiquities*, 9.7.3.

3. M *Sotah* 7:8; emphasis added; in Herbert Danby, trans., *The Mishnah* (London: Oxford University Press, 1933), 301.

4. See John A. Tvedtnes, "King Benjamin and the Feast of Tabernacles," in *By Study and Also By Faith,* ed. John M. Lundquist and Stephen D. Ricks (Salt Lake City: Deseret Book and FARMS, 1990), 2:197–221; Terrence L. Szink and John W. Welch, "King Benjamin's Speech in the Context of Ancient Israelite Festivals," in *King Benjamin's Speech: "That Ye May Learn Wisdom,"* ed. John W. Welch and Stephen D. Ricks (Provo, Utah: FARMS, 1998), 147–223; Stephen D. Ricks, "The Coronation of Kings," in *Reexploring the Book of Mormon,* ed. John W. Welch (Salt Lake City: Deseret Book and FARMS, 1992), 124–26.

26

BENJAMIN'S TOWER AND OLD TESTAMENT PILLARS

*"He caused a tower to be erected, that thereby
his people might hear the words which he should
speak unto them." (Mosiah 2:7)*

While scholars are uncertain about the precise nature of the *ʿammud*[1] (see the previous article), it is clear that it was something other than a pillar. Roland de Vaux imagines the king "standing on a pedestal" where presumably he worshipped God.[2] Gerhard von Rad, commenting on the pillars in 2 Kings, sees them as some kind of high, narrow platform: "The king would have had to be visible to the crowd which had gathered for the solemnities, so that one may probably think of some sort of pillar-like platform."[3]

The biblical Hebrew literally says that the king or priestly leader stood on a "standing thing." Only later did the Greek LXX translation promote the specific idea that the *ʿammud* was precisely a pillar *(stylos)*. Thus, once again King Benjamin's text is consistent with the broader Hebrew term, which can easily refer to any kind of platform or, indeed, to a tower.

Moreover, scholars are uncertain about the purpose of the *ʿammud*. Kraus speculates that the king was lifted onto the platform in order to receive "the homage of the congregation."[4] But a careful reexamination of the Bible finds that the *ʿammud* always stood in or by the temple as the king or

100

leader officiated at times of coronation, lawgiving, covenant renewal, or temple dedication. Thus Geo Widengren has insightfully concluded: "At least towards the end of the pre-exilic period, but possibly from the beginning of that period, the king when reading to his people on a solemn occasion from the book of the law and acting as the mediator of the covenant making between Yahweh and the people had his place on a platform or a dais."[5]

Accordingly, the use of the tower by King Benjamin was especially pertinent, inasmuch as his speech involved so many of these elements of an ancient Israelite solemn assembly: a coronation proclamation (see Mosiah 2:30), a stipulation of covenant between the new king and the people (see Mosiah 2:31), a renewal of the basic covenant between God and the people (see Mosiah 5:5), and the consecration of the king and appointment of priests (see Mosiah 6:3). Thus again, the biblical texts give a picture whose focus is sharpened by the Book of Mormon text.

Reflection on Benjamin's tower draws another possible connection to mind. The word *ʿammud* is used in other Old Testament texts to describe the pillar of light (or fire) and the pillar of cloud that stood before the Tabernacle, signaling God's presence at that holy sanctuary.[6] Is it possible that Benjamin's tower, standing beside the temple of Zarahemla, in turn signified the pillar of God's presence? If so, does this explain why Benjamin was so careful at the beginning of his speech to disclaim any implication that he was "more than a mortal man" (Mosiah 2:10; compare 2:26)?

The tower built by Benjamin was evidently more than just a way to communicate to the people. It was a rich symbolic part of ancient Israelite tradition in which the king stood on a platform at the temple to officiate between God and his people.

Research by John W. Welch, Terry L. Szink, and others, origi-nally published as a FARMS Update in Insights *(October 1995): 2.*

NOTES

1. See T. R. Hobbs, 2 *Kings,* Word Biblical Commentary (Waco: Word Books, 1985), 13:142, is "uncertain" but suggests "some kind of column, podium, or platform."

2. Roland de Vaux, *Ancient Israel* (New York: McGraw-Hill, 1965), 1:102–3.

3. Gerhard von Rad, "The Royal Ritual in Judah," in *The Problem of the Hexateuch and Other Essays,* trans. E. W. Trueman Dicken (New York: McGraw-Hill, 1966), 224.

4. Hans-Joachim Kraus, *Worship in Israel: A Cultic History of the Old Testament,* trans. Geoffrey Buswell (Richmond: John Knox, 1966), 224.

5. Geo Widengren, "King and Covenant," *Journal of Semitic Studies* 2 (1957): 10; it should also be noted that in modern Judaism the Torah is to be read from a raised platform called a *bimah* which is to be placed in the center of the synagogue. Some have connected this structure with the platforms in the temples. See "Bimah," in *Encyclopaedia Judaica* (Jerusalem: Keter, 1971), 4:1002–6.

6. See Henri Frankfort, *Kingship and the Gods: A Study of Ancient Near Eastern Religion as the Integration of Society and Nature* (Chicago: University of Chicago Press, 1948), 245–46.

27

UNINTENTIONAL SIN IN BENJAMIN'S DISCOURSE

"His blood atoneth for the sins of those . . .
who have ignorantly sinned." (Mosiah 3:11)

In explaining the atonement of Jesus Christ, King Benjamin pointedly states that in addition to atoning for the fall of Adam, "his blood atoneth for the sins of those . . . who have died not knowing the will of God concerning them, or who have *ignorantly* sinned" (Mosiah 3:11). For modern readers, the notion of sinning unintentionally may seem illogical. Isn't sin a conscious violation of a commandment of God? If someone transgresses a law of God in ignorance, is there any guilt or culpability that calls for repentance?

Although the modern mind tends to see sin essentially as a bad choice or an evil intent, the ancient mind included many other dimensions in its concept of sin, such as defilement, accident, error, or misjudgment. Impurity could result, for example, from any direct or indirect contact with a corpse, even if the person was unaware of the contact (see Numbers 19:14). Likewise, mistakenly touching the ark of the covenant was erroneous, even if the person had good intentions (see 2 Samuel 6:6–7). In Old Testament times, the concept of sin embraced many nuances of erring, disobeying, missing the mark, bending, rebelling, straying, wandering, or otherwise being at fault, whether consciously or unconsciously.[1]

In Numbers 15:27–29, the law of Moses prescribes what should be done "if any soul sin through ignorance." The transgressor must bring a goat for a sin offering and "the priest shall make an atonement for the soul that sinneth ignorantly" (15:28). By way of contrast, if a person who "despised the word of the Lord" sins "presumptuously," that person shall be cut off (Numbers 15:30–31). Indeed, inadvertence was "a key criterion in all expiatory sacrifice. A deliberate, brazen sinner is barred from the sanctuary."[2]

With this background, we may better understand why Benjamin so expressly stated that the atonement of Jesus Christ would atone for the sins of those who "ignorantly sinned." Benjamin's people would naturally have wondered, as he described the workings of the promised atonement, whether its efficacy would cover all categories of sin or only certain types of transgressions. They were told that Christ's atonement would automatically cover the fall of Adam and sins committed in ignorance. Although modern theologies would think of inadvertent sins as being only marginally significant, they stood at the crux of the concept of expiation and atonement in the ancient system of sacrifices. At the same time, Benjamin also pronounced a resounding eternal wo upon the unrepentant who transgress the law of God knowingly, who come out "in open rebellion against God" (Mosiah 2:37; see Mosiah 2:33; 3:12). Forgiveness for intentional misconduct depends on a full change of heart.

Moreover, Mosiah 3 recognizes two types of ignorant sins: (1) some people live and die unaware of the will of

God concerning them (3:11) as revealed in the written law of Moses (3:14) and thereby transgress the law, while (2) other people presumably know the law of God in some form but still commit sins accidentally or in ignorance of the law's true meaning or application.

Interestingly, other ancient people similarly spoke of various types of ignorant sins. The Dead Sea Scrolls punished "a single inadvertent sin" by a small fine (1QS, col. 9, lines 1–2); repeated error was apparently not tolerated. Inadvertence could be due to carelessness or misjudgment, but it could also come from ignorance of the "hidden matters" embedded in the law of Moses known only to the Qumran sect. Of course, one who openly "rebels" against the revealed portions of the law obvious to everyone was very stringently punished (1QS, col. 8, lines 17–18; see 4Q159).[3]

Unintentional sin was of much greater concern to ancient people than it is to us today. Although we worry very little about such sins, this is only because we know that Christ's infinite sacrifice has atoned for them. Even though we are now less concerned with unintentional sins, Benjamin's words remind us that we should not remain ignorant of or ungrateful for this aspect of Christ's atonement.

Research by John W. Welch, originally published as a FARMS Update in Insights *(April 1996): 2.*

NOTES

1. See Gerhard Kittel, ed., *Theological Dictionary of the New Testament* (Grand Rapids, Mich.: Eerdmans, 1964), 1:269–79.

2. Jacob Milgrom, *Leviticus 1–16* (New York: Doubleday, 1991), 228.

3. See Gary A. Anderson, "Intentional and Unintentional Sin in the Dead Sea Scrolls," in *Pomegranates and Golden Bells: Studies in Biblical, Jewish, and Near Eastern Ritual, Law, and Literature in Honor of Jacob Milgrom*, ed. David P. Wright, David N. Freedman, and Avi Hurvitz (Winona Lake, Ind.: Eisenbrauns, 1995), 55.

28

ON THE RIGHT OR LEFT:
BENJAMIN AND THE SCAPEGOAT

"Ye shall be called the children of Christ . . .
and there is no other head whereby ye can
be made free." (Mosiah 5:7–8)

Over the years, scholars have found in King Benjamin's speech much that is at home in the ancient Israelite autumn festivals surrounding the Day of Atonement.[1] An essential part of that day was the scapegoat ritual.

As prescribed in Leviticus 16, two goats were set before the high priest. From an urn, he drew two lots to determine which goat was to be declared "for the Lord" and which "for Azazel," a term which most likely referred to a desert-dwelling demon.[2] The high priest then placed the lots on the heads of the goats. According to rabbinic writings, if the lot "for the Lord" came up in the priest's left hand, he was permitted to place that lot on the goat on the right so that the Lord's goat would always be on the right hand while Azazel's would be on the left.[3] The goat for the Lord was then sacrificed and its blood was used to purge the temple. The high priest transferred Israel's sins to the other goat, and it was then taken out into the desert.

Such factors have prompted further examination of Mosiah 5:7–12. In these verses, Benjamin speaks in terms of a dichotomy that is similar to the paradigm of the two goats. He gives his people a name (see 5:7–8), for they, like the goats, must either be "called by the name of Christ" (for the Lord) and "be found at the right hand of God" (5:9), or they "must be called by some other name" and find themselves "on the left hand of God" (5:10, 12).

Verse 8 contains an unusual mention of a "head" that makes one free: "And there is no other head whereby ye can be made free." When Benjamin spoke the word "head," one might imagine that he looked to his right at the head of the sacrificial animal that symbolized Christ and whose blood would be used in purifying the people.

In the course of his speech Benjamin used the term "evil spirit(s)" four times (Mosiah 2:32, 37; 3:6; 4:14). Perhaps this "evil spirit" is to be connected with Azazel. Indeed, three of these references are associated with sins of rebellion and quarreling, the types of sins the scapegoat carried away to Azazel. In the third (see Mosiah 3:6), Benjamin prophesied that evil spirits will be "cast out" by Jesus, perhaps an event that was foreshadowed by the scapegoat being cast out by the high priest.

Just as the goat carrying the sins of Israel was driven away, so any individual who might break the covenant was, in Benjamin's words, to be "consigned to an awful . . . state of misery and endless torment" (Mosiah 3:25), and lost in a "worthless and fallen state" of "nothingness" (Mosiah 4:5). Such a transgressor would ultimately be driven away and cast out (see Mosiah 5:10–14). The dramatic banishment of the goat of Azazel into an empty wilderness must have vividly portrayed the fallen and miserable fate of such a transgressor.

Had Benjamin said that the sinner would be driven out like a goat instead of an ass, these connections with the Day of Atonement would appear even stronger. But it was not critical among Israel's neighbors in the ancient Near East what animal was used in such rituals.[4]

Thus, elements in Benjamin's address seem to presuppose the scapegoat ritual. Through such a ceremony, Benjamin's people would have understood that anyone who received the name of the Lord was consecrated to be sacrificed to God, giving emphatic meaning to their own irrevocable covenant to serve God "with all [their] *whole souls*" (Mosiah 2:21) and to be diligent "even unto the *end* of [their] life" (Mosiah 4:6).

Research by Terrence L. Szink and John W. Welch, originally published as a FARMS Update in Insights *(January 1995): 2.*

NOTES

1. See John A. Tvedtnes, "King Benjamin and the Feast of Tabernacles," in *By Study and Also by Faith,* ed. John M. Lundquist and Stephen D. Ricks (Salt Lake City: Deseret Book, 1990), 2:197–221; Terrence L. Szink and John W. Welch, "King Benjamin's Speech in the Context of Ancient Israelite Festivals," in *King Benjamin's Speech: "That Ye May Learn Wisdom,"* ed. John W. Welch and Stephen D. Ricks (Provo, Utah: FARMS, 1998), 147–223; Welch, "The Temple in the Book of Mormon: The Temples at the Cities of Nephi, Zarahemla, and Bountiful," in *Temples of the Ancient World,* ed. Donald W. Parry (Salt Lake City: Deseret Book, 1994), 352–58.

2. Jacob Milgrom, *Leviticus 1–16* (New York: Doubleday, 1991), 1020–21; see Hayim Tawil, "ʿAzazel the Prince of the Steppe: A Comparative Study," *Zeitschrift für die Alttestamentliche Wissenschaft* 92 (1980): 43–59.

3. See Babylonian Talmud, *Yoma* 40b.

4. See Delbert R. Hillers, *Covenant: The History of a Biblical Idea* (Baltimore: Johns Hopkins, 1969), 40–41.

29

very good

DEMOCRATIZING FORCES IN KING BENJAMIN'S SPEECH

*"And it came to pass that there was not one
soul, except it were little children, but who had
entered into the covenant and had taken upon
them the name of Christ." (Mosiah 6:2)*

Recently, numerous dimensions of King Benjamin's masterful speech have been studied and explored to a far greater extent than ever before, both in regard to elements within the speech itself and with respect to its influence in subsequent Nephite generations. These expansive studies have appeared in the recent volume, entitled *King Benjamin's Speech: "That Ye May Learn Wisdom,"* along with a more popular abridgment of that volume, entitled *Benjamin's Speech Made Simple.*[1] In particular, one line of investigation introduced in that volume has led us to appreciate the many ways in which Benjamin's speech paved the way, theologically and politically, for the democratization of the government and politics that flowered in the land of Zarahemla only thirty years after Benjamin's death.

King Benjamin was known by Nephite historians as one of the best kings they had ever had, and no other Nephite king was remembered in so many positive ways (see Words of Mormon 1:13–18). Benjamin unified his people in the land of Zarahemla at a critical time in their history and gave them the spiritual strength they needed to flourish for the next several generations; his influential words and deeds produced an important era of religious and political strength for the next one hundred years.[2]

Although he was a multifaceted man and must have been many things to many people, he was remembered primarily for his righteous and equitable reign. As the records disclose, Benjamin was a faithful, inspired, just, frugal, loving, humble, articulate, and courageous ruler. About thirty years after his death, his son and successor, Mosiah, declared to the Nephites, "If ye could have men for your kings who would do even as my father Benjamin did for this people—I say unto you, if this could always be the case, then it would be expedient that ye should always have kings to rule over you" (Mosiah 29:13). The contrast that Mosiah draws between his father, Benjamin, and the wicked King Noah is not only explicitly stated in Mosiah's abdication speech in Mosiah 29, but is also powerfully accentuated by the structure of the book of Mosiah, which places Benjamin at the beginning in parallel with Mosiah at the end and then positions Noah and Abinadi at the overall chiastic center of the book.[3] In so doing, Mosiah clearly signals to his readers that the origins of his democratizing reforms had their roots and their justification in Benjamin's speech.

King Benjamin prepared the way for democratic developments in many ways. Personally, he was kind and generous toward all his subjects (see Mosiah 2:10–12). He eschewed oppression and prohibited slavery (see Mosiah 2:13–14). He established economic policies that broke down class distinctions by requiring everyone to give to the poor regardless of the person's status as a widow, orphan, or foreigner (see Mosiah 4:14–28).[4] These steps would have required his people to rethink many of their social structures, financial credit and debt-collection mechanisms, and other cultural attitudes, all of which moved the society along in the direction of becoming more egalitarian.

Moreover, Benjamin accomplished all of this while ruling over a diverse population of Nephites and Mulekites, a complex situation that was increasingly challenging as the population in Zarahemla became even more diverse upon the arrival of groups led by Alma the Elder and King Limhi soon after Benjamin's death. In such an atmosphere, Benjamin quite distinctly moved his people more in the direction of respecting individuality, individual responsibility, and individual rewards and punishments. His was a delicate union, trying to hold together two peoples having very different backgrounds and probably retaining a considerable degree of cultural identity and political distinctness.[5]

Whenever two different cultures such as these come together, the leader of the conglomeration faces certain alternatives: either he can prefer the organic social structure of one of the two groups and impose that regime on the newly merged population, or he can break down old class privileges or social structures and move more toward a political system that places greater emphasis on each individual in the society so as to build a new sense of political identity and civic duty based on individual status and participation.[6] It would appear that Benjamin set in motion the latter option, as elements of the old order began fading out: for example, direct male descendants in Jacob's lineage ceased to be available to control the records and priestly functions assigned to Jacob (see Omni 1:25), and the "holy men" and "the prophets" who once worked at Benjamin's side to ensure orthodoxy (Words of Mormon 1:17–18) are not mentioned again and seem to step back into a less significant role. Even the priests who normally surrounded the king (see Mosiah 6:3; see also Noah's priests, Mosiah 11:5) soon diminished in social prominence to the point that special interest groups, such as Alma's and Nehor's, were allowed to appoint and define the rights and duties of their own individual priests and followers (see Mosiah 26:8; Alma 1:6). In that environment, Alma the Younger could teach in the next generation that "many" men (and perhaps *any* man) could be ordained to the high priesthood so long as they were exceedingly faithful, repentant, and righteous before God (see Alma 13:10). These factors indicate movement in Nephite society toward a less centrally structured and more individualistic polity. The initial decision in this direction made by King Benjamin was a strong step taken by a strong leader: only an effective and powerful leader could have made such a change that would have favored the populist poor and would have probably unsettled members of the upper class.[7]

Despite Benjamin's long and successful reign as a highly revered king, within a generation after his death the Nephites not only implemented his egalitarian policies but went further than perhaps even Benjamin could have imagined. They abandoned the idea of kingship altogether and moved on to a more democratic form of government led by a chief judge and other judges empowered by "the voice of the people," with other key responsibilities divided among a few specialized religious, military, and administrative leaders (see Mosiah 29).

Such a change in the fundamental structure of a society is usually accompanied by great upheavals and radical social restructuring. Dislodging a royal family, divesting aristocratic property owners, and unseating entrenched officials usually involves demagoguery and disruption, if not violence and revolution. But the transition from kingship to democracy in Zarahemla was accomplished relatively easily. The ruling Nephites themselves engineered and favored the change in government (see Mosiah 29:4–37), and the change was accepted readily by a majority of all enfranchised people in the land (see Mosiah 29:37–41).

While it is true that a civil uprising soon followed, led by the so-called kingmen under Amlici who opposed the new regime (see Alma 2–3), ideologically most of the people easily embraced the idea and the ideals of democratization.

The question thus becomes: How is one to explain this remarkably smooth transition? For the nineteen reasons listed below, the answer would seem to be found primarily in King Benjamin's speech. Thirty-three years before the inauguration of the reign of judges, Benjamin's speech paved the way, perhaps unwittingly, for the obsolescence of the monarchy. Ironically, at a coronation ceremony installing his own son Mosiah as king, Benjamin's generous and progressive theology planted seeds that would have contributed significantly to the evolution of his son's kingship into a more democratic form of government. Consider the following factors:

Profound Equality

Benjamin taught powerfully that he as king was no better than any other person in the society (see Mosiah 2:10–11). He told his people that he too was of the dust, an extraordinary concession for any king to make (see Mosiah 2:26). Although his people may have understood this more as an expression of personal humility than as a plank in a political manifesto, the notion that all people in the land were of the dust and were therefore fundamentally equal to each other would have had a strong potential for leveling political attitudes and strengthening democratic tendencies within that society.

Universal Humiliation

One of the elements of an ancient New Year festival, which also happens to appear in Benjamin's speech, was the ritual humiliation of the king,[8] during which he fell to the earth.[9] Some scholars have suggested that the king in Israel underwent a similar type of annual humiliation.[10] Notably, Benjamin had all the people participate in this *proskynesis*. In Mosiah 4:1–3, they all fell to the earth, as normally the king alone would have done, having "viewed themselves in their own carnal state, even less than the dust of the earth" (Mosiah 4:2). By participating in the kingly ritual of humiliation, every person in the crowd would have felt an increased sense of societal equality and involvement.

Royal Diminution

Benjamin's concept of kingship was remarkably modest, even for an Israelite. The so-called "Paragraph of the King" in Deuteronomy 17 imposed a remarkable set of limitations on the lawful power of any king in Israel, assuring that he remained as "one from among thy brethren" (Deuteronomy 17:15) and did not become a demigod as kings became in most other ancient civilizations. Benjamin made sure that his people understood that the only real king was God, the king of heaven and creator of the universe; and if the people owed Benjamin any thanks or praise, then how much more should they render that thanks to their Heavenly King (see Mosiah 2:19). Not only did these declarations keep King Benjamin at the same level as his people, but they also placed all of those people on par with the king in the ritual and moral functions of giving offerings of thanks to God.

Universal elevation

Another important element of Israelite royal ideology was viewing the king as arising from the dust to exaltation.[11] God told the Israelite king Baasha that divine power had raised him to kingship from the dust: "I exalted thee out of the dust, and made thee prince over my people Israel" (1 Kings 16:2). The king's total dependence on God as his source of strength and legitimacy was accentuated by the king's reduction to the status of dust. Accordingly, when Benjamin not only brought himself to the dust (see Mosiah 2:26), but also affirmed that all people are of the dust and therefore belong entirely to God who created them and are dependent upon God for their daily breath and everything that they have and are (see Mosiah 2:20–21; 4:21), Benjamin drew all his people into the realm of royal ideology. He positioned them to be raised in status just as his son, the new monarch, would also be elevated. Like kings or queens, the people asked for forgiveness, and "the Spirit of the Lord came upon them, and they were filled with joy" (Mosiah 4:3), and ultimately they were raised to the level of being sons and daughters of God (see Mosiah 5:7).

Direct Participation in the Political Covenant

The operative power that raised the Israelite king from the dust to his elevated position was the power of covenant. In traditional Israelite coronations, only the king entered into the covenant with God and thereby became his son. Davidic kings, as a type or shadow of the Messiah, were told by God upon their coronation, "I [have] set my king upon my holy hill of Zion. I will declare the decree: the Lord hath said unto me, Thou art my Son; this day have I begotten thee" (Psalm 2:6–7). The covenant instilled in the king a position of authority or favor. In the coronation of Benjamin's son, however, not only the new king but every person in the kingdom was allowed to enter into the covenant (see Mosiah 5:2–7). Modern readers may have a hard time appreciating how egalitarian this simple, symbolic gesture must have seemed in the minds of the people who were allowed to receive this royal privilege from Benjamin. By affording all people in his land participation in this covenant status at the time of his son's coronation, Benjamin again reduced the distance between king and people, thereby facilitating the transition from kingship to democracy.

Hearing the Voice of the People

When the people answered King Benjamin, "they all cried aloud with one voice" (Mosiah 4:2), confessing their need for the atonement of Jesus Christ and expressing their faith and loyalty toward the Son of God, who created heaven and earth. By allowing the people to express aloud their allegiance to the Lord God Omnipotent, Benjamin also acknowledged the importance of hearing from the voice of the people both in political and religious affairs. Prior to this time, nothing in the Nephite records indicates that "the voice of the people" had been previously consulted. We may see in Benjamin's speech, therefore, an important instance (if not the inaugural appearance) of the "voice of the people," a significant element of Nephite politics under the reign of the judges (see Mosiah 29:25–26; Alma 2:7).

Direct Participation in the Religious Covenant

Also relevant is the fact that King Benjamin allowed all of his people to enter into the covenant in Mosiah 5, promising to obey the commandments of God that he should give to them. Benjamin's assembly, of course, was not the first in ancient Israel to renew the covenant between God and his people. In Joshua 24, for example, Joshua exhorted the people to choose Jehovah and to "serve him in sincerity and in truth" (Joshua 24:14–15), to which "the people answered and said, God forbid that we should forsake the Lord, . . . we will serve the Lord" (Joshua 24:16, 21). On other occasions, however, the people of Israel were simply gathered together to hear the words of the law read to them, after which a covenant renewal may or may not have occurred (see, for example, Deuteronomy 31:12–13). By allowing all of his people—every man, woman, and child—to participate in a direct covenant renewal, not merely a reminder of a covenant previously made, Benjamin intensified the individualistic involvement of his people in the religious and public process.

Recognition of Freedom

Benjamin's people at first viewed themselves as "even less than the dust of the earth" (Mosiah 4:2), but through the force and effect of their covenant they became spiritually begotten, free, and empowered (see Mosiah 3:17; 5:7–8). Freedom in the ancient world was a rare and precious commodity. Only the rich and the powerful had much latitude in being able to come and go as they pleased. Other people, including slaves, debtors, day laborers, peasant farmers, and simple craftsmen, had little political (let alone economic) capacity to go, to do, to say, to believe, or to effectively think whatever they wanted. With Benjamin's impressive covenant, however, came the declaration, "And under this head ye are made free, and there is no other head whereby ye can be made free" (Mosiah 5:8). This double declaration of the free status of his people would have hit these covenantors as a bold declaration of independence. It would have moved their world view a major step toward democracy.

Dispensing the New Name

In a world in which a new coronation name was typically given exclusively to the ascending monarch,[12] it is politically significant that Benjamin decided to give the new name, revealed in connection with his son's coronation, to every person in the crowd (see Mosiah 3:17; 5:7–8). Benjamin recognized that this move was unique—even remarkably daring. In giving the people a new name, he said that they would thereby "be distinguished above all the people which the Lord God hath brought out of the land of Jerusalem" (Mosiah 1:11). Not only was the new name distinctive and unique, but if these people knew anything about traditional coronation ceremonies, they must have been staggered beyond imagination to find themselves the privileged recipients of the new name and the ones who took upon themselves this new name. By dispensing the blessing of the new name as universally as he did, Benjamin countered the humiliation of the king and the people to the dust with the elevation of the people to a privileged status. Again, all of this must have comprised a significant step in the direction of democratizing the prevailing Nephite political atmosphere.

Divine Adoption of All the People

Based on several scriptures, one may well conclude that "as part of the enthronement procedure the divine adoption of the king" occurred.[13] For example, the Lord spoke of Solomon, "I will be his father, and he shall be my son" (2 Samuel 7:14). Whereas the traditional procedure resulted in only the king being designated as "son," Benjamin's covenant ended with the pronouncement, "because of the covenant which ye have made ye shall be called the children of Christ, his sons, and his daughters; for behold, this day he hath spiritually begotten you" (Mosiah 5:7). As we have previously observed, "What was once reserved for kings at coronation has now been extended in Nephite culture to the people generally."[14]

Standing on the Right Hand

As a result of the covenant, the king in Israel stood in a special position with respect to God: he stood on the right hand of God. Psalm 110, a royal coronation psalm, speaks to the king of Israel and affirms his sonship to God, with the Lord announcing to the king, "Sit thou at my right hand, until I make thine enemies thy footstool" (Psalm 110:1). In Benjamin's case, by giving his people the name by which they shall be called, Benjamin made it possible for all to "be found at the right hand of God" (Mosiah 5:9). He shared with all his people the cherished place of honor traditionally reserved for the king alone.

Sharing Royal Duties

In ancient Israel, it was typically the obligation of the king to care for the poor. Kings of Babylon boasted that they were guardians over the poor, the widows, and the orphans. Similarly, in ancient Israel, a king was recognized as a just ruler if he afforded or provided social justice for all. With Benjamin's speech, the obligation to assure social justice in his kingdom was placed upon all people, both the rich and the poor (see Mosiah 4:21–30). The demanding obligations of helping those in need of help, giving of one's substance to those who stand in need, and not turning the beggar out to perish (see Mosiah 4:16) were shouldered by all the people, who in effect were asked to assume a burden normally considered to be a preeminently royal obligation.

Civil and Economic Equality

By prohibiting slavery in the land of Zarahemla (see Mosiah 2:13), Benjamin decreed an innovative policy that protected the poor, relieved the indebted, and afforded the lower classes significant civil protection against various forms of economic and social servitude (see Mosiah 4:21–26). Assuming that Benjamin's move was a novel edict (which seems likely because various forms of slavery and bond servitude were permitted but regulated under the law of Moses; see Exodus 21:20; Leviticus 25:6; Isaiah 24:2), Benjamin's policy must have emboldened the lower classes and started the people in Zarahemla thinking about new social arrangements based on a much stronger concept of citizen equality. Benjamin correctly sensed the motivations or policies underlying the lenient rules that regulated and limited the institution of slavery or servitude under the law of Moses, namely that all people belonged to God and therefore could not rightly belong to a slave master, and similarly that God had freed Israel from bondage in Egypt and therefore it was unbecoming for them to turn around and make permanent slaves one of another. By taking these purposes one step further, by not allowing his people (Nephites or Mulekites) in any way (not even for a term of years) to make slaves one of another (see Mosiah 2:13), Benjamin moved his society a major step closer to the ideal of removing economic and social "inequality" from the land (Mosiah 29:32).

Record Distribution

Benjamin caused the words of his speech to be written and then "sent [them] forth among those that were not under the sound of his voice, that they might also receive his words" (Mosiah 2:8–9). According to the Paragraph of the King (see Deuteronomy 17:18), only the king and the priests were typically required to have a copy of the law and to read it all the days of their lives. When King Benjamin distributed to many of his people a copy of his speech, which imposed covenantal obligations with the force and effect of law within his kingdom and under God, he transferred the evidence or testimony of that covenant into the hands of the common man. One may suspect that this action had a significant leveling effect in the society. No longer did each person need to go to the palace or the temple to find a stele posting the prevailing law of the land. Like the king, each person could read in this document all the days of his life.[15]

Name Recorded

With each coronation, the name of the new king was recorded or inscribed prominently in the land. Names of new pharaohs were chiseled onto the walls and pillars of temples in ancient Egypt, and royal names were added to king lists in ancient Mesopotamia. In the case of Benjamin's ceremony, every man, woman, and child had their name recorded in the book of the covenant as they entered into this sacred covenant relationship with God.

A New Census

At the beginning of Benjamin's assembly, the decision was made not to number the people. The traditional census was not taken. The rationale given for this departure from normal procedure was "they had multiplied exceedingly" and were so great "that they did not number them" (Mosiah 2:2). Of course, they *could* have numbered them, for they took down all of their names at the end of the ceremony, but for some reason they decided not to number them at that time. Perhaps Benjamin delayed the "numbering" of his people until after the covenant had been made because under the old system, the people would have been "numbered" by tribes and by families, as one encounters, for example, in Numbers 1:17–54. The last thing that Benjamin wanted at this point was for his people to be divided against each other. Some groups or families were undoubtedly larger or more influential than others; competition among families or tribes over political power or social privileges could have become highly problematical for his son Mosiah as a new ruler. To avert this divisiveness,

Benjamin waited to "number" his people until they all stood under a single "head," not under family or tribal heads (see Mosiah 5:8; 6:1–2). This leveling of the society and breaking down the old social structure must have been extremely conspicuous to Benjamin's people, all of whom had gathered around the temple according to their families, each man with his family in his tent (see Mosiah 2:5). We may well imagine that extended family groups and tribal organizations of Mulekites, Nephites, Jacobites, Josephites, and Zoramites would have come to the assembly with their traditional banners, precincts, and loyalties ready to be counted and to assert their conventional presence.

Shared Risks

Kingship brought with it certain risks, particularly that of being swept away in the event that the ruler ever broke the covenant. Just as the king had been elevated from the dust by God, God would return an unrighteous king to the dust and utterly sweep him out of the house, as if by a woman sweeping the dirt out her home (compare 1 Kings 16:3). Similarly, Benjamin placed on his people, in the event that they should fall into wickedness, the awful prospects of being cast out, of the Lord having no place in them, of never-ending torment, and of having their names utterly blotted out (see Mosiah 2:37, 39; 5:11, 14).

Individual Responsibility

In shifting to the people the responsibility for their own spiritual destiny before God, Benjamin used traditional Israelite theology to his political advantage. For many years, the law of Moses had placed personal responsibility on the shoulders of each individual: "The fathers shall not be put to death for the children, neither shall the children be put to death for the fathers: every man shall be put to death for his own sin" (Deuteronomy 24:16). Thus, it was not particularly innovative when Benjamin placed an individual "wo" on each person who was inclined to obey the evil spirit, for "the same drinketh damnation to his own soul" (Mosiah 2:33). Nor was it new when he said that "none shall be found blameless" (Mosiah 3:21) after each person in every nation had been warned and taught of the Lord. But to place this theology so prominently in the midst of a political coronation setting probably added a new democratic element to the Nephite political awareness. This theological point manifested itself politically in the law reform of King Mosiah, who understood equality as requiring that each citizen would have "an equal chance . . . to answer for their own sins" and would no longer be accountable for the iniquities of their king (Mosiah 29:38; see vv. 31–37).

Dissemination of Blessings

Great blessings, however, were also promised to the king in the ancient world. In particular, the Psalms expect that the foes of the king will "bow before him; and his enemies shall lick the dust" (Psalm 72:9). Along the same lines, Benjamin promised his son Mosiah and his people that one of the blessings of obedience was that "your enemies shall have no power over you" (Mosiah 2:31). In other words, the promise of victory over enemies and resurrection from the dust, common themes from Near Eastern enthronement ceremonies, were extended by Benjamin to the common people as well as to the new king in Zarahemla.

Conclusion

When one examines the structure of the book of Mosiah, the first chapter beginning at the height of the reign of kings and the last chapter ending with the commencement of the reign of the judges, the progression of events in this era of Nephite history seems obvious. Benjamin's speech paved the way for the coming of the reign of judges. In many respects, Benjamin's speech may be the best royal and religious text to be found anywhere in world literature that shows both king and common folk sharing all of the crucial elements in the traditional ancient set of the interconnected themes of kingship, coronation, covenant, and being raised from the dust to eternal life. Perhaps openly sharing these previously restricted elements, along with publicly disclosing sacred revelations that would normally have been retained among the prophetic elite, contributed to the overwhelming, united reaction of the people who were deeply moved on this occasion by spiritual feelings of love and appreciation for their old and new kings.[16] All this leads to the conclusion that the ultimate elimination of kingship and the subsequent inauguration of the reign of judges by King Mosiah was already a political inevitability embedded in the spirit of this age, propelled forward decisively by the expansive steps taken by King Benjamin in his powerful and masterful oration.

Research by John W. Welch, 1998. Originally presented at a FARMS Brown Bag Lecture, April 8, 1998.

NOTES

1. See John W. Welch and Stephen D. Ricks, eds., *King Benjamin's Speech: "That Ye May Learn Wisdom,"* ed. John W. Welch and Stephen D. Ricks (Provo, Utah: FARMS, 1998); and *Benjamin's Speech Made Simple* (Provo, Utah: FARMS, 1999).

2. See John W. Welch, "Benjamin, the Man: His Place in Nephite History," in *King Benjamin's Speech,* 23–54.

3. See John W. Welch, "Chiasmus in the Book of Mormon," *BYU Studies* 10/1 (1969): 69–84, especially 82.

4. The law of Moses, of course, prohibited people from oppressing those who fit into these specific categories (see Exodus 22:21–24), who were also allowed to glean in the fields (see Deuteronomy 24:19–22); Benjamin, however, required his people to impart of their substance to all those who were in need regardless of their status as widows, orphans, or resident aliens.

5. See Welch, "Benjamin, the Man," 48–49.

6. I am grateful to Noel B. Reynolds for this observation and line of analysis.

7. See John W. Welch, "A Masterful Oration," in *King Benjamin's Speech*, 58.

8. See Helmer Ringgren, "Enthronement Festival or Covenant Renewal?" *Biblical Research* 7 (1962): 45.

9. For more information on this topic, see Terrence L. Szink and John W. Welch, "King Benjamin's Speech in the Context of Ancient Israelite Festivals," in *King Benjamin's Speech*, 147–223; first discussed by Hugh W. Nibley, *An Approach to the Book of Mormon*, 3rd ed. (Salt Lake City: Deseret Book and FARMS, 1988), 304.

10. See Aubrey R. Johnson, *Sacral Kingship in Ancient Israel* (Cardiff: University of Wales Press, 1955), 22–25; John H. Eaton, *Kingship and the Psalms*, 2nd ed. (Sheffield: Journal for the Study of the Old Testament, 1986), 133–34; Helmer Ringgren, *Israelite Religion*, trans. David E. Green (Philadelphia: Fortress, 1966), 236–37.

11. See Walter Brueggemann, "From Dust to Kingship," *Zeitschrift für die alttestamentlische Wissenschaft* 84/1 (1972): 1–18.

12. See Stephen D. Ricks, "Kingship, Coronation, and Covenant in Mosiah 1–6," in *King Benjamin's Speech*, 252–53.

13. Ricks, "Kingship, Coronation, and Covenant," 253.

14. Ibid., 254.

15. Scholars speak of the democratizing of Egyptian religion, which similarly occurred as their burial texts were moved, first from the pyramids onto coffins, and then from coffins into the Book of the Dead, which all people could afford to purchase for their burial. No longer could the aristocracy alone enjoy the privilege of possessing the text necessary for a full burial.

16. See Welch, "A Masterful Oration," 59.

30

AS A GARMENT
IN A HOT FURNACE

"The life of king Noah shall be valued even
as a garment in a hot furnace." (Mosiah 12:3)

In Mosiah 12:3, Abinadi prophesied "that the life of king Noah shall be valued even as a garment in a hot furnace." Noah's priests reported the words a little differently, "thy life shall be as a garment in a furnace of fire" (Mosiah 12:10). The prophecy was fulfilled when King Noah was burned to death (see Mosiah 19:20).

Mark J. Morrise has shown that Abinadi's words fit the pattern of a simile curse, in which the subject of the curse is likened to a specific event;[1] Morrise provides many examples, such as the following from an Aramaic treaty of approximately 750 B.C.:

Just as this was is burned by fire, so shall Arpad be burned.

Hugh Nibley suggested that Abinadi borrowed from the simile curse in Isaiah 50:9, 11 (cited in 2 Nephi 7:9, 11): "Who is he that shall condemn me? lo, they all shall wax old as a garment; the moth shall eat them up. . . . Behold, all ye that kindle a fire, that compass yourselves about with sparks: walk in the light of your fire, and in the sparks that ye have kindled."[2]

But the Isaiah parallel is only a partial one, for verse 11

127

(which mentions fire) has nothing to do with the garment, which is consumed by the moth, not the fire. If there are parallels to be found, one might expect them to include both the garment and the fire and possibly the furnace. Yet no such complete parallels are forthcoming from the Old Testament or other ancient Near Eastern literature. Nevertheless, there are some partial parallels.

The law of Moses provides that a garment visibly tainted by the plague is to be burned (see Leviticus 13:52, 57; compare Jude 1:23). While the Lord knew about germs, the ancient Israelites did not. Therefore, the burning of garments to prevent the spread of disease would not have been reasonable before the nineteenth century, when people learned that microorganisms caused diseases. But the burning of a man's possessions after his death is very common in "primitive" cultures throughout the world. Typically, all his personal possessions would be brought into his house (usually a rather insubstantial structure in such societies), which would then be set on fire. In this way, the deceased would not be able to find his possessions and would be free to move on to the world of spirits. In such cases, we have the garment and the fire, but not the furnace.

A ceremonial burning of worn-out priestly clothing took place in the Jerusalem temple of Christ's time during the Feast of Tabernacles. Located above the court of the women were huge cups in which olive oil was burned; these garments served as wicks. Just as priests who developed bodily infirmities were disqualified from performing priestly functions under the law of Moses (see Leviticus 21:17–23), so, too, their worn clothing became unsuited for temple service.[3]

Proverbs 6:27 asks, "Can a man take fire in his bosom, and his clothes not be burned?" The answer is that this can happen only if he is righteous and the Lord intervenes to protect him. A number of ancient Jewish texts speak of how Abraham was tossed into a fiery furnace to be burned. One of these accounts notes that all but his "lower garments" (i.e., undergarments) were removed and that, while the cords that bound him were burned, these undergarments were not (see *Book of Jasher* 12:27). Similarly, when Daniel's three friends were tossed into the fiery furnace, fully clothed (see Daniel 3:21), their clothing sustained no fire or smoke damage (see Daniel 3:27).

In the Book of Mormon, the three Nephites were thrice "cast into a furnace and received no harm" (3 Nephi 28:21; see Mormon 8:24). Three times the Bible compares Israel's deliverance from Egypt to rescue from a furnace of iron (see Deuteronomy 4:20; 1 Kings 8:51; Jeremiah 11:4). Indeed, the righteous are purified as silver or gold in the furnace (see Psalm 12:6; Proverbs 17:3; 27:21; Isaiah 48:10 [see 1 Nephi 20:10]; 1 Corinthians 3:12–15). On the other hand, the wicked are considered dross, to be melted down in the furnace (see Ezekiel 22:18–22). Jesus said that he would send forth angels to gather up the wicked and "cast them into a furnace of fire" (Matthew 13:41–42, 49–50). Of course, this does not necessarily mean a literal furnace. The wicked of Sodom and Gomorrah were destroyed by fire from heaven and "the smoke of the country went up as the smoke of a furnace" (Genesis 19:28).

A number of pseudepigraphic texts speak of a heavenly river of fire into which the dead are made to pass. The righteous cross the river without injury and approach the throne of God, while the wicked are burned or tortured in the fire.[4] This reminds us of the declaration in Genesis 14:35 JST that "the sons of God should be tried so as by fire." In 2 Nephi 30:10, we read, "the wicked will he destroy; and he will spare his people, yea, even if it so be that he must destroy the wicked by fire." Lehi and Nephi, in their vision of the tree of life, "saw that the justice of God did also divide the wicked from the righteous; and the brightness thereof was like unto the brightness of a flaming fire, which ascendeth up unto God forever and ever, and hath no end" (1 Nephi 15:30).[5] On the other hand, "were the wicked, in their sins, under the necessity of walking into the presence of the Father and the Son . . . their condition would be more excruciating and unendurable than to dwell in the lake that burns with fire and brimstone."[6] Elder Orson Pratt declared:

> I have often heard blasphemers and drunkards and abominable characters say, I really hope I shall at last get to heaven. If they get there, they will be in the most miserable place they could be in. Were they to behold the face of God, or the angels, it would kindle in them a flame of unquenchable fire; it would be the very worst place a wicked man could get into: he would much rather go and dwell in hell with the Devil and his host.[7]

The Book of Mormon prophet Moroni probably had this idea in mind when he wrote to the wicked:

> Ye would be more miserable to dwell with a holy and just God, under a consciousness of your filthiness before him, than ye would to dwell with the damned souls in hell. For behold, when ye shall be brought to see your nakedness before God; and also the glory of God, and the holiness of Jesus Christ, it will kindle a flame of unquenchable fire upon you. (Mormon 9:4–5; see also Mosiah 2:38; 3:25, 27; compare Jacob 6:9–10)

It seems that Abinadi's curse of King Noah, with the specific mention of fire, was intended to indicate the very serious nature of Noah's sins. Like the diseased garment in Leviticus 13:52, 57 and the useless garment in Isaiah 14:19–20 (another simile curse), he is not to be honored with burial. Instead, he will suffer death by fire, which is the ultimate punishment of the wicked.

Research by John A. Tvedtnes, originally published in the Journal of Book of Mormon Studies *6/1 (1997): 76–79.*

NOTES

1. See Mark J. Morrise, "Simile Curses in the Ancient Near East, Old Testament, and Book of Mormon," *Journal of Book of Mormon Studies* 2/1 (1993): 124–38. His discussion of Mosiah 12:3, 10–12 is found on page 135.

2. Hugh W. Nibley, *The Prophetic Book of Mormon*, ed. John W. Welch (Salt Lake City: Deseret Book and FARMS, 1989), 305.

3. Jewish tradition indicates that priestly garments could not be consumed by fire and sometimes protected their wearers from harm. See the discussion in John A. Tvedtnes, "Priestly Clothing in Bible Times," in *Temples of the Ancient World*, ed. Donald W. Parry (Salt Lake City: Deseret Book and FARMS, 1994), 659–61.

4. See *Testament of Isaac* 5:21–29; *Sibylline Oracles* 2:196–213, 252–308, 313–18, 330–38; Ethiopic *Apocalypse of Peter*; compare Zechariah 3:2.

5. Joseph Smith taught that "God Almighty Himself dwells in eternal fire . . . all corruption is devoured by the fire. 'Our God is a consuming fire' [Hebrews 12:29; compare Deuteronomy 4:24]. . . . Immortality dwells in everlasting burnings. . . . All men who are immortal dwell in everlasting burnings" (*History of the Church*, 6:366). While the wicked suffer "a torment as the lake of fire and brimstone" (ibid., 6:317), the righteous dwell in flames (see ibid., 6:51–52). Those who are exalted become, in the resurrection, kings and priests to God, as the other gods before them, and are "able to dwell in everlasting burnings, and to sit in glory, as do those who sit enthroned in everlasting power" (ibid., 6:306; see 6:476 and *Journal of Discourses*, 8:92).

6. *Journal of Discourses*, 8:153–54.

7. Ibid., 7:89.

31

HIS STEWARDSHIP WAS FULFILLED

"Ye see that ye have not power to slay me,
therefore I finish my message." (Mosiah 13:7)

When Abinadi testified before King Noah and his priests, they "attempted to lay their hands on him" (Mosiah 13:2), but he warned them, "Touch me not, for God shall smite you if ye lay your hands upon me, for I have not delivered the message which the Lord sent me to deliver" (Mosiah 13:3). Knowing that "the Spirit of the Lord was upon him," "the people of king Noah durst not lay their hands on him" (Mosiah 13:5), and Abinadi went on to tell them about the coming of the Messiah. "I finish my message," he declared, "and then it matters not whither I go, if it so be that I am saved" (Mosiah 13:9). Only after he had delivered the words of the Lord were they able to slay him (see Mosiah 17:1).

A similar story is found in the pseudepigraphic book known as *4 Baruch* or "The Things Omitted from Jeremiah the Prophet."[1] "And as Jeremiah was saying these things about the Son of God, that he is coming into the world, the people became angry and said, 'These (once) again are the words spoken by Isaiah the son of Amos, saying, "I saw God and the son of God." Come, therefore, and let us not kill him by that (same) death [as Isaiah], but let's stone him with stones'" (*4 Baruch* 9:21–22).[2] But Jeremiah declared, "they will not kill me until I have described to you everything that I saw" (*4 Baruch* 9:24). He then asked the Lord to protect him, and his life was spared by divine intervention when the Lord blinded their eyes and made them think that a large stone was Jeremiah. "Jeremiah delivered all the mysteries that he had seen . . . and then he simply stood in the midst of the people, desiring to bring his stewardship to an end" (*4 Baruch* 9:29). The people then "saw him, [and] they immediately ran at him with many stones, and his stewardship was fulfilled" (*4 Baruch* 9:31).

On several occasions, as Jesus testified of himself and his relationship with the Father, those who heard him sought to slay him. On two of these occasions, he simply went "through the midst of them" and escaped unharmed (Luke 4:30; compare John 8:58–59). On two other occasions, we read that "no man laid hands on him, because his hour was not yet come" (John 7:30; see 8:20; compare John 2:4; 7:6, 8). Only when he had completed his mortal ministry did he declare that "the hour is come; [and] the Son of man is betrayed into the hands of sinners" (Mark 14:41; compare John 12:23; 13:1; 17:1).

These ancient accounts from the Book of Mormon, *4 Baruch,* and the New Testament reflect a consistent attitude found among the words of Jesus Christ and his early prophets. Interestingly, in October 1844, Brigham Young articulated this as a divine principle: "The Lord never let a prophet fall on the earth until he had accomplished his work."[3]

Research by John A. Tvedtnes, originally published in the Journal of Book of Mormon Studies *5/2 (1996): 169–70.*

NOTES

1. The text used herein is the English translation by S. E. Robinson, in *The Old Testament Pseudepigrapha,* ed. James H. Charlesworth (Garden City, N.Y.: Doubleday, 1985), 2:418–25.

2. Similarly, when Lehi told the people about his vision "of the coming of a Messiah, and also the redemption of the world . . . the Jews . . . were angry with him; yea, even as with the prophets of old, whom they had cast out, and stoned, and slain; and they also sought his life, that they might take it away" (1 Nephi 1:19–20; compare Helaman 8:22). The Lord saved Lehi by telling him to flee Jerusalem. In this, Lehi's story resembles that of Abinadi in Mosiah 11:26. When Nephi was threatened by his brothers, the Lord protected him as he protected Abinadi, by making it impossible for them to lay their hands on him until he had finished speaking (1 Nephi 17:48–55; compare Lehi in 1 Nephi 2:13–14).

3. *History of the Church,* 7:302.

32 good

EVIDENCE FOR TENTS
IN THE BOOK OF MORMON

*"And it came to pass that when Alma could pursue the
Amlicites no longer he caused that his people should
pitch their tents in the valley of Gideon." (Alma 2:20)*

One of the minor points made in recent criticisms of the
Book of Mormon is the claim that there is no evidence
of a tent-making or tent-using tradition in Mesoamerica
and no available material for making the tents that the
Book of Mormon mentions. Actually, Mesoamericanist literature makes it clear that tents were in regular use by
Aztec armies at the time of the Spanish conquest, and there
is good reason to suppose that they were used by other
peoples and in earlier times (including Nephite times) in
Mesoamerica.

When the Spaniards saw the Aztec tents, they immediately labelled them *tiendas*, "tents." Ross Hassig, the authority on Aztec warfare, notes, "The [Aztec military] camp
itself was constructed of tents and huts [*xahcalli*] made of
woven grass mats."[1] Durán, whose *Historia de las Indias de
Nueva España* is a fundamental source on Aztec war customs,
also reports tents. Durán arrived in New Spain in 1542, only
twenty-one years after the Conquest. He reports, for example, that the combined armies of the Mexicans prepared
for an expedition against the city of Tepeaca by getting their
encampment set up, "pitching their tents and huts [*armando*

135

sus tiendas y jacales]—that is what they call their war tents—very nicely ordered and arranged."[2]

"And one day's journey before they arrived [at their destination], they sent ahead those charged with logistics to the place where they were going to set up the camp, and they pitched the tents *[tiendas]* and erected the huts *[chozas]*."[3]

In preparation for war, Montezuma ordered surrounding cities to furnish stores of food and "sleeping mats *[petates]* to make tents *[tiendas]* . . . in which they would dwell [while] in the field."[4]

Bernal Diaz mentions that the Aztec soldiers "erect[ed] their huts" in the field,[5] and John Sorenson distinguishes at least five types of field military shelters from the literature, several of them labelled *tiendas,* "tents," by the Spaniards.[6]

Durán's *Historia* describes tents in detail. He mentions at least six kinds of field military shelters:

- *casas pajizas,* houses of straw;
- *chozas,* huts of unspecified material but suitable for leaders to occupy;
- *jacales* (from Nahuátl *xahcalli*), huts; some were collapsible and movable; it is unclear how these differed from chozas; perhaps the latter were made from materials such as brush scrounged in the field, while the jacales may have been formed from mats;
- *tiendas,* tents; made of mats, or sometimes perhaps of cloth, given the normal Spanish sense of the term *tiendas;* some were good enough to house leaders;
- *casas de petates,* literally "houses of mats"; the cheap, light, portable mats could be combined with a framework of, say, spears, to make a simple tent;
- *cuarteles,* quarters, barracks; perhaps commandeered housing, or perhaps collapsible multiperson shelters.

Such military housing should not surprise us. After all, every army in the world has had to find culturally and ecologically effective ways to cope with the problem of shelter in the field. As long as there are armies, there must be cross-cultural equivalents of "tents." The only questions in relation to a specific culture have to do with form, materials, and terminology.

For an added witness, we can look in the Motul dictionary, a classic sixteenth-century work that scholars automatically turn to for supplementary light on pre-Spanish Yucatec Maya language and culture. The definition for the Maya word *pazel* is *"choza o tienda en el campo, o casilla pequeña de paja"* (hut or tent for use in the field, or small straw booth).[7]

Mesoamerican farmers have long and widely used a similar type of hut. For example, the Zoques of Santa Maria Chimalapa in the Isthmus of Tehuantepec still construct "very small *chozas* of palm fronds and grass, almost level with the ground, where they sleep during the days when they work in the fields" away from home.[8]

There is no archaeological evidence for tents among the Aztecs—just accounts in historical documents. What archaeological evidence one could expect that would establish the presence of overnight *tiendas, chozas,* or *jacales,* even among the Aztecs less than five centuries ago, is not at all clear. Then what hope has an archaeologist of finding the still slimmer traces of a temporary encampment dated two thousand years before that, the time of the Nephites? Until archaeologists come up with an operational solution to this dilemma, it seems sensible to accept the Book of Mormon as documentary evidence of the use of tents in the first century B.C. on a par with Durán's testimony for the sixteenth century A.D.

Research by John L. Sorenson, originally published as a FARMS Update in Insights *(May 1994): 2.*

NOTES

1. Ross Hassig, *Aztec Warfare* (Norman: University of Oklahoma Press, 1988), 73.

2. Fray Diego Durán, *Historia de las Indias de Nueva España e Islas de Tierra Firme* Tomo II, Biblioteca Porrua 37 (México: Editorial Porrua, 1967), 2:157. The translations are Sorenson's; pages refer to the Porrua edition.

3. Ibid., 2:180.

4. Ibid., 2:156.

5. Cited in Sorenson, *An Ancient American Setting for the Book of Mormon* (Salt Lake City: Deseret Book and FARMS, 1985), 161.

6. See John L. Sorenson, "Viva Zapato! Hurray for the Shoe," review of "Does the Shoe Fit? A Critique of the Limited Tehuantepec Geography," by Deanne G. Matheny, *Review of Books on the Book of Mormon* 6/1 (1994): 333–34.

7. *Diccionario de Motul. Maya, Español, atribuido a Fray Antonio de Ciudad Real . . . Parte 2,* ed. Juán Martinez Hernandez (Mérida: Tipográfica Yucateca, 1929), 732.

8. Carlos Muñoz M., *Crónica de Santa Maria Chimalapa: en las selvas del Istmo de Tehuantepec* (San Luis Potosí: Molina, 1977), 14.

33

REVISITING THE
LAND OF JERUSALEM

*"And behold, [Christ] shall be born of Mary, at
Jerusalem . . . the land of our forefathers." (Alma 7:10)*

For more than 160 years, beginning at least with the
1833 publication of Alexander Campbell's *Delusions*,
countless critics have claimed that the Book of Mormon's
use of the phrase *land of Jerusalem* was a major error and
proof that the book was false. They have especially criticized the use of this phrase in reference to the place where
Christ would be born. That phrase was not used in the
Bible nor in the Apocrypha. Therefore, the critics have
concluded, it was an example of Joseph Smith's ignorance
and evidence that he had tried to perpetrate a fraud.[1] For
anyone honestly concerned with the authenticity of the
Book of Mormon, there was little to argue about after
Hugh Nibley showed in 1957 that one of the Amarna letters, written in the thirteenth century B.C. and discovered
in 1887, recounted the capture of "a city of the land of
Jerusalem, Bet-Ninib."[2] Predictably, this evidence, along
with further evidence of the general usage of this type of
terminology in the Old World[3] has been ignored by critics
of the Book of Mormon.

Now from the Dead Sea Scrolls comes an even more
specific occurrence of the phrase *land of Jerusalem* that gives

insight into its usage and meaning—in a text that indirectly links the phrase to the Jerusalem of Lehi's time.

Robert Eisenmann and Michael Wise, in *The Dead Sea Scrolls Uncovered,* discuss one document that they have provisionally named "Pseudo-Jeremiah" *(4Q385).* The beginning of the damaged text reads as follows: ". . . Jeremiah the Prophet before the Lord [. . . wh]o were taken captive from the land of Jerusalem" (fragment 1, lines 1–2).[4]

In their discussion of this text, Eisenmann and Wise elaborate on the significance of the phrase *land of Jerusalem,* which they see as an equivalent for Judah *(Yehud):* "Another interesting reference is to the 'land of Jerusalem' in Line 2 of Fragment 1. This greatly enhances the sense of historicity of the whole, since Judah or 'Yehud' (the name of the area on coins from the Persian period) by this time consisted of little more than Jerusalem and its immediate environs."[5]

Based on the evidence from Qumran, and in the words of Eisenmann and Wise, we can conclude that consistent usage of such language among a people of Israel who fled Jerusalem at the time of Jeremiah also "greatly enhances the sense of historicity" of the Book of Mormon.

Critics of the Book of Mormon will not likely give up this argument, despite the evidence. This is not surprising, after all, because the part of their argument that the phrase was not known in Joseph Smith's day was correct. Virtually all opponents of the Book of Mormon have to assume, *a priori,* that the text is a purely human nineteenth-century document in order to justify their rejection of the text. In the case of *land of Jerusalem,* since the phrase could not be explained as being part of Joseph's information environment and since it was not known in biblical literature, they incorrectly concluded that Joseph must have been wrong. Trying to prove a negative, they argued from silence and puffed this supposed error into what they believed was one of their highest polemical mountains of evidence against the Book of Mormon.

The phrase *was not* current in Joseph's day, but, unknown to him, it was an accurate usage for the day in which he claimed the book was written. Thus, despite the critics' best efforts, Joseph's supposed "error" becomes one more evidence of the Book of Mormon's authenticity.

Research by Gordon C. Thomasson, originally published as a FARMS Update in Insights *(March 1994): 2.*

NOTES

1. For a thorough overview of this argument, see Daniel C. Peterson, "Chattanooga Cheapshot, or The Gall of Bitterness," review of *Everything You Ever Wanted to Know about Mormonism,* by John Ankerberg and John Weldon, *Review of Books on the Book of Mormon* 5 (1993): 62–78.

2. Hugh W. Nibley, *An Approach to the Book of Mormon,* 3rd ed. (Salt Lake City: Deseret Book and FARMS, 1988), 101.

3. See Robert F. Smith, "The Land of Jerusalem: The Place of Jesus' Birth," in *Reexploring the Book of Mormon,* ed. John W. Welch (Salt Lake City: Deseret Book and FARMS, 1992),170–72.

4. Robert H. Eisenmann and Michael Wise, *The Dead Sea Scrolls Uncovered* (Shaftesbury, Eng.: Element, 1992), 58.

5. Ibid., 57.

34

BLESSING GOD AFTER EATING ONE'S FILL

"And it came to pass that Alma ate bread and
was filled; and he blessed Amulek and his house,
and he gave thanks unto God." (Alma 8:22)

The Christian practice of saying grace before meals probably owes its origin to the blessing Jesus offered at the last supper when he gave bread and wine to his disciples in remembrance of his body and blood. In Matthew 26:26 we read, "And as they were eating, Jesus took bread, and blessed it, and brake it, and gave it to the disciples, and said, Take, eat; this is my body." But the word *it*, which appears three times in the King James Version of the Bible, is not present in the Greek text. Possibly Jesus was following the Jewish practice of blessing God, not the bread and wine, on the eve of the Sabbath. Indeed, the Roman Catholic Mass is still based on the wording of the Jewish prayer, "Blessed art thou, O Lord, our God, king of the universe, who has brought forth bread from the ground."[1]

In Judaism, while a brief blessing is recited before eating, a series of longer blessings, the *birkat ha-mazon*, follows the meal. Four blessings come after the consumption of bread, while separate blessings are offered for other foods, depending on their nature and origin. The basis for this practice is Deuteronomy 8:10:

> When thou hast eaten and art full,
> then thou shalt bless the Lord thy God
> for the good land which he hath given thee.

This observance is also found in a Dead Sea Scroll poem, which Gaster calls *Invitation to Grace after Meals;* this poem paraphrases the language in the first part of Deuteronomy 8:10. It says, "whenso they eat and are filled," noting that this is when men should speak of wisdom and think of the law given by God.[2]

Blessing after meals is mentioned in Mishnah *Berakhot* 3:3 and *Sukkah* 2:5. The latter notes that when Rabbi Zadok ate only a small portion of food, he didn't say the blessing afterward, probably because Deuteronomy 8:10 calls for a blessing only if one has eaten and is full. The amount that one must eat in order to say "common grace" for a group of people is discussed in Mishnah *Berakhot* 7:2–3, wherein the formula for the blessing varies according to how many are present. In each case, however, it is the Lord who is blessed. Grace after meals is also noted in several passages of the Zohar.[3]

Compare this practice with the wording of Alma 8:22: "And it came to pass that Alma ate bread and was filled; and he blessed Amulek and his house, and he gave thanks unto God." Here, too, the blessing and thanks to God are offered only after being "filled." One might object that it is Amulek's household, and not God, being blessed. But the context of Deuteronomy 8:10 is gratitude to God "for the good land which he hath given thee" and hence perfectly in line with Alma's giving "thanks unto God." It is, in fact, God who does the real blessing, which is the context in which Deuteronomy 14:29 speaks of "eat[ing] and be[ing] satisfied." Deuteronomy 6:10–11 and 8:12–14 warn against eating and being full and yet being ungrateful to God. As for Alma's blessing of Amulek's family after having eaten and being filled, a parallel can be found in the biblical story of Isaac, who desired to eat before blessing his son (see Genesis 27:4, 7, 10, 19, 25, 31, 33).

John W. Welch has noted that an early Christian document, Didache 10:1–2, 5, enjoins prayer "after being filled" during communion.[4] In this connection, it is interesting to see that similar thoughts are expressed on both occasions when the resurrected Christ blessed the sacrament for the Nephites. In 3 Nephi 18:8–18 we read that the Nephites partook of the bread and wine and "were filled" (3 Nephi 18:9), after which Jesus instructed them to pray. 3 Nephi 20:9 contains the slight variation that "when the multitude had all eaten and drunk, behold, they were filled with the Spirit; and they did cry out with one voice, and gave glory to Jesus, whom they both saw and heard." In this case, the people were filled not with the bread and wine, but with the Spirit.[5] Nevertheless, it is interesting that they "gave glory to Jesus" on this occasion.

Hugh Nibley compared the latter passage with the description of Christ's blessing the sacrament for his Old World disciples, as found in an early Coptic document called the *Gospel of the Twelve Apostles*.[6] The text reads, "His [Jesus'] blessing fell upon [shope] the bread in the apostles' hands. And all the people ate and were filled. They *gave praise* to God."[7] Here, again, the pattern is retained. Having eaten their fill, they praised God. Blessing God after eating one's fill is another illustration from the Book of Mormon that the Nephites did, indeed, follow the law of Moses.

The value of all this information as evidence for the Book of Mormon is increased by the fact that the practice is mentioned only in passing, as one would expect for an authentic record that takes such things for granted.

Research by Angela M. Crowell and John A. Tvedtnes, originally published in the Journal of Book of Mormon Studies 6/2 *(1997): 251–54.*

NOTES

1. The sacramental prayers found in the Book of Mormon (Moroni 4:3; 5:2) and repeated in Doctrine and Covenants 20:77, 79 may have been unique to the Nephites. When the revelation now in Doctrine and Covenants 20 was first published in the Book of Commandments in 1833, the prayers were not included; instead, reference was made to the Book of Mormon page on which they were found. For a discussion of the development of the sacramental prayers among the Nephites, see "Our Nephite Sacrament Prayers," in *Reexploring the Book of Mormon,* ed. John W. Welch (Salt Lake City: Deseret Book and FARMS, 1992), 286–89, and John W. Welch, "Benjamin's Covenant as a Precursor of the Sacrament Prayers," in *King Benjamin's Speech: "That Ye May Learn Wisdom,"* ed. John W. Welch and Stephen D. Ricks (Provo, Utah: FARMS, 1998), 295–314.

2. Taken from Theodor H. Gaster, trans., *The Dead Sea Scriptures,* 3rd ed. (Garden City, N.Y.: Doubleday, 1976), 219–21. The text also admonishes the reader to "bless ye the Lord" (line 17), but the thought is separated from the Deuteronomy 8:10 quotation by three other lines and hence may not derive from that scriptural passage.

3. According to Zohar *Exodus* 153a–b, Rabbi Hiya comments on Deuteronomy 8:10: "Should a man then bless the Lord only after he has filled his belly? Nay, even if one eats but a morsel and counts it as a meal, that is called eating to satisfaction." Rabbi Hezekiah added that even an intoxicated person, who is usually barred from saying prayers, "is allowed to say the grace after meals." Maurice Simon and Paul P. Levertoff, trans., *The Zohar* (New York: Bennet, 1958), 4:37–38. Zohar *Exodus* 218a says, "Whoever pronounces the after-meal benediction must do so devotedly, and in a joyful mood unmingled with any tinge of sadness, inasmuch as in giving thanks he is giving of his own to

someone else" (ibid., 4:242). Grace after meals is also discussed briefly in Zohar *Exodus* 157a and *Numbers* 186b.

4. John W. Welch, "From Presence to Practice: Jesus, the Sacrament Prayers, the Priesthood, and Church Discipline in 3 Nephi 18 and Moroni 2–6," *Journal of Book of Mormon Studies* 5/1 (1996): 134.

5. In Jesus' sermon to the Nephites at the temple in Bountiful, those who hunger and thirst after righteousness "shall be filled with the Holy Ghost" (3 Nephi 12:6).

6. The text was published in Eugene Revillout, *Les Apocryphes Coptes, Première Partie, Les évangiles des douze apôtres et de Saint Barthélemy*, vol. 2 of Patrologia Orientalis (Paris: Firmin-Didot, 1907–13).

7. Here we quote Hugh W. Nibley's English translation of Revillout, *Les Apocryphes Coptes*, 2:134–35, in Nibley, *The Prophetic Book of Mormon* (Salt Lake City: Deseret Book and FARMS, 1989), 421.

35 good

THE LAWS OF ESHNUNNA
AND NEPHITE ECONOMICS

"And the judge received for his wages according to his time . . . according to the law which was given. . . . A senum of silver was equal to a senine of gold, and either for a measure of barley." (Alma 11:3, 7)

In order for ancient economies to work effectively, kings spelled out the value of various commodities and established exchange ratios, especially between consumable goods and precious metals. For example, the Laws of Eshnunna, promulgated in Babylonia probably during the early eighteenth century B.C., instituted a system of weights and measures.

The following initial provisions stand at the head of Eshnunna's ancient law code:

1 kor of barley [she'um] is (priced) at [ana] 1 shekel of silver;

3 qa of "best oil" are (priced) at 1 shekel of silver;

1 seah (and) 2 qa of sesame oil are (priced) at 1 shekel of silver [and so on]. . . .

The hire for a wagon together with its oxen and its driver is 1 massiktum (and) 4 seah of barley. If it is (paid in) silver, the hire is one third of a shekel. He shall drive it the whole day.[1]

These laws in the kingdom of Eshnunna allowed people to deal confidently with barley, silver, oil, lard, wool, salt, bitumen, and refined and unrefined copper—an immense step forward from the former bartering system.

147

Several parallels exist between these foundational parts of the law code of Eshnunna and King Mosiah's economic system found in Alma 11:3–19. First, their basic forms are comparable. For example, the standard phrasing "One kor of barley is (priced) at one shekel of silver" resembles "A senum of silver was equal to a senine of gold" (Alma 11:7).

Second, the primary conversion in ancient Babylonia was between barley and silver. Nine other provisions convert various additional commodities into silver values, followed by three more provisions that convert others into measures of barley. Thus, precious metal and grain measures were convertible into each other. The law of Mosiah featured the same conversion capability: the basic measure for either gold or silver was equated with "a measure of barley" (Alma 11:7).

Third, in Babylonia the basic commodity valuation system allowed traders to deal in a variety of commodities, all convertible into silver or barley. Similarly, Mosiah's system allowed traders to expand from silver, gold, or barley into "a measure of every kind of grain" (Alma 11:7).

Fourth, both economic systems were instituted by kings for similar announced reasons. The Laws of Eshnunna began with a royal superscription that probably proclaimed this standardization as instrumental in establishing justice, eliminating enmity, and protecting the weak. Likewise, King Mosiah enacted his laws expressly to establish peace and equality in the land (see Mosiah 29:38, 40).

Fifth, the ideal, practical motivation behind the Laws of Eshnunna seems to have been to undergird the rental market and to standardize values on daily wages and the computation of various damages and penalties. Similarly, a motivation for the economic part of King Mosiah's reforms was to provide a standard system under the new reign of judges for the payment of judges on a daily basis: "a senine of gold for a day, or a senum of silver" (Alma 11:3).

In enacting his law, King Mosiah "did not reckon after the manner of the Jews who were at Jerusalem" (Alma 11:4), but he still utilized a system that drew on elements known in the ancient Near East. Such similarities between the Laws of Eshnunna (discovered and translated in the mid–twentieth century) and Mosiah's economic system show yet another way in which the Book of Mormon presents a truly complex civilization with roots in ancient society.

Research by John W. Welch, originally published as a FARMS Update in Insights *(December 1998): 2.*

NOTE

1. James B. Pritchard, ed., *Ancient Near Eastern Texts Relating to the Old Testament* (Princeton: Princeton University Press, 1950), 161; see also Martha T. Roth, *Law Collections from Mesopotamia and Asia Minor* (Atlanta: Scholars, 1995), 59.

36

NOTES ON KORIHOR
AND LANGUAGE

"Behold, ye cannot know of things
which ye do not see." (Alma 30:15)

The story of Korihor is often cited as an example of how the Book of Mormon can be used to identify the enemies of the Church, as well as a paradigm for how to deal with them. I would suggest that the story itself is very subtly textured and has much to say about the very nature of such paradigms. Note first the recurrence of words with linguistic connotations: *sign, denote, utterance, testify, flattering words,* etc. At issue is the role of language in maintaining order and power within a community, and what steps can be taken to counter one who would undermine that order, that language.

Korihor is less concerned with the truth of the traditionally received teachings than he is with the role those traditions play in maintaining structures of dominion within the society. In binding "themselves down under the foolish ordinances and performances," he tells the high priest, they are "brought down according to thy words" (Alma 30:23). Authority is shown to be the power to determine the boundaries of the language, to establish the words that will constitute communal discourse. Inasmuch as the use of other words places one outside of the linguistically constituted community, Korihor sees this as a way of escape from the constraints imposed by orthodox discourse. We can see this in a pattern that is repeated four times: "*Ye say* that this people is a free people. Behold, *I say* they are in bondage" (Alma 30:24). Note the effort, not to disprove, but to question the solidity and knowability of the received prophecies: "They are foolish traditions of your fathers. How do ye know of their surety? Behold, ye cannot know of things which ye do not see" (Alma 30:14–15). "This derangement of your minds comes because of the traditions of your fathers" (Alma 30:16). The ground is linguistically prepared for their "delusions."

In what follows, however, we can see the consequences of radical doubt concerning the authority of language's structure. For one thing, it is impossible to escape dependence on some linguistic structure or other, which will be authoritative in its own sphere. Alma points this out when he asks Korihor, "What evidence have ye? . . . I say unto you that ye have none, save it be your word only" (Alma 30:40). And Korihor's language, no less than that of the tradition, is subject to the critique he offers.

That being the case, listen to the overtones of the following request: "If thou wilt show me a sign, that I may be convinced that there is a God, yea, show unto me that he hath power, and then I will be convinced of the truth of thy words" (Alma 30:43). For all his questioning the value and authority of an arbitrary linguistic system, a system that he claims represents only the interplay of strivings for power, in the end such a system is what he himself asks for, a system of signs that will bring to bear God's power upon him. Alma's response, of course, is not to deny the basic value of signs, of linguistic communication, but only to point out that such signs have already been given. The way he presents his argument is particularly appropriate: "The scriptures are laid before thee, yea, and all things denote there is a God; yea; even the earth, and all things . . . do witness that there is a supreme Creator" (Alma 30:44). God himself is the referent of all things in the prophetic tradition of the scriptures. The received linguistic structure does not serve primarily to maintain power, but to testify to the power of God as supreme creator. Even the earth and the planets in their regular, traditional structure serve as "witnesses."

True enough, a certain power is maintained by all this. But in trying to tear down that power, and thereby "liberate" the people, Korihor likewise tears down the order in which the powers of society are held, thus leading to such things as murder, robbery, theft, and adultery (see Alma 30:10), working toward the disintegration of the community. And all the while, he never manages to escape the linguistic constraints he had found so repulsive. Rather than escaping from power, it turns out that "the devil has power over [him]" (Alma 30:42). Rather than liberating the people through abolition of linguistic constraint, he becomes "the means of bringing many souls down to destruction, by [his] lying and by [his] flattering words" (Alma 30:47).

He himself is nothing but a "means," a sign through which is communicated the language of doubt. "He [the devil] taught me that which I should say" (Alma 30:53). It is therefore appropriate that when God does, through Alma, declare the sign he will give, it is Korihor's dumbness. When a person really takes seriously the desire to find liberation from language's constraints, it soon enough becomes impossible for him to say anything at all, at least if he tries to be consistent. And it is only fair that this should be his sign from God, the revelation of the futility and danger of his quest. As Alma asks him, "Would ye that he should afflict others, to show unto thee a sign?" (Alma 30:51).

Speech and language are a given; Korihor is no more free of their constraints than anyone he presumes to liberate. And yet, the aims to which that language may be put can differ, along with the effects that flow from conformity or nonconformity to the received standard. And so the scripture is quoted at the beginning of the chapter: "Choose ye this day, whom ye will serve" (Alma 30:8). The various dimensions and contingencies of that choice, of course, remain to be investigated, but the story of Korihor gives us, in the language it uses, a good paradigm in which to start dealing with it.

Research by Robert E. Clark, originally published in the Journal of Book of Mormon Studies *2/1 (1993): 198–200.*

37

Cursing a Litigant with Speechlessness

"In the name of God, ye shall be struck dumb,
that ye shall no more have utterance." (Alma 30:49)

Alma's curse on Korihor, "In the name of God, ye shall be struck dumb, that ye shall no more have utterance" (Alma 30:49), resembles an ancient Greek practice of cursing a litigant with speechlessness. When the curse materialized, divine disapproval was so clear that Korihor was compelled to yield the case.

Such curses were common in the ancient Mediterranean world, especially in the legal sphere. In recent decades, more than a hundred Greek and Roman binding spells—curses inscribed on small lead sheets that were folded up and pierced with a nail—have been recovered from tombs, temples, and especially wells near the law courts, where they were placed in hopes that a deity from the underworld would receive and act upon them. These spells are known as *defixiones* because their words and powers were intended to "defix" (restrain or hinder) an opponent. In ancient Greece, those targeted by these spells could be commercial, athletic, or romantic rivals, or adversaries in litigation.[1]

The largest body of Greek binding spells deals with litigation, with sixty-seven different *defixiones* invoking curses on legal opponents. The earliest of these date to the fifth century B.C. Eleven of them ask the gods to bind the tongue of a legal opponent so he would lose the lawsuit.[2]

Evidence suggests that occasionally these curses were apparently fulfilled. For example, a third-century-B.C. *stela* (an inscribed stone slab) from the Greek island of Delos expresses the gratitude of a victorious litigant who believed he had been helped in court by a god: "For you bound the sinful men who had prepared the lawsuit, secretly making the tongue silent in the mouth, from which [tongue] no one heard a word or an accusation, which is the helpmate in a trial. But as it turned out by divine providence, they confessed themselves to be like god-stricken statues or stones."[3]

The speechlessness of Korihor, and to an extent the stunning of Sherem, was precisely the kind of sign or restraint that people in the ancient Mediterranean world expected a god to manifest in a judicial setting when false accusations or unfair ploys placed an opponent at a distinct disadvantage.

Stricken litigants often erected confession stelae. The inscriptions apparently were "a confession of guilt, to which the author has been forced by the punishing intervention of the deity, often manifested by illness or accident."[4] In hopes of appeasing the offended god, a punished litigant would inscribe on the stela a clear profession of his newly admitted faith in the deity and would warn others not to disdain the gods.

The trials of Sherem and Korihor show these same trends of confession. Sherem recanted his public teachings, confessed the truth of the god who had intervened against him, admitted his error, and expressed concern that he would never be able to appease that god (see Jacob 7:17–19). Korihor's confession acknowledged the power of God, probably to assure those concerned in Zarahemla that the curse would not afflict any others, as well as to terminate the dispute (see Alma 30:51). Such reactions are similar to the responses of others in the ancient world whose judicial perfidy had been exposed and quashed by the intervention of a god responding to the restraining curse of a beleaguered litigant.

Research by John W. Welch, originally published as a FARMS Update in Insights *(October 1998): 2.*

NOTES

1. See Christopher A. Faraone, "The Agonistic Context of Early Greek Binding Spells," in *Magika Hiera: Ancient Greek Magic and Religion,* ed. Christopher A. Faraone and Dirk Obbink (New York: Oxford University Press, 1991), 11.

2. See A. Audollent, *Defixionum Tabellae* (Paris: n.p., 1904), nos. 22–24, 26–29, 31, 33–34, 37.

3. Faraone, "Early Greek Binding Spells," 19.

4. H. S. Versnel, "Beyond Cursing: The Appeal to Justice in Judicial Prayers," in *Magika Hiera,* 75.

38

ALMA'S USE OF *STATE* IN THE BOOK OF MORMON

*"The spirits of those who are righteous are received
into a state of happiness, which is called paradise,
a state of rest, a state of peace." (Alma 40:12)*

Joseph Smith claimed the Book of Mormon was a product of multiple ancient authors. Recent studies of the words and phrases used by the book's various writers have provided evidence of this claim.[1] The following notes on how the word *state*[2] is employed in the Book of Mormon suggest that Alma the Younger can be singled out as a distinct author within the record.

Statistical Significance

Eleven individuals in the Book of Mormon used the word *state*.[3] Only Alma used the word to any degree of *potential* statistical significance.[4] However, even though an author's use of a word might potentially qualify for statistical significance, any statistical model that could be employed to determine such significance would necessarily assume normal or similar topic distribution within the Book of Mormon. Because the different writers treated diverse subjects, there is no statistical way to compare the probability of the different authors' use of *state*. Therefore, it is nearly impossible to prove *objectively* that an author's word usage is statistically significant on the basis of word frequency alone.

Aside from the challenges of this statistical qualification, it is still possible to see Alma as a distinct author in the Book of Mormon. This can be done by examining his use of *state* in contrast with other writers on three fronts: unusual concentrations of the word, resumptive rewording with *state*, and shared topic comparison.

Unusual Concentrations of the Word *State*

All but two of the eleven writers who used *state* did so infrequently and sporadically. In contrast, the recorded writings of Alma and in one case, Lehi, contain passages that display unusual concentrations of the word *state*. For example, Lehi uses the word four times in three verses when describing Adam and Eve's paradisiacal existence in 2 Nephi 2:21–23. A far more impressive concentration of *state* appears in Alma 40, where Alma is teaching Corianton about the postmortal existence.

> Now, concerning the *state* of the soul between death and the resurrection. . . .
>
> . . . the spirits of those who are righteous are received into a *state* of happiness, which is called paradise, a *state* of rest, a *state* of peace. . . .
>
> Now this is the *state* of the souls of the wicked, yea, in darkness, and a *state* of awful, fearful looking for the fiery indignation of the wrath of God upon them; thus they remain in this *state,* as well as the righteous in paradise, until the time of their resurrection.
>
> Now, there are some that have understood that this *state* of happiness and this *state* of misery of the soul, before the resurrection, was a first resurrection. (Alma 40:11–12, 14–15)

Here in just four verses Alma employs the word nine times. Even more remarkable is the concentration in chapter 41 where in just two verses Alma uses *state* six times:

And now, my son, all men that are in a *state* of nature, or I would say, in a carnal *state*, are in the gall of bitterness and in the bonds of iniquity; they are without God in the world, and they have gone contrary to the nature of God; therefore, they are in a *state* contrary to the nature of happiness.

And now behold, is the meaning of the word restoration to take a thing of a natural *state* and place it in an unnatural *state*, or to place it in a *state* opposite to its nature? (Alma 41:11–12)

In chapter 42 Alma clusters his use of *state* again where it occurs six times in verses 10–13. It is consistent with a work that claims to be written by multiple authors to find one of these authors displaying an unusual usage of a particular word when the other writers do not.

Resumptive[5] Rewording with *State*

In several instances Alma displays a tendency to with *state*. For example, in discussing the preparatory nature of mortal existence after the fall, Alma writes: "And thus we see, that there was a *time* granted unto man to repent, yea, a probationary *time*, a *time* to repent and serve God" (Alma 42:4). Resuming this thought six verses later, Alma renames this as a probationary *state*—it "became a *state* for them to prepare; it became a preparatory *state*" (Alma 42:10). Again three verses later he repeats this rewording with "Therefore, according to justice, the plan of redemption could not be brought about, only on conditions of repentance of men in this probationary *state*, yea, this preparatory *state*" (Alma 42:13).

Another example of Alma's tendency to reword with *state* is found approximately one hundred pages earlier. While visiting Gideon, Alma hoped to "find that ye were not in the *awful dilemma* that our brethren were in at Zarahemla" (Alma 7:3). Three verses later Alma defines the dilemma when he resumes the thought with, "I trust that ye are not in a *state of so much unbelief* as were your brethren" (Alma 7:6). After discoursing about the atonement he returns again to this topic and combines the two earlier phrases: "For as I said unto you from the beginning, that I had much desire that ye were not in the *state of dilemma* like your brethren, even so I have found that my desires have been gratified" (Alma 7:18). No other author in the Book of Mormon rewords with *state*—in this Alma stands completely unique.

When only one writer displays this kind of preference for a particular term when restating, especially a nonessential word like *state,* the reasonable reaction is to believe that this writer is distinct within the larger work authored by other individuals.

Shared Topic Comparison

As noted above, because of the varied topics that the different writers of the Book of Mormon address, it is difficult to make statistical comparisons of their use of any given word. On the other hand, a comparison is available between those passages where multiple writers address the same topic. One such topic is the concept of agency. It is here that Alma's preference for *state* distinguishes him most clearly from the other writers of the Book of Mormon.

Because it is reasonable to expect that any given topic will generate some common language to describe it, it comes as no surprise that each of the four writers who addressed agency—Lehi, Jacob, Alma, and Samuel—all used some form of the words *act* and *choose*.[6] Yet when each passage is further analyzed, Alma's use of *state* again distinguishes him from other Book of Mormon writers.

Wherefore, he gave commandments unto men, they having first transgressed the first commandments as to things which were temporal, and becoming as Gods, knowing good from evil, placing themselves in a *state* to *act*, or being placed in a *state* to *act* according to their wills and pleasures. . . .

. . . in the first place being left to *choose* good or evil; therefore they having *chosen* good, and exercising exceedingly great faith, are called with a holy calling. (Alma 12:31; 13:3)

It is significant to note that both Lehi and Jacob used *state* elsewhere in their writings, so their capacity to have done so in passages relating to agency is not in question.[7] Further, the presence of *state* is not the only difference between Alma and the others. Lehi, Jacob, and Samuel each include references to the word *free* when discussing agency.[8] Alma does not.

Of tangential interest, there is marked contrast between Alma and Joseph Smith when their writings about agency are compared.[9] In Doctrine and Covenants 93:30–31, Joseph revealed that "all truth is independent *in that sphere* in which God has placed it, to *act for itself*, as all intelligence also; otherwise there is no existence. Behold, here is the agency of man." In comparison with Alma's passage in Alma 12:31, Joseph Smith writes about a *sphere* in which agency exists, while Alma writes of a *state* of agency; their meanings are the same, but the language is decidedly different. Further, Alma only describes the principle, while Joseph actually names it as agency. In fact, every major passage concerning the agency of man in the Doctrine and Covenants is marked with the words *agency, agent,* or *agents.*[10] In direct distinction, the Book of Mormon does not have a single reference to these words. This suggests that the use of *state* in the Book of Mormon was a feature of the original text and not simply introduced by Joseph Smith.

Clearly Alma's distinction from his Book of Mormon counterparts is shown in the context of agency. He not only displays his preference for *state* uniquely when addressing this topic, but he also elected not to use a key word that the other three authors employed.

Conclusion

Alma certainly stands distinct from the other authors in the Book of Mormon when his use of *state* is analyzed. Alma's unique concentration of *state*, his tendency to re-word with *state*, and his distinctive treatment of a shared topic involving *state* all point to him as a unique writer within the Book of Mormon. This is perfectly consistent with Joseph's claims about the Book of Mormon. Also, the differences between the Book of Mormon and the other scriptures produced by Joseph Smith in relation to the use of *state* are also what one would expect to find in the various publications of a prophet who both translated other's writings and received his own prophetic material.

Research by Philip A. Allred, originally published in the Journal of Book of Mormon Studies *5/1 (1996): 140–46.*

NOTES

1. See John W. Welch et al., "Words and Phrases," in *Reexploring the Book of Mormon,* ed. John W. Welch (Salt Lake City: Deseret Book and FARMS, 1992), 282–85; Roger R. Keller, "Mormon and Moroni as Authors and Abridgers," in ibid., 269–71; John L. Hilton, "Wordprints and the Book of Mormon," in ibid., 221–26; and Welch, "Three Accounts of Alma's Conversion," in ibid., 150–53.

2. "The condition of a person or thing, as with respect to circumstances or attributes," *Webster's Encyclopedic Unabridged Dictionary of the English Language* (1989), s.v. "state."

3. Abinadi, Alma the Younger, Amulek, Benjamin, Jacob, Lehi, the Lord, Mormon, Moroni, Nephi, and an angelic visitor to Nephi all employed the word *state;* compare Eldin Ricks, *Eldin Ricks's Thorough Concordance of the LDS Standard Works* (Provo, Utah: FARMS, 1995), 691–92.

4. An author must display at least one use of the word per one thousand total words. Alma is the only author whose use of *state* qualifies in this preliminary way (Alma used *state* 35 times in 19,137 total words, which equals nearly 2 instances per 1,000 words). The idea for this comparative figure is drawn from Roger R. Keller's article entitled "Law and Commandments in the Book of Mormon" (FARMS, 1991).

5. This is not to be equated with epanaleptic repetition, which is specifically employed for digressions within a single sentence; see Larry G. Childs, "Epanalepsis in the Book of Mormon" (FARMS, 1986).

6. See 2 Nephi 2:26–27; 10:23; Alma 12:31; 13:3; and Helaman 14:30–31.

7. See 2 Nephi 2:21–23 and 9:27 respectively.

8. See 2 Nephi 2:26–27 (three times); 2 Nephi 10:23; and Helaman 14:30 (two times).

9. Comparisons between the four major works that Joseph Smith brought forth further suggest multiple authorship of the Book of Mormon. While the Book of Mormon contains the term seventy-seven times (See Ricks, *Thorough Concordance,* 691–92), the books of Abraham and Moses, as well as the entire Joseph Smith Translation of the Bible lack even a single use of *state.* Of interest also, the Doctrine and Covenants contains the word only three times (71:1; 93:38; 130:9) and the Joseph Smith History employs the word only once (Joseph Smith—History 1:29). In addition, Joseph Smith's wording in Joseph Smith—History 1:29, in which he synonymously couples *state* with *standing,* is interesting because the word *standing* only appears twice in the Book of Mormon and neither time with *state;* see Mosiah 4:11 and Alma 13:5.

10. See Doctrine and Covenants 29:35–39; 58:27–28; 93:30–31; and 101:78. Moses 4:3 and 7:32 also contain references to agency and Moses 6:56 refers to agents.

39

CITIES AND LANDS IN THE BOOK OF MORMON

*"They called the name of the city, or
the land, Nephihah." (Alma 50:14)*

Throughout the Book of Mormon, the terms *city* and *land* seem to be interchangeable. There is a city of Nephi and a land of Nephi, a city of Zarahemla and a land of Zarahemla, and so forth. Evidently, each city controlled a certain territory or land that was designated from the name of the city. This is especially clear in Alma 50:14, where we read of the construction of a new site: "They called the name of the city, or the land, Nephihah."

The pattern followed by the Nephites (and by the Lamanites when they became sedentary) was evidently brought from the Old World. In ancient Israel, the cities were places of refuge for farmers in surrounding villages. In time of war, the peasants could flee to the protection of the city walls, where arms were stored for defense. This is precisely what we find described in Mosiah 9:14–16.

In the law of Moses, cities assigned to the Levites were required to have pastures extending two thousand cubits (roughly three thousand feet) outside the walls (see Numbers 35:5). Because of this, the rabbis took the word *place* in Exodus 16:29 to mean a walled city, and restricted inhabitants to a maximum two thousand cubits' walk on the Sabbath, giving us the "Sabbath day's journey" of Acts 1:12.[1]

Archaeological excavations in the fields surrounding the ancient site of Gezer disclosed six stones from the second century B.C. on which the words *border of Gezer* were inscribed in Hebrew and Greek. Clearly, biblical cities, like those of the Book of Mormon, controlled nearby land. Hence, we read of "the king of Ai, and his people, and his city, and his land" (Joshua 8:1) and of the city of Hebron, its suburbs (perhaps "pasturage"), fields, and villages (see 1 Chronicles 6:55–56).

It should therefore not be surprising to find that cities are sometimes called by the term *land* in the Bible. Tappuah is called a *land* in Joshua 17:8, but a *city* in Joshua 16:8 (see v. 9). Jeremiah prophesied that Jerusalem would become "a land not inhabited" (Jeremiah 6:8; compare 15:5–7).

The Mesha or Moabite stela of the ninth century B.C. provides contemporary archaeological evidence for the interchange of *city* and *land*. The text, reporting the rebellion of Mesha, king of Moab, against Israel, lists a number of "lands" which are known from the Bible to be cities. Internal evidence also implies that they are cities, since Mesha noted that he had "built" these lands.

The reason that lands were named after their principal cities was that some cities controlled other nearby sites. In the account of the assignment of lands to the tribes under Joshua, we frequently read of "cities with their villages."[2] In some cases, a known city is named and is said to have other cities, towns, or villages under its dominion. Thus, we read of "Heshbon and all her cities" (Joshua 13:17), "Ekron, with her towns and her villages" (Joshua 15:45), "Megiddo and her towns" (Joshua 17:11), and "Ashdod with her towns and her villages" (Joshua 15:47).

Clay tablets written in the fourteenth century B.C. and found at El-Amarna in Egypt use the term *land* for Canaanite sites known to have been ancient cities. For example, one text speaks of the "town of Rubutu,"[3] while

165

another mentions the "land of Rubutu."[4] The first of these also speaks of the "land of Shechem" and "the land of the town of Gath-carmel" (both ancient cities) and says of Jerusalem, "this land belongs to the king." A third text mentions the lands of Gezer, Ashkelon, and Jerusalem.[5]

Lehi and Nephi seem to have known the designation of Jerusalem as both a city and the land it governed.[6] The phrase *land of Jerusalem* is found in 1 Nephi 3:9–10; 7:2. We read that Lehi dwelt "at Jerusalem in all his days" (1 Nephi 1:4), but he evidently did not live in the city of that name. After coming to Jerusalem, where Laman visited Laban in his house (see 1 Nephi 3:11, 23), Lehi's sons, thinking to purchase the brass plates from Laban, "went down to the land of [their] inheritance" (1 Nephi 3:22) to gather up their wealth. They then "went up again" to Jerusalem (1 Nephi 3:23) and offered their wealth in exchange for the plates. Laban chased them away and, after a time, they returned to "the walls of Jerusalem" (1 Nephi 4:4), and Nephi "crept into the city and went forth towards the house of Laban" (1 Nephi 4:5). From this, it appears that Lehi dwelt in the "land" of Jerusalem, but not in the city itself, as did Laban.

Though the term *land of Jerusalem* is not found in the Bible, it is known from one of the Dead Sea Scrolls attributed to the prophet Jeremiah and denominated 4Q385^b.[7] The importance of Jerusalem as a political capital of the kingdom of Judah is demonstrated by a Babylonian text recounting Nebuchadrezzar II's siege of Jerusalem, in which it is called "the city of Judah."[8] Alma 7:10 contains a prophecy that Christ would be born in "Jerusalem which is the land of our forefathers." Critics of the Book of Mormon typically use this as evidence of error in the text and conclude that it invalidates the book as an authentic ancient document. They attribute the error to Joseph Smith, whom they believe to be the author of the Book of Mormon. This presupposes, however, that Joseph Smith was ignorant of the fact that Jesus was born in Bethlehem, not Jerusalem, which is hardly likely. It is much easier to believe that the denomination of Jerusalem as a "land" was deliberate. In view of the evidence we have seen thus far, this was perfectly in keeping with ancient Near Eastern tradition. Even were it not so, there would be nothing wrong with Alma, author of the passage, using Nephite geographical terminology to denote the place of Jesus' birth. To the Nephites, whose society revolved around cities controlling larger lands, it would have been perfectly logical to place Bethlehem in the land of Jerusalem.

But there is evidence that, even in the Old World, Bethlehem was considered to be part of the "land of Jerusalem." One of the Amarna texts speaks of "a town in the land of Jerusalem" named *Bît-NINIB*. Some scholars give the name as *Bît-Lahmi*, which is the Canaanite equivalent of the Hebrew name rendered *Beth-lehem* in English Bibles.[9]

We conclude that Lehi's descendants in the New World followed authentic Old World custom in denominating each land by the principal city in the land.[10] This kind of detail lends evidence to the authenticity and antiquity of the Book of Mormon text.

Research by John A. Tvedtnes, originally published in the Journal of Book of Mormon Studies 4/2 (1995): 147–50.

NOTES

1. Exodus 16:29 reads, "Abide ye every man in his place, let no man go out of his place on the seventh day." The "Sabbath limit" of two thousand cubits is defined in Mishnah, *ʿEruvin* 4:3; 5:7, and *Sotah* 5:3 (which refers to Numbers 35:4–5). Other references to the "Sabbath limit" are found in Mishnah, *Shabbat*

23:3–4; ʿEruvin 3:4; 4:2–3, 11; 5:4–5; 7:11; 8:1; 10:2; Beẓah 4:2; Rosh ha-Shanah 4:8, Ketubbot 2:10; Nedarim 7:5; Makkot 2:7.

2. Joshua 15:36; see 13:23, 28; 15:32, 41, 44, 46–47, 51, 54, 57, 59–60, 62; 16:9; 18:24, 28; 19:6–8, 15–16, 22, 30–31, 38–39, 48; 21:12. Sometimes the word *daughters* was used in the Hebrew text to mean villages, in the sense of satellites (Exodus 21:25, 32; 2 Chronicles 28:18; Nehemiah 11:25, 27, 30–31).

3. El-Amarna 289, in James B. Pritchard, *The Ancient Near Eastern Texts Relating to the Old Testament* (Princeton: Princeton University Press, 1969), 489; see Taanach tablet 1, in ibid., 490.

4. El-Amarna 290, in ibid., 489.

5. See El-Amarna 287, in ibid., 488.

6. Hugh W. Nibley discussed this subject in *Lehi in the Desert; The World of the Jaredites; There Were Jaredites* (Salt Lake City: Deseret Book and FARMS, 1988), 6–7, and in *An Approach to the Book of Mormon*, 3rd ed. (Salt Lake City: Deseret Book and FARMS, 1988), 101–2.

7. See Geza Vermes, *The Complete Dead Sea Scrolls in English* (New York: Penguin, 1997), 566.

8. Pritchard, *Ancient Near Eastern Texts*, 564.

9. See El-Amarna 290, in Pritchard, ibid. 489, where the name is rendered *Bit-Lahmi*.

10. For examples and discussion of the word pair *city/land*, see Kevin L. Barney, "Poetic Diction and Parallel Word Pairs in the Book of Mormon," *Journal of Book of Mormon Studies* 4/2 (1995): 37–38.

40

EYEWITNESS DESCRIPTIONS
OF MESOAMERICAN SWORDS

*"And it came to pass that thousands . . .
did take up their swords in the defence of
their freedom, that they might not
come into bondage." (Alma 62:5)*

Recent scholarship on Book of Mormon warfare suggests that the Mesoamerican weapon, the *macuahuitl*, fits the criteria for the Book of Mormon "sword."[1] Recent critics of this position have argued that the comparison is faulty. The *macuahuitl*, they argue, was merely a club studded with obsidian. "Such flexible interpretations," insists one recent critic, "suggest a lack of methodological rigor on the part of those already certain of the Book of Mormon's ancient historicity."[2] It is noteworthy that early chroniclers of Mesoamerican culture such as Duran and Clavijero unashamedly describe this weapon as a sword. Modern Mesoamerican historians commonly use similar terminology.[3] In order to shed additional light on the issue I have provided extracts from Spanish accounts of those who encountered this weapon in battle. As these examples clearly demonstrate, these witnesses almost universally describe the *macuahuitl* as a "sword," and in some cases these same witnesses distinguish between several kinds of swords.

169

Christopher Columbus

The Admiral thanked God for having shown him in a moment samples of all the goods of that country without exertion or exposing his men to any danger. He ordered such things to be taken as he judged most handsome and valuable, such as . . . *long wooden swords* with a groove on each side where the edge should be, in which cutting edges of flint were fixed with thread and bitumen (*these swords cut naked men as if they were of steel*).[4]

Bernal Diaz

Many bands of Indians came along the coast from the town of Champoton, as it is called, wearing cotton armour to the knees, and carrying bows and arrows, lances and shields, *swords which appeared to be two-handed*, slings and stones.

Then they attacked us hand to hand, some with lances and some shooting arrows, and others with their *two-handed cutting swords*.

They were carrying their usual weapons: bows, arrows, lances of various sizes, some of which were as large as ours; shields, *swords single and double handed*, and slings and stones.

Then they attacked us with their *two-handed cutting swords*.

When we met the enemy bands and companies, . . . they were armed with large bows and arrows, spears and shields, *swords like our two-handed swords*, and slings and stones.

They carried *two-handed swords*, shields, lances, and feather plumes. Their *swords*, which were as long as *broadswords*, were made of flint which cut worse than a knife, and the blades were so set that one could neither break them nor pull them out.

They put up so good a defence that they wounded some of our horses with their *swords* and lances.

These Indians put up a good fight with their arrows and fire-hardened darts, and did wonders with their *two-handed swords*.

But the passage was very difficult, for the Indians' shooting was extremely good, and they did us great damage with their spears and *broadswords*.

We did not dare break our formations, however, for any of our soldiers who was bold enough to break ranks and pursue their *swordmen* or captains was immediately wounded and in great danger.

While we were at grips with this great army and their *dreadful broadswords*, many of the most powerful among the enemy seem to have decided to capture a horse. They began with a furious attack, and laid hands on a good mare well trained both for sport and battle. Her rider, Pedro de Moron, was a fine horseman; and as he charged with three other horsemen into the enemy ranks—they had been instructed to charge together for mutual support—some of them seized his lance so that he could not use it, and others slashed at him with their *broadswords*, wounding him severely. Then they slashed at his mare, cutting her head at the neck so that it only hung by the skin. The mare fell dead, and if his mounted comrades had not come to Moron's rescue, he would probably have been killed also.

Their *swordsmen* and spearmen pressed us hard, and closed with us bravely, shouting and yelling as they came.

Their charging *swordsmen* were repelled by stout thrusts from our *swords*, and did not close in on us so often as in the previous battle.

Then their *swordsmen* made a sudden attack on the fourth side, in the positive certainty that they would be able to carry off some of our men for sacrifice. But God provided otherwise.

Cortes gave them a mild answer. . . ."When I remember seeing us surrounded by so many companies of the enemy, and watching the play of their *broadswords* at such close quarters, even now I am terrified. When they killed the mare with a single *sword-stroke* we were defeated and lost, and at that same moment I was more aware of your matchless courage than ever before."

Montezuma had two houses stocked with every sort of weapon; many of them were richly adorned with gold and precious stones. There were shields large and small, and *a sort of broadsword, and two-handed swords set with flint blades that cut much better than our swords.*

Then they described the weapons which the Mexicans used: . . . flint-edged *two-handed swords.*

At a difficult pass they attacked us with their *broadswords*, killing two of our soldiers and one horse, and wounding almost all the rest.

And the dogs fought back furiously, dealing us wounds and death with their lances and their *two-handed swords.*

The Tlascalans became like very lions. With their *swords*, their *two-handed blades*, and other weapons which they had just captured, they fought most valiantly and well.

Some of their captains carried scythe-like lances made from the swords they had captured from us during the slaughter on the causeway; others had long straight gleaming lances, which were also made from captured swords. Then there were archers and warriors with double-headed javelins, and with slings and stones, and their *two-handed swords.*

The soldier Olea had been badly wounded by three *sword-cuts* and was losing blood.

The ensigns waved their banners and standards, and all carried bows and arrows, *two-handed swords*, javelins, and spear-throwers. Some also had *double-edged swords* and long or short lances.

The Mexicans had erected many barricades and ramparts, so that it was impossible to cross except by swimming. Whenever an attempt was made hosts of warriors were waiting for our men with arrows and slings and their *various kinds of swords* and lances.

Many Indians were attacking us, with swords captured when Cortes was defeated or with flint-edged *broadswords*, trying to prevent us from rescuing the launch.[5]

Antonio de Solis y Rivadeneyra

They had likewise long *Swords*, which they used with both Hands, as we do our Scimitars or Falchions, made of Wood, in which they fixed sharp Flints.[6]

Andres de Tapia

As the Spaniards tried to capture one of them to find out where they were from, the Indians with two blows of their *swords* killed two horses, and also wounded two Spaniards, and so defended themselves that not one of them was taken alive.

The marqués ordered all the arms taken out of the arsenal we have mentioned, which were bows and arrows, spears and slings, and *wooden swords* with flint blades. There were about five hundred cartloads, and he had them burned.[7]

Juan Diaz

This Indian gave us signs of a place with many islands where there were caravels and men like ourselves, except they had large ears, and he said they had *swords* and shields, and that there were many other provinces there.[8]

Hernan Cortes

Two horsemen who had gone on in front of me perceived several Indians wearing the feathers which they are accustomed to wear in time of war, together with *swords* and shields.[9]

They had neither arrows, darts nor stones with which to resist us, and they were fighting against our allies armed with *swords* and shields.[10]

Francisco de Auguilar

They used . . . cudgels and *swords* and a great many bows and arrows. . . . One Indian at a single stroke cut open the whole neck of Cristóbal de Olid's horse, killing the horse. The Indian on the other side slashed at the second horseman and the blow cut through the horse's pastern, whereupon this horse also fell dead.

As soon as this sentry gave the alarm, they all ran out with their weapons to cut us off, following us with great fury, shooting arrows, spears and stones, and wounding us with their *swords*. Here many Spaniards fell, some dead and some wounded, and others without any injury who fainted away from fright.[11]

The Anonymous Conquistador

They have *swords* that are like *broadswords*, but their hilts are not quite so long and are three fingers wide; they are made of wood with grooves into which they fit hard stone blades which cut like a Tolosa blade. One day an Indian I saw in combat with a mounted horseman struck the horse in the chest, cutting through to the inside and killing the horse on the spot. On the same day I saw another Indian give a horse a *sword* thrust in the neck that laid the horse dead at his feet.

In another part they cut the stones for knives and *swords*, which is something very interesting to see, and they also make *swords* and shields.[12]

Research by Matthew Roper, originally published in the Journal of Book of Mormon Studies *5/1 (1996): 150–58; for more information on Mesoamerican swords, see his "Swords and 'Cimeters' in the Book of Mormon,"* Journal of Book of Mormon Studies *8/1 (1999): 34–43.*

NOTES

1. See John L. Sorenson, *An Ancient American Setting for the Book of Mormon* (Salt Lake City: Deseret Book and FARMS, 1985), 262–63; William J. Hamblin and A. Brent Merrill, "Swords in the Book of Mormon," in *Warfare in the Book of Mormon*, ed. Stephen D. Ricks and William J. Hamblin (Salt Lake City: Deseret Book and FARMS, 1990), 329–51; John L. Sorenson, "Viva Zapato! Hurray for the Shoe!" review of "Does the Shoe Fit? A Critique of the Limited Tehuantepec Geography," by Deanne G. Matheny, *Review of Books on the Book of Mormon* 6/1 (1994): 324–31; William J. Hamblin, "An Apologist for the Critics: Brent Lee Metcalfe's Assumptions and Methodologies," review of "Apologetic and Critical Assumptions about Book of Mormon Historicity," by Brent L. Metcalfe, *Review of Books on the Book of Mormon* 6/1 (1994): 481–83; and most recently Matthew Roper, "Swords and 'Cimeters' in the Book of Mormon," *Journal of Book of Mormon Studies* 8/1 (1999): 35–43.

2. Brent Lee Metcalfe, "Apologetic and Critical Assumptions about Book of Mormon Historicity," *Dialogue* 26/3 (1993): 161 n. 27.

3. See Hubert H. Bancroft, *The Native Races of the Pacific States* (San Francisco: Bancroft, 1883), 2:409–10; Philip Drucker, *La Venta, Tabasco: A Study of Olmec Ceramics and Art*, Smithsonian Institution Bureau of American Ethnology, no. 153 (Washington, D.C.: U.S. Government Printing Office, 1952), 202; Maurice Collis, *Cortés and Montezuma* (New York: Avon Books, 1954), 41, 91, 94, 97, 202; Jon M. White, *Cortés and the Downfall of the Aztec Empire* (New York: St. Martin's, 1971), 115; Ross Hassig, *Aztec Warfare: Imperial Expansion and Political Control* (Norman: University of Oklahoma Press, 1988), 33, 45, 50, 75, 80–86, 90, 92, 96, 101–2, 111, 116, 121, 143, 172, 290 n. 67; Ross Hassig, *War and Society in Ancient Mesoamerica* (Berkeley and Los Angeles: University of California Press, 1992), 7, 112–14, 122–23, 126–27, 137–39, 150–51, 153, 160, 162, 172–73,

177; Hugh Thomas, *Conquest: Montezuma, Cortés, and the Fall of Old Mexico* (New York: Simon & Schuster, 1993), 237.

4. Samuel E. Morison, trans. and ed., *Journals and Other Documents on the Life and Voyages of Christopher Columbus* (New York: Heritage, 1963), 327; italics added.

5. Bernal Díaz, *The Conquest of New Spain,* trans. J. M. Cohen (London: Folio Society, 1974), 22, 29, 72, 75, 125–26, 127, 130, 133, 138, 180, 197, 260–61, 262, 292–94, 304, 321, 328.

6. Antonio de Solís y Rivadeneyra, cited in Hassig, *Aztec Warfare*, 15.

7. Andrés de Tapia, untitled account, in *The Conquistadors: First-Person Accounts of the Conquest of Mexico,* ed. and trans. Patricia de Fuentes (New York: Orion, 1963), 29, 42.

8. Juan Díaz, untitled account, in *The Conquistadors,* 9.

9. Hernando Cortés, Second Letter, 30 October 1520, in *Hernando Cortés: Five Letters, 1519–1526,* trans. J. Bayard Morris (1928; reprint, New York: Norton, 1991), 41.

10. Hernando Cortés, Third Letter, 15 May 1522, in *Hernando Cortés,* 224.

11. Francisco de Auguilar, untitled account, in *The Conquistadors,* 139–40, 155.

12. The Anonymous Conquistador, untitled account, in ibid., 169, 179.

41

New Technology
and Ancient Voyages

"Hagoth, he being an exceedingly curious man,
therefore he went forth and built him an exceedingly
large ship . . . and launched it forth . . . and whither
she did go we know not." (Alma 63:5, 8)

The potential of advanced scientific techniques for giving us new information about ancient history has
sometimes been overhyped, yet real advantages are becoming apparent. Interestingly, however, the findings are more
likely to produce fascinating new questions than to settle
old ones neatly.

A recent example comes from study of the genetic
(DNA) makeup of cotton. Half a century ago botanical
studies revealed that the common New World species that
yielded the cotton fibers used in the civilizations of Peru
and Mesoamerica had resulted from a combination of an
Old World species with some American wild type. Those
who believed that voyagers crossed the ocean from Asia to
America, including prominent botanists, argued that the
most likely way this genetic joining of cottons took place
was that humans in boats brought cotton seeds with them.

Subsequently, radiocarbon dating of archaeological
specimens showed that cotton was in use in Mesoamerica
at such an early date (on the order of seven thousand years
ago) that introduction of Old World cotton by any voyage

seemed out of the question. Today, DNA analysis has confirmed that indeed cotton has been growing in this hemisphere for so long that the only logical means for it to have arrived in the New World so early was by natural accident—probably by floating on the ocean.

But a new study comes up with a new question. Botanist Jonathan Wendel and colleagues at Iowa State University have shown from an investigation of the DNA composition of cotton species worldwide (in Africa, Australia, and America) that indeed interhemispheric sharing had to have taken place long ago, before human hands could have been involved. But they also found one species that grows in the Isthmus of Tehuantepec area in southern Mexico that shows an unexplained hybridization with or descent from an African cotton. The botanists cannot establish a mechanism for this connection, although it may have happened "during the last several thousand years."[1]

Note that recent evidence from linguistics[2] and art[3] may indicate some kind of voyaging connection between Egypt and southern Mexico, perhaps less than three thousand years ago. Such a voyage or voyages might have introduced the African cotton characteristics. One possibility for such a voyage that occurs to Latter-day Saints in terms of the Book of Mormon is the ship that brought Mulek to the promised land, although other possibilities exist.

Incidentally, the Iowa State study of cotton also demonstrated that a native species found in Hawaii was directly linked genetically with the most common domesticated cotton of Mexico. A voyage by humans from Mesoamerica into Polynesia may be the explanation. Even more mysterious is the fact that Wendel's data show that a unique cotton on the Galapagos Islands west of South America is directly tied to a species in Baja California, thousands of miles to the north! David H. Kelley of the University of Calgary has demonstrated from language, myth, and calendar data that a voyaging party from western Mexico must have reached Polynesia, possibly by way of South America, a couple of thousand years ago.[4]

Other recent applications of new technologies to old questions appear to produce both answers and questions about voyaging from southeast Asia to the Americas and about the use of drugs native to the Americas among ancient Egyptians.

Research by John L. Sorenson, originally published as a FARMS Update in Insights *(December 1996): 2.*

NOTES

1. See Jonathan F. Wendel, Andrew Schnabel, and Tosak Seelanan, "An Unusual Ribosomal DNA Sequence from Gossypium gossypioides Reveals Ancient, Cryptic, Intergenomic Introgression," *Molecular Phylogenetics and Evolution* 4/3 (1995): 298–313.

2. See John L. Sorenson, "Old World People in the New? (Part 2)," *Insights* (June 1995): 2.

3. See Rafique A. Jairazbhoy, *Ancient Egyptian Survivals in the Pacific* (London: Karnak House, 1990) and *Rameses III: Father of Ancient America* (London: Karnak House, 1992).

4. See "Tane and Sina: A Uto-Aztecan Astronomical Cult in Polynesia," in *Circumpacifica, Band II: Ozeanien, Miszellen,* ed. Bruno Illius and Matthias Laubscher (Frankfurt: Peterlang, 1990), 137–56.

42

ROLLERCOASTER ECONOMICS

*"And so great was the prosperity of the church, and
so many the blessings which were poured out upon the
people, that even the high priests and the teachers were
themselves astonished beyond measure." (Helaman 3:25)*

The ups and downs of Nephite economy readily catch the
attention of most first-time readers of the Book of
Mormon. From one year to the next, the Nephites could go
from abundant riches to abject poverty, and just as quickly
they could rise again from humiliating poverty to wealthy
prosperity. Why was their economy so volatile?

A chart of the economic swings of the Nephites looks
like a rollercoaster. Its cycles are erratic, and its fluctuations are often rapid and extreme, ranging from eras of
turbulence and turmoil to extended periods of peace and
prosperity. For example, the fifteenth year of the judges
saw extreme war (see Alma 28:2); while the sixteenth and
seventeenth years, profound peace (see Alma 30:5). The
sixtieth through sixty-second years saw the Nephites lose
half of all their holdings (see Helaman 4:10–12); yet the
sixty-third year was exceptionally prosperous for what
the Nephite historian considered a "long" time (Helaman
6:9, 17); nevertheless troubles again developed already in
the sixty-seventh year, and only five years after that there
was extensive famine and poverty (see Helaman 11:4–5).

Triggering these swings were many shifts in the righteousness and wickedness of the people; but behind the

180

scenes, several other conditions accompanied and exaggerated this economic instability. Among the many factors that might be considered and explored are the following:

1. The Nephite economy had a very simple agricultural base. Modern people easily forget how exposed and vulnerable ancient farmers were. Plows and other implements were primitive to nonexistent, farmers had no commerical fertilizers or pesticides, and crop rotation was rare, so soils soon became depleted. With limited irrigation, crop success depended on the weather from season to season. Thus, when Abinadi issued the following curses in the name of the Lord, he raised serious threats of constant concern: "I will send forth hail . . . [and] the east wind; and insects shall pester their land" (Mosiah 12:6); and when Nephi closed the heavens in the seventy-second year of the judges, this immediately started a severe four-year famine (see Helaman 11:3–6). In small, simple agricultural villages, putting seed into the ground each year was an act of faith, for the harvest was always an uncertainty.

2. The Nephites, like most ancient people, apparently had little ability to store food or to produce an excess of basic commodities. Food storage requires such things as durable containers, refrigeration or preservatives, and a surplus of food. Grains keep, meat can be cured, and fruit can be dried, but most other food stuffs are perishable. On one rare occasion the Nephites retreated into a fortified position with provisions for seven years (see 3 Nephi 3:20–4:4), but when they finished they had only livestock, grain, and precious metals left (see 3 Nephi 6:1–2). After a short period of occupation by Lamanite soldiers, the food supply in the city of Antiparah was apparently soon depleted, for provisioning was a major factor in the military strategy around that city (see Alma 56:29–31). So we

get the picture that food storage was probably difficult, further increasing the vulnerability of the economy to change.

3. The Nephite economy usually functioned with limited trade. Extended commercial contacts between the Nephites and other groups of people were the exception, not the rule. When the Nephites and Lamanites were finally able in the sixty-fourth year of the judges to travel and trade freely, immediate prosperity resulted (see Helaman 6:9), but it did not last. Travel was generally discouraged, especially into the land northward. Transportation was limited; trips often meant hunger and hardship (see Mosiah 9:3). Under such conditions, surplus could not easily be shipped from one area to another to relieve destitution or crop failures.

4. Ancient economies were heavily beset by the ravages of war. Most ancient cities lived in constant fear of being overrun by invading armies or harassed by robber bands. Zarahemla was no exception: at one point the city was easily conquered in a single invasion (see Helaman 4:5). Fighting for one's very existence in sustained campaigns placed heavy strains on these already fragile economies. Besides costing time away from planting and harvesting crops, wars claimed the lives of scarce workers and leaders. The deaths of captain Moroni, Pahoran, Helaman, and Shiblon in rapid succesion at the end of the war years against Amalickiah (see Alma 62:52–Helaman 1:2) left the city of Zarahemla without an obvious leader in Helaman 1.

5. The small size of the Nephite population during the first century B.C. further extended its susceptibility to economic pressures. There was no cushion to absorb the immediate demands that inevitably arose. To show how disruptive even small political elements could become, the case of the king-men is instructive: in the end, a group of only four thousand men were able to set the Nephite

capital city in disarray and nearly topple its government and economy (see Alma 51:19).

6. Obviously, the government did little to regulate the economy in Nephite society. The currency was relatively simple; as in most ancient economies, it took a king's decree to establish a system of weights and measures (see Alma 11:4), and they could be arbitrarily changed under each new government. There was no central power or bureaucracy to organize and protect the accumulation of wealth, except perhaps for the benefit of a few corrupt groups. No economic indicators were monitored, no economic forecasting was available. No one had the ability to monitor or manipulate supply and demand, no national debt existed to take up the slack. No banks, Federal Reserve Board, or other institutions were there to stabilize and protect the economy. Superstition about good days and bad drove economic decisions far more than business sense.

7. Moreover, under these circumstances it must have been extremely easy for a few to get a monopoly on certain precious commodities. The main items with trading value were scarce but transportable: the text mentions such things as gold, silver, pearls, costly apparel, and fine cloth. As fashions shifted, the few people who happened to have the most desirable commodities were suddenly considered very rich. That is not to say that those people stayed rich, however. If there is one lesson economists believe they have learned, it is that it is nearly impossible for monopolies to exist for very long because there is hardly anything for which a substitute cannot be found. As the price of the good in short supply increases, people start looking more intently for substitutes, and they almost always find them. This merely adds to the fluctuations of the markets. Similar developments are taking place in the highly volatile and unstructured economies in Eastern Europe today.

8. Nephite society seems to have placed great economic value on things with little intrinsic or practical value: gold, silver, precious stones, pearls, and fine fabrics. What drove the highest price were consumables and tangible personal property. Never, however, is land mentioned as the basis of wealth in the Book of Mormon. Perhaps because land was plentiful it was therefore of little commercial value, or perhaps it was basically inalienable, being a lineage or village possession; moreover, the people probably considered land as belonging to God or to the entire community, not to private individuals, and thus it did not distinguish the upper class from the poor. This, however, meant that wealth could be easily lost or destroyed, devalued or rendered useless, moved or stolen, buried up in tombs, or consumed in ritual celebrations—leaving the people without those markers of wealth and contributing again to the volatility of their economy.

9. During the period of the judges, Nephite society became quite fluid. Subgroups organized rather easily. Some, like Alma's group, formed a religious coalition to aid and support one another, but most others sought political (i.e., economic) advantage. The Zoramites broke away to Antionum and created a new society deeply divided in its class structure (see Alma 31:3; 32:2–3). Nehor's group, as well as the dissenters who tried to desert from the city of Morianton, the kingmen, and many other subgroups formed. Each of these groups became relatively self-contained and exclusivistic. Such social conditions further breed economic instability and recession, for social uncertainty leads people to place less importance on long-term economic growth, and fragmentation reduces the number of trading parties available to those who have specialized in the production of particular commodities.

10. Finally, the religious views of the Nephites strongly discouraged the accumulation of wealth or "getting gain." Leaders and prophets such as Nephi (see 2 Nephi 28), Jacob (see Jacob 2:11–22), Benjamin (see Mosiah 4:13–28), Alma the Elder as well as his son, Alma the Younger (see Mosiah 18:24–29; Alma 1:26–33), Abinadi (see Mosiah 12:29), Samuel the Lamanite (see Helaman 13:28–39), and many others spoke out strongly against the hoarding of wealth. While generosity can actually increase the total wealth of a community, as Lindon Robison has recently demonstrated, favorable economic effects of generosity occur only to the extent that the entire community shares basically the same ethic of care and generosity toward each other.[1] If they do not, then the Nephite attitudes toward giving liberally to the poor tend to dissipate the wealth of the righteous, while concentrating the remaining economic power in the hands of the unrighteous, thus contributing further toward volatility and the inevitable collision of values in the larger society.

These and probably many other factors help us to understand why and how the Nephite society was so highly susceptable to the economic fluctuations that came as blessings or punishments from the Lord. These were the result of many causes, both the result of conscious choices on their part, and of other factors beyond their control, let alone their awareness. People in modern societies, on the other hand, find themselves insulated in many ways from the vicissitudes of the simple economies of ancient societies, which probably makes it harder for modern readers to understand the Nephite condition and to appreciate all of the influences that impressed them to be dependent spiritually upon the Lord.

Research by John W. Welch, 1993; discussed at a FARMS brown bag lecture.

NOTE

1. See Lindon J. Robison, "Economic Insights from the Book of Mormon," *Journal of Book of Mormon Studies* 1/1 (1992): 35–53. In a letter to the author, Robison wrote: "Still, religious tenets regarding wealth did not vary and thus cannot be used to explain cycles unless one is referring to the cycles of religious adherence to the religious tenets. . . . The wickedness of the people produced many of the observed causes including the failure of governments, the reduction of trade, the subdivision of the population into groups without caring or respect for each other, and under investments of public goods. But for all of these, the underlying problem was an absence of charity" (p. 4).

43

CHALLENGING CONVENTIONAL VIEWS OF METAL

"And behold, there was all manner of gold in both these
lands, and of silver, and of precious ore of every kind;
and there were also curious workmen, who did work
all kinds of ore and did refine it." (Helaman 6:11)

Orthodox archaeologists have for many years supposed that metals were not used in Mesoamerica, the probable area where Book of Mormon events took place, until nearly five hundred years after the scripture says the Nephites were destroyed. Of course the Book of Mormon briefly mentions the use of metal among the Nephites (although by the time of its mention in Mosiah 11:8, metal was "precious"). Previous attempts to refute the prevailing view have had little effect. Renewed research has revealed a substantial body of data on the subject that was previously ignored.

An intensive survey of the literature reporting archaeological and metallurgical investigations in the area, made possible by a donation from Mark Cannon, now shows that between fifty and one hundred specimens from about forty sites predate the A.D. 900 "metal curtain" claimed by the archaeologists.[1] In some cases the actual status of a piece proves hard to pin down from published statements, but at least two-thirds of the total were found by experienced archaeologists whose reports seem reliable. These known fragments date back to at least 100 B.C.

Typically when one of these "anomalous" specimens has been reported, the accompanying statement goes something like this: "Since we know that metals date only after A.D. 900, in all probability this specimen was intruded into our archaeological feature by latecomers to the site, or else the site itself is later than it otherwise seems." In one famous case, metal fragments were found in a cache constructed beneath a stela at Copan, Honduras, dated A.D. 782 by its inscription. A respected analyst suggested that the objects "were gathered together and inserted into the vault (much later), perhaps by a band of pilgrims visiting the deserted ceremonial center." In fact this scenario directly contradicts the judgment of the excavator. The suggestion that ragtag visitors would dig beneath a massive stela at an abandoned site to find the cache put there by those who erected the monument and then put pieces of scarce copper in among earlier artifacts instead of looting the deposit is unsupported by a single known case of similar behavior. Yet logic little more compelling than this is not infrequent in the reports.

There is another line of evidence that supports the idea that metal was in use earlier than usually thought. Works of art—human figures carved on stone or in ceramic—show what are quite surely metal objects. The dates range as early as 300 B.C.

Even more compelling is linguistic evidence. Based on words that are similar in different Mesoamerican languages current in recent centuries, linguists have reconstructed "protolanguages" that consist of words that apparently were in use centuries ago. Differences between similar terms in present-day languages are understandable to linguistic scientists if there was a word in the protolanguage from which the present terms descended, but such variations are puzzling if there was not. Linguists can also make reasonable estimates of the time it took for these variations to develop.[2] In five major language families of Mexico and Guatemala, terms for metal have been reconstructed, and in each case the date given to account for the divergences in the daughter tongues exceeds 1000 B.C. This means that speakers of the parent languages way back then had a word for metal. That they would all have had a word without having any metal seems highly unlikely. If archaeologists have good luck, they will someday find pieces of metal that date as early as the names do.

This research makes clear that there is more information about Mesoamerican metal than had been previously brought together, and that information suggests that metal was used before the experts have said it was.

At least two methodological lessons are taught by the study of "old" source materials such as those examined in this project: (1) "Everyone knows" can be a convenient excuse for going along with prevailing views that seem to challenge scripture (or texts), even though deeper digging may counter that challenge; (2) we may be too prone to accept unthinkingly "expert" answers to serious issues, even, perhaps, in our reading of the scriptural text.

Research by John L. Sorenson, originally published as a FARMS Update in Insights *(May 1992): 2.*

NOTES

1. See John L. Sorenson, "Metals and Metallurgy Relating to the Book of Mormon Text" (FARMS, 1992).

2. As discussed in John L. Sorenson, *An Ancient American Setting for the Book of Mormon* (Salt Lake City: Deseret Book and FARMS, 1985), 71–73.

44

SECRET COMBINATIONS REVISITED

*"And it came to pass on the other hand, that
the Nephites did . . . join with them in their
secret murders and combinations." (Helaman 6:38)*

It has long been contended by critics of the Book of Mormon that its "Gadianton robbers" are merely nineteenth-century Freemasons, transparently disguised.[1] As one of their chief arguments for that notion, such writers as David Persuitte and Robert Hullinger have pointed out that the Book of Mormon refers to the Gadianton robbers using the same phrase, "secret combination," with which contemporary newspapers referred to the Masons during the great anti-Masonic agitation of the late 1820s.[2]

One can easily demonstrate, though, that the word *combination* was commonly used, in the nineteenth century and earlier, in the sense of "conspiracy." Thus, its use for the robbers of Gadianton seems to bear little real significance for the question of Book of Mormon authorship, proving at best that the text's English vocabulary is most likely that of a nineteenth-century American. But this was never in doubt.

However, in a 1989 article, Dan Vogel took the argument even further. "At the time of the Book of Mormon's publication," he claimed, "the term 'secret combinations' was used almost exclusively to refer to Freemasonry."[3] According to this view—which soon tends to lose its modest "almost"—it is the phrase as a whole that uniquely denotes Freemasonry and, so, points to a nineteenth-century origin for the Book of Mormon as well as to the real identity of the (presumably fictional) Gadianton robbers.

The obvious problem with such a view is that it is difficult to see why the joining of a common adjective like *secret* to a common term of the day like *combination* should be regarded as a technical piece of esoteric jargon so distinctive as to constitute a definitive test of authorship or a conclusive refutation of the Book of Mormon's historical authenticity. The evidence supporting Vogel's claim, furthermore, seems to have been drawn from an overly narrow sampling of documents and to be, simply, too sparse to sustain him. I noted this in 1990:

> Vogel's own evidence—which consists of seven anti-Masonic newspaper quotations—merely demonstrates what has been known for many years, that the phrase was indeed sometimes employed in reference to Masons. But this is a far cry from demonstrating that such was its exclusive use. . . .
>
> What is needed, before one can confidently declare that the phrase "secret combination" was never used in non-Masonic contexts in the 1820s and 1830s, is a careful search of documents from that period of American history that have nothing to do with the controversy surrounding the Masons. This has not yet been done.[4]

I made a small effort in that direction for my 1990 article, but the results, while they were interesting and suggested that Vogel was probably wrong, remained inconclusive. A computerized search of available nineteenth-century federal and state court opinions revealed ten occurrences of the phrase *secret combination(s),* not one of which referred to the Masons. Unfortunately, though, the earliest of these dated only to 1850, fully two decades after the publication of the

Book of Mormon. This lack of pre-1850 references was, I believe, a merely accidental effect of the fact that court decisions of the first half of the nineteenth century remain largely uncomputerized and so could not be easily searched. Following a somewhat different research direction, I located a passionate 1831 attack on bar associations, by a Massachusetts journalist named Frederick Robinson, in which such phrases as "secret bar association," "secret brotherhood of the bar," "combination," "conspiracy," "secret society," and "secret fraternity" all appeared in close proximity. It seemed mere bad luck that the precise phrase "secret combination" did not actually occur.[5]

However, the fact remained that a non-Masonic occurrence of the precise phrase "secret combination" had not been located prior to 1850. At this point, though, I elected to retire from the issue. I am a medieval Islamicist, not an American historian. I could only say in parting that the conservative character of legal language, coupled with the fact that the phrase *secret combination(s)* occurred at least ten times in court decisions issued between 1850 and 1898, certainly suggested that exploration of older court materials would likely find earlier occurrences of the phrase.[6] And there remained the tens of thousands of pages of nonlegal writing from Jacksonian America, which I had neither the time nor the patience to comb. "Can anyone doubt," I wrote rather resignedly, "that a more extensive search in period writings will locate precisely that phrase?"[7]

I have now quite unintentionally located precisely that phrase, *secret combination,* used in a plainly non-Masonic context, in a letter from late 1826. This establishes that the phrase was being used to refer to things other than Freemasonry before Joseph Smith obtained the plates from which he translated the Book of Mormon, as well as after.

The 1828 presidential campaign sank to depths that make today's "dirty campaigning" seem like a church choir rehearsal. For example, Charles Hammond, the editor of the *Cincinnati Gazette* and a fervent partisan of Henry Clay, advanced the claim that Clay's rival, Andrew Jackson, had never actually been legally married to his wife. Hammond was strident and shrill in his accusations. "Ought a convicted adulteress and her paramour husband to be placed in the highest offices of this free and Christian land?" he demanded. This was just one of many brutal charges and countercharges traded during the election campaign—a leading Clay newspaper was the Washington *National Journal*—but it was particularly resented by General Jackson. And when his wife died at the end of the campaign, Jackson held Clay personally responsible. "A being so gentle and so virtuous," he said, "slander might wound but could not dishonor." Indeed, Jackson had long felt that Clay was behind such attacks. Even "the aged and virtuous female," he had written to Sam Houston on 15 December 1826, could not escape "his secrete [sic] combination of base slander."[8]

The importance of this passage should be obvious. Here, as I have said, we have a non-Masonic occurrence of the term *secret combination* from the period immediately prior to the translation of the Book of Mormon. Indeed, the individual using the phrase, General Andrew Jackson, was himself a very prominent Mason.[9] Had he known the phrase as referring uniquely to Freemasonry, or even as predominantly associated with Freemasonry, it seems highly unlikely that he would have used it in this pejorative way against a despised opponent. Yet by the date of Jackson's letter to Houston, 15 December 1826, the hysteria surrounding the murder or disappearance of William Morgan—which Brodie and others have imagined to be reflected in the Book of Mormon, and during which, we are told, the phrase *secret combination* referred exclusively to Freemasonry—was already approximately three months old.[10]

Thus we can now say without fear of contradiction that non-Masons could be accused of involvement in "secret combinations" both before and after the publication of the Book of Mormon, and even, most particularly, during the anti-Masonic hysteria of the late 1820s.

It is not often that so neat a refutation of a historical claim presents itself. Yet, since my own desultory readings on American history and politics have supplied this counterexample, one can confidently predict that a true search of period writings would furnish many more. The claim that the Book of Mormon's "secret combinations"—simply because they are called "secret combinations"—necessarily betray their origins in nineteenth-century anti-Masonic paranoia can now be definitively laid to rest.

Research by Daniel C. Peterson, originally published in the Journal of Book of Mormon Studies *1/1 (1992): 184–88.*

NOTES

1. For a survey and preliminary evaluation of the arguments advanced for this proposition, see Daniel C. Peterson, "Notes on 'Gadianton Masonry,'" in *Warfare in the Book of Mormon,* ed. Stephen D. Ricks and William J. Hamblin (Salt Lake City: Deseret Book and FARMS, 1990), 174–224; see also "'Secret Combinations,'" in *Reexploring the Book of Mormon,* ed. John W. Welch (Salt Lake City: Deseret Book and FARMS, 1992), 227–29.

2. See Robert N. Hullinger, *Mormon Answer to Skepticism: Why Joseph Smith Wrote the Book of Mormon* (St. Louis: Clayton, 1980), 114, nn. 30 and 31.

3. Dan Vogel, "Mormonism's 'Anti-Masonick Bible,'" *John Whitmer Historical Association Journal* 9 (1989): 18.

4. Peterson, "Notes on 'Gadianton Masonry,'" 191.

5. See ibid., 195–97.

6. See ibid., 191–93.

7. Ibid., 197.

8. Quoted in Robert V. Remini, *Henry Clay: Statesman for the Union* (New York: W. W. Norton, 1991), 340; original spelling retained.

9. Henry Clay was also a Mason, although by this time he was not particularly active in the organization. See Remini, *Henry Clay*, 333–34.

10. See Remini, *Henry Clay*, 332–33; Fawn M. Brodie, *No Man Knows My History: The Life of Joseph Smith*, 2nd ed. (New York: Knopf, 1975), 63.

45

THE MARKETPLACE

*"[Nephi's tower] was in the garden of Nephi, which
was by the highway which led to the chief market,
which was in the city of Zarahemla." (Helaman 7:10)*

In relating the story of the prophet Nephi's praying on his
tower after returning to his home in Zarahemla from the
land northward, Mormon adds a seemingly immaterial
description of the tower's location when he places it "in the
garden of Nephi, which was by the highway which led to the
chief market" (Helaman 7:10). Significantly, this is the only
place in the Book of Mormon where the word *market* appears.

One hardly notices the words *chief market* in this
particular chapter, and upon deeper perusal of the verse,
the use of the two words at first seems unnecessary. Why
add this description? If Joseph Smith were authoring the
book, there would be no need to include such a description.
In fact, any unusual word or description could jeopardize
the integrity of the work. After all, the native Americans
with whom he was familiar had no marketplaces!

We can, however, draw several conclusions from Mormon's inclusion of the phrase *chief market*. First, the
description was important to include, since he was limited
for space and therefore would have included only words,
phrases, and events that he felt were significant.[1] Also, this
description signifies that cities in this time period not only

had more than one market, but that one of the markets was either larger or more significant than the others.

If we look at Mesoamerica, the area most current Latter-day Saint scholars believe is the land of the Book of Mormon, we find that reference to a market (marketplace) is not only proper but crucial to Mormon's description of Nephi's praying and its effect upon the people. Some two million Maya live in Mesoamerica today. They hold close to their old ways, practicing their traditional skills of farming and craftwork and seldom marrying outside the Maya natives. The marketplace is a continuing and important part of their culture. Most Mesoamerican scholars acknowledge the existence of marketplaces in ancient Mesoamerica. J. Eric Thompson comments, "The present-day markets of highland Guatemala are enchanting, colorful, and thought-provoking, but they are but pale shadows of the markets in pre-Columbian times."[2] Willey indicates that "the high development of the market as an institution and the rise of specialized merchants is distinctively Mesoamerican," and "markets were emphasized in native Mesoamerica as they are today."[3]

The ancient Mesoamerican markets were probably held out in the open. They were generally located in the main plaza or courtyards next to the temples, just as they are located near churches today. In most of these markets, the merchants would have little cover over their stalls other than those made of straw or wood. This material, of course, would not endure the ravages of time to tell us the precise size and placement of their markets.

Many scholars also acknowledge the existence of main or central (chief) marketplaces as well as satellite or smaller markets in large towns or cities. A decade ago John L. Sorenson cited statements supporting this concept by Richard Blanton and Stephen Kowaleski, Rene Millon, George Corogill, Paula H. and G. R. Krotser, and Edward Calnek.[4]

Other scholars have noted the same phenomenon. Nash, commenting on present-day life in middle America, states, "Around the major market are a series of market places" which "specialize in a given produce or commodity and . . . carry a reduced selection of the goods available in the central market."[5] According to Morley and Brainerd, "the most important economic institution of the ancient Maya was the centralized market."[6] Ross Hassig's research reveals "the possibility of a central market" near Monte Alban's north slope.[7] William Sanders notes at Tlatelolco, "aside from the main market there were numerous local food markets all over the city."[8] After a four-year study of the settlement pattern of the Maya city of Sayil comprising a site of some 4.5 square kilometers, Sabloff and Tourtellot developed a map of the site, displaying what they believe "might have been the central marketplace."[9]

Bernal Diaz's account of the "great market" of Tlatelolco is probably the earliest firsthand description of a Mesoamerican market. Diaz gives a very vivid account, including the size and complexity of the markets, the variety of goods found therein, and even descriptions of the judges and constables who supervised these activities. His fellow soldiers, who had been in many parts of the world, commented that "they had never seen a market so well laid out, so large, so orderly, and so full of people." Interestingly, in this same dialogue Diaz also comments on the beauty and number of Montezuma's gardens and describes the courts and enclosures on the road to the market.[10]

I have walked on market day on the rocky gravel road leading to the chief market in San Juan Chamula, Guatemala. Early in the morning the road was busy. Men and women were on their way to sell and purchase wares. Many walked barefoot, proudly carrying their goods on their heads or backs. Some had children tagging along.

This experience gave me the distinct feeling of being in another time period. This market, like the one in Diaz's account, was well organized. It also had its constables. This was not a market for the tourists, but one for the natives. This activity was important to their way of life, just as it had been in the days of Cortez, and just as it must have been in the early time period of the Book of Mormon people.

To stand on the road leading to a marketplace can be an especially moving experience when one is observing a routine that has been followed for millennia. It was easy for me to envision Nephi's garden on the road to the chief market and the attention that a prayer offered from his prayer tower would attract. Thus Mormon, being intimately familiar with the markets of his day, surely knew that his description of Nephi's garden and tower as being on the road to the chief market was very important in adequately conveying the impression of the large number of people who would hear Nephi praying and who would quickly assemble to hear him speak.

Again, we find the small details in the Book of Mormon consistent with modern-day findings. In addition, this easily overlooked yet very significant information lends credence to the modern-day placement of the Book of Mormon city of Zarahemla in Mesoamerica.

Research by Wallace E. Hunt Jr., originally published in the Journal of Book of Mormon Studies 4/2 (1995): 138–41.

NOTES

1. To demonstrate the significance of his severe abridgment, Mormon stated four times that in abridging the Nephite records, he wrote less than a "hundredth part" (Words of Mormon 1:5; Helaman 3:14; 3 Nephi 5:8; 26:6).

2. J. Eric S. Thompson, *The Rise and Fall of Maya Civilization,* 2nd ed. (Norman: University of Oklahoma Press, 1966), 222.

3. Gordon R. Willey, Gordon F. Ekholm, and René F. Millon, "The Patterns of Farming Life and Civilization," in *Handbook of Middle American Indians* (Austin: University of Texas Press, 1964), 1:461–62.

4. John L. Sorenson, "Nephi's Garden and Chief Market," FARMS Update, *Insights* (April 1985): 2; reprinted in *Reexploring the Book of Mormon,* ed. John W. Welch (Salt Lake City: Deseret Book and FARMS, 1992), 236–37.

5. Manning Nash, "Indian Economies," in *Handbook of Middle American Indians* (1969), 6:87.

6. Sylvanus G. Morley and George W. Brainerd, *The Ancient Maya,* 4th ed. (Stanford: Stanford University Press, 1983), 249.

7. Ross Hassig, *War and Society in Ancient Mesoamerica* (Berkeley and Los Angeles: University of California Press, 1992), 35.

8. William T. Sanders, "Settlement Patterns in Central Mexico," in *Handbook of Middle American Indians* (1973), 10:27.

9. Jeremy A. Sabloff and Gair Tourtellot, "Beyond Temples and Places: Recent Settlement Pattern Research at the Ancient Maya City of Sayil (1983–85)," in *New Theories on the Ancient Maya,* ed. Elin C. Danien and Robert J. Sharer (Philadelphia: University of Pennsylvania Museum, 1992), 159.

10. Bernal Díaz, *The Conquest of New Spain,* trans. J. M. Cohen (London: Penguin, 1963), 231–35.

46 *good*

HEBRAIC CONDITIONALS
IN THE BOOK OF MORMON

*"Yea and if he saith unto the earth move and
it is moved." (Helaman 12:13, 1830 edition)*

Recent research has yielded another interesting clue about the language of the Nephites and about the manner in which it was translated into English. By comparing the original manuscript of the Book of Mormon to the subsequent printed versions, Royal Skousen has found that the original English-language text of the Book of Mormon contained expressions that are uncharacteristic of English.[1] One such expression is a Hebrew-like conditional clause.

In English, it is common to express a conditional idea in the following manner: *"if* you come, *then* I will come," with *then* being optional. In Hebrew this same idea is expressed in another manner: *"if* you come, *and* I will come." This structure makes perfect sense in Hebrew but is not found in English. When Joseph Smith translated 1 Nephi 17:50, he dictated: *"if* he should command me that I should say unto this water be thou earth, *and* it shall be earth." This non-English construction was removed by Oliver Cowdery as he copied the original manuscript to produce the printer's manuscript. He deleted the word *and*, making the text read better in English. The sentence now reads: *"if* he should command me that I should say unto this water, be thou earth, it should be earth."

Thirteen other occurrences of this Hebraic conditional were printed in the first edition of the Book of Mormon and then later removed by Joseph Smith in his grammatical editing in preparation for the second edition of the Book of Mormon, published in 1837 in Kirtland, Ohio. One of these instances is the famous passage in Moroni 10:4, which originally read: "and *if* ye shall ask with a sincere heart with real intent having faith in Christ *and* he will manifest the truth of it unto you by the power of the Holy Ghost" (1830 ed., p. 586). In the 1837 and all subsequent editions, the *and*s in conditional clauses like this one have been dropped to express the idea appropriately in English.

This use of *and* is not due to scribal error. Strong evidence of this is found in Helaman 12:13–21, where the *if/and* expression occurred seven times in the 1830 edition (p. 440):

13 yea and *if* he saith unto the earth move *and* it is moved

14 yea *if* he say unto the earth thou shalt go back that it lengthen out the day for many hours *and* it is done

16 and behold also *if* he saith unto the waters of the great deep be thou dried up *and* it is done

17 behold *if* he saith unto this mountain be thou raised up and come over and fall upon that city that it be buried up *and* behold it is done

19 and *if* the Lord shall say be thou accursed that no man shall find thee from this time henceforth and forever *and* behold no man getteth it henceforth and forever

20 and behold *if* the Lord shall say unto a man because of thine iniquities thou shalt be accursed forever *and* it shall be done

21 and *if* the Lord shall say because of thine iniquities thou shalt be cut off from my presence *and* he will cause that it shall be so

This type of structure is perfectly acceptable in Hebrew, but these verses were changed in 1837 to make the book read more smoothly and convey the proper meaning in English.

These observations support the idea that Joseph Smith's translation was a literal one and not simply a reflection of either his own dialect or the style of early modern English found in the King James Version of the Bible. They also support the idea that the language from which the book was translated into English was Hebrew or Hebrew-like.

Research by Royal Skousen, originally published as a FARMS Update in Insights *(December 1997): 2.*

NOTE

1. See Royal Skousen, "The Original Language of the Book of Mormon: Upstate New York Dialect, King James English, or Hebrew?" *Journal of Book of Mormon Studies* 3/1 (1994): 28–38; see also Skousen, "Translating the Book of Mormon: Evidence from the Original Manuscript," in *Book of Mormon Authorship Revisited,* ed. Noel B. Reynolds (Provo, Utah: FARMS, 1997), 61–93.

47

"THUS SAITH THE LORD": PROPHETIC LANGUAGE IN SAMUEL'S SPEECH

"Therefore, thus saith the Lord: Because of the hardness
of the hearts of the people of the Nephites, except they repent
I will take away my word from them." (Helaman 13:8)

Ancient scriptures contain a number of revelatory speech forms or formulaic expressions which are unique to the prophetic writings.[1] That is to say, the prophetic speech forms are present in sections of scripture where God reveals his word directly to the prophets (i.e., Isaiah, Amos, Nephi, Joseph Smith). As might be expected, the same prophetic forms are also present in the Book of Mormon, for it, too, consists of prophetic writings.

To demonstrate the usage of prophetic language in the Book of Mormon, we will take a brief look at the prophetic writings of Samuel the Lamanite (Helaman 13–15). Six speech forms will be identified:

1. Messenger Formula. "Thus saith the Lord" (found thirty-nine times in the Book of Mormon, e.g., 1 Nephi 20:17; Mosiah 3:24; Alma 8:17). Samuel twice used the expression *saith the Lord* (Helaman 13:8, 11). The formula introduces oracular language, and hence is often found at the beginning of a pericope or section. Either God or a prophet is the speaker of the messenger formula. Its purpose is to indicate the origin and authority of the revelation.[2]

2. Proclamation Formula. "Listen to the words of Christ" (Moroni 8:8) or "Hearken to the word of the Lord" (Jacob 2:27; see Helaman 12:23) or "Hear the words of Jesus" (3 Nephi 30:1). Samuel told his audience to "hearken unto the words which the Lord saith" (Helaman 13:21). Similar to the messenger formula, the proclamation formula is often found at the beginning of a revelation or announcement. It is used as an emphatic summons to hear the word of the Lord.

3. Oath Formula. "As the Lord liveth" (1 Nephi 3:15, 4:32; 2 Nephi 9:16; see 25:20). The declaration is added to a testimony to accentuate the words of the speaker. For instance, Samuel stated: "As surely as the Lord liveth shall these things be, saith the Lord" (Helaman 15:17; compare Helaman 13:26).

4. Woe Oracle. An accusation form usually found as part of a judgment speech. Some forty examples of the woe oracle are attested in the Book of Mormon (see 1 Nephi 1:13; 2 Nephi 9:27; 2 Nephi 15:21). The characteristic woe oracle consists of the accusation, the addressee, the intent of the accusation, and the promise of judgment. The prophet Samuel uttered a number of woe oracles against the Nephites (see Helaman 13:11–12, 14–17, 24; 15:2–3). Helaman 13:16–17, for example, contains the following elements:

Accusation: Yea, and wo
Addressee: be unto all the cities which are in the land round about
Intent: because of the wickedness and abominations which are in them
Promise of Judgment: And behold, a curse shall come upon the land, saith the Lord of Hosts

5. Announcement Formula. "I say unto you." The revelation formula is well attested in the Book of Mormon. The

Lord speaks to his audience (an individual or group) in the first person (see 3 Nephi 12:22; 20:15), or a prophet speaks to his audience using the formula, adding authority and emphasis to the revelation. The formula is found at the beginning of a clause, often accompanied with the particles *yea, behold,* or *therefore.* Samuel employs the formula three times (see Helaman 15:6, 12, 14).

6. *Revelation Formula.* "The word [of the Lord] came unto me, saying" (Jacob 2:11; see Alma 43:24; Ether 13:20). At the beginning of Samuel's ministry to the Nephites, "behold, the voice of the Lord came unto him" (Helaman 13:3). Samuel told the Nephites that they would cry unto the Lord, "O that we had repented in the day that the word of the Lord came unto us" (Helaman 13:36).

Six prophetic speech forms present in Samuel's speech—the messenger formula, the proclamation formula, the oath formula, the woe oracle, the announcement formula, and the revelation formula—are indicative of prophetic authority and prerogative. These speech forms and others dealing with the commission and divine workings of a prophet are also present in other sections of the Book of Mormon. It is hoped that this brief report will give birth to additional and in-depth studies on the topic of prophetic language in the Book of Mormon.

Research by Donald W. Parry, originally published in the Journal of Book of Mormon Studies *1/1 (1992): 181–83.*

NOTES

1. For a complete study on the subject, see David E. Aune, *Prophecy in Early Christianity and the Ancient Mediterranean World* (Grand Rapids: Eerdmans, 1983), 88–101.

2. Modern prophets have commented concerning the import of this expression; see, for example, Joseph Smith, *Teachings of the*

Prophet Joseph Smith, comp. Joseph Fielding Smith (Salt Lake City: Deseret Book, 1979), 136; *Journal of Discourses,* 23:370–72; 22:291–92; *Discourses of Brigham Young,* comp. John A. Widtsoe (Salt Lake City: Deseret Book, 1971), 38, 330.

48

MORE ON THE
HANGING OF ZEMNARIHAH

*"And their leader, Zemnarihah, was taken
and hanged upon a tree." (3 Nephi 4:28)*

The Book of Mormon details the execution of a leader of
the Gadianton robber band in the following words:

> And their leader, Zemnarihah, was taken and hanged
> upon a tree, yea, even upon the top thereof until he was
> dead. And when they had hanged him until he was dead
> they did fell the tree to the earth, and did cry with a loud
> voice, saying: May the Lord preserve his people in righ-
> teousness and in holiness of heart, that they may cause to
> be felled to the earth all who shall seek to slay them
> because of power and secret combinations, even as this
> man hath been felled to the earth. (3 Nephi 4:28–29)

In the law of Moses, stoning was the usual method of
execution for Israelites guilty of sin. Nevertheless, there is
evidently provision for hanging in Deuteronomy 21:22–23:
"And if a man have committed a sin worthy of death, and he
be to be put to death, and thou hang him on a tree: His body
shall not remain all night upon the tree, but thou shalt in any
wise bury him that day."[1] Most early rabbis understood this
to mean that the bodies of stoned malefactors were subsequently hanged for public display to warn others. Some of
them held that only blasphemers and idol worshippers were
to be hanged.[2] But one of the Dead Sea Scrolls supports the

use of hanging for certain crimes and may shed light on why Zemnarihah was hanged rather than stoned. The *Temple Scroll* calls for execution by hanging for the crime of treason:

> If there were to be a spy against his people who betrays his people to a foreign nation or causes evil against his people, you shall hang him from a tree and he will die. . . . If there were a man with a sin punishable by death and he escapes amongst the nations and curses his people [and] the children of Israel, he also you shall hang on the tree and he will die. Their corpses shall not spend the night on the tree; instead you shall bury them that day because they are cursed by God and man, those hanged on a tree; thus you shall not defile the land which I give you for inheritance.[3]

The Gadianton band led by Zemnarihah consisted of "dissenters" who had turned against the Nephites (see Helaman 11:24–26; 3 Nephi 1:27–28). Giddianhi, Zemnarihah's predecessor as leader of the band, admitted that his people had dissented from the Nephites (see 3 Nephi 3:9–11). It is also of interest that Giddianhi swore "with an oath" to destroy the Nephites (3 Nephi 3:8), clearly cursing the people as also mentioned in the *Temple Scroll*.

During the great war with the Lamanites, the Nephites regularly executed dissenters who refused to defend their country against enemy invasion (see Alma 51:15, 19–20; 62:6–10). Later, members of the Gadianton band were also executed if they did not renounce their evil ways and rejoin the Nephite nation (see 3 Nephi 5:4–5). We are not told how these traitors were executed, but the story of Zemnarihah, along with the evidence of the *Temple Scroll*, suggests that they may have been hanged.[4]

Research by John A. Tvedtnes, originally published as a FARMS Update in Insights *(April 1997): 2.*

NOTES

1. John W. Welch has noted that Jewish law required that the tree on which a criminal was hanged be cut down and buried with the body, and he noted that the hanging was principally to suit the punishment to the crime. He further demonstrated the execrational nature of Zemnarihah's execution. See "The Execution of Zemnarihah," in *Reexploring the Book of Mormon*, ed. John W. Welch (Salt Lake City: Deseret Book and FARMS, 1992), 250–52, and his sources.

2. See Abraham Chill, *The Mitzvot: The Commandments and Their Rationale* (Jerusalem: Keter, 1974), 450–51, and his references.

3. *Temple Scroll (11Q19)*, col. 64, lines 6–13, in Florentino García Martínez, *The Dead Sea Scrolls Translated*, 2nd ed. (Leiden: Brill, 1996), 178.

4. Some have wondered if Nehor may have been hanged, since Alma 1:15 speaks of him acknowledging his faults "between the heavens and the earth." However, this may have reference to the fact that he had been taken "upon the top of the hill Manti." In any event, we are merely told that "he suffered an ignominious death."

49

WORD GROUPS IN
THE BOOK OF MORMON

*"Lamanites . . . were converted unto the true faith;
and they would not depart from it, for they were firm,
and steadfast, and immovable." (3 Nephi 6:14)*

An early issue of the *Journal of Book of Mormon Studies* included Kevin L. Barney's article on word pairs—a common feature in the Hebrew poetry of the Old Testament—in the Book of Mormon.[1] As Barney explained, word pairs are generally synonymous or antithetic and were used as the basic building blocks for parallel lines, often in repeating or formulaic fashion. For example, two words frequently paired together in the Psalms and elsewhere in the Old Testament in the creation of parallel lines are *earth* and *world:*

> The *earth* is the Lord's, and the fulness thereof;
> > the *world,* and they that dwell therein. (Psalm 24:1)

> Their line is gone out throughout all the *earth,*
> > and their words to the end of the *world.* (Psalm 19:4)

The relationship between the words in a pair became sufficiently strong that these words were often juxtaposed in prose settings.

The same phenomenon underlying word pairs could also lead to more extensive groupings of words. For example, consider Isaiah 1:8:

> And the daughter of Zion is left
> like a *booth* in a vineyard,
> like a *lodge* in a cucumber field,
> like a besieged *city*.[2]

Here the words *booth* and *lodge* would have sufficed, both to fill out the poetic line and to get the message across, but the prophet added a third word, *city*. There was a time when some scholars would have assumed that the part of the line containing the unnecessary third word ("like a besieged city") had been added after the fact; today, however, it is widely recognized that such tricola are an authentic means of expression in Hebrew poetry. Thus, although word pairs are by far the most common phenomenon, many passages also reflect what we might call *word triplets*.

A word triplet is the simplest example of what I refer to as a *word group*. More extensive groupings can include four, five, six, or more words. One scholar noted twenty-five such examples in Isaiah alone.[3]

Word groups tend to fall into certain categories. Perhaps the most common categories include animals, the implements of war, precious metals and jewels, plants and trees, and agricultural items. For instance, a precious-metals word group from Job 28:1–6 includes silver, gold, iron, brass, stone, sapphire, and gold (again), and an implements-of-war group from Job 41:26–29 includes sword, spear, dart, javelin (KJV "habergeon"), arrow, slingstone, club (KJV "dart" is incorrect), and another type of spear (a different Hebrew word).

I first noted the possible presence of word groups in the Book of Mormon in connection with 3 Nephi 6:14. It struck me, when reading that passage, that the words "firm, and steadfast, and immovable" seemed to be a quote from Lehi's words to his son Lemuel in 1 Nephi 2:10. It seemed beyond coincidence that Mormon, who abridged the record in 3 Nephi, should have used the same three words employed by Lehi.[4] Either Mormon was quoting Lehi's words or the combined use of these words was common among the Nephites. Investigating further, I found word pairs such as "firm and steadfast" (Helaman 15:8), and "steadfast and immovable" (Mosiah 5:15; Alma 1:25). But the parallels run deeper. Both Alma 1:25 and 3 Nephi 6:14 note that the people were steadfast and immovable in "keep[ing] the commandments of God [the Lord]," thus reflecting Lehi's words in 1 Nephi 2:10. Equally significant is that Helaman 15:8 and 3 Nephi 6:14 refer to being steadfast in/unto the [true] faith, and both passages are describing converted Lamanites. Remember that Lehi used the words *firm, steadfast, and immovable* to admonish Lemuel, one of the ancestors of the Lamanites, to be faithful.

This made me wonder about other word groups, such as *temples, sanctuaries,* and *synagogues* in Alma 16:13 and the variants *synagogues, houses, temples,* and *sanctuaries* (see Alma 23:2); *houses, streets, hills, temples, synagogues* (see Alma 26:29); *synagogues, houses,* and *streets* (see Alma 32:1); and *temples, synagogues,* and *sanctuaries* (Helaman 3:9, 14). In his sermon, Jesus used the word pair *synagogues/streets* (see Matthew 6:2, 5; 3 Nephi 13:2, 5), while *houses/streets* appears in Isaiah 15:3 and *hills/streets* in Isaiah 5:25. The words are in a parallel construction in both Isaiah passages.

It may be perfectly natural to couple *old/young,* but when combined with other pairs, the effect is startling. Consider, for example, Alma 1:30, "both old and young, both bond and free, both male and female." The same group of three pairs is used in Alma 11:44, which adds a fourth pair, "both the wicked and the righteous." Similar is the passage in Alma 5:49, which speaks of "both old and young, both bond and free . . . the aged, and also the middle aged, and the rising generation." It seems more than coincidental that only the record kept by Alma the Younger employs the grouping of pairs *old/young, bond/free.*

While no other writers use the pair *bond/free,* Nephi wrote of "both old and young, both male and female" (1 Nephi 8:27). King Benjamin addressed his words to "all ye old men, and also ye young men, and you little children who can understand my words" (Mosiah 2:40). Such passages are similar to Joel 2:28 (also cited in Acts 2:17), where we have the double pairing: *your sons* and *your daughters, your old men, your young men.*

Zeniff, speaking of the war between his people and the Lamanites, described his people in terms of "women and children . . . old men . . . and . . . young men" (Mosiah 10:9). Mormon, also describing a war with the Lamanites, spoke of how the enemy spared "neither old nor young; and they delight in everything save that which is good; and the suffering of our women and our children" (Moroni 9:19). This kind of pairing in describing victims of warfare is also found in the Bible. Isaiah wrote of the Egyptian and Ethiopian "captives, young and old, naked and barefoot" who would be taken by the Assyrians (Isaiah 20:4). In 2 Chronicles 36:17, we read of the Babylonian attack on Jerusalem that "the king of the Chaldees . . . slew their young men with the sword . . . and had no compassion upon young man or maiden, old man, or him that stooped for age." The same slaughter is described in several other Bible passages. Through Jeremiah, the Lord declared that he would "break in pieces man and woman . . . old and young . . . the young man and the maid" (Jeremiah 51:22). "The young and the old lie on the ground in the streets: my virgins and my young men are fallen by the sword" (Lamentations 2:21). Jeremiah's younger contemporary, Ezekiel, wrote, "Slay utterly old and young, both maids, and little children, and women" (Ezekiel 9:6). A later Persian king ordered the destruction of "all Jews, both young and old, little children and women" (Esther 3:13). Also of interest is the description given in Joshua 6:21 of the destruction of Jericho by the Israelites: "And they utterly destroyed all that was in the city, both man and woman, young and old, and ox, and sheep, and ass, with the edge of the sword."

The addition of animal groups to human pairs is also found in Psalm 148:10–12, "Beasts, and all cattle; creeping things, and flying fowl: Kings of the earth, and all people; princes, and all judges of the earth: Both young men, and maidens; old men, and children," and in Exodus 10:9, "We will go with our young and with our old, with our sons and with our daughters, with our flocks and with our herds." The latter, taken from the account of the Israelite exodus from Egypt, is similar to the exodus of the people of Limhi described in Mosiah 22:2:

> And it came to pass that they could find no way to deliver themselves out of bondage, except it were to take their women and children, and their flocks, and their herds, and their tents, and depart into the wilderness; for the Lamanites being so numerous, it was impossible for the people of Limhi to contend with them, thinking to deliver themselves out of bondage by the sword.

The combination *flocks/herds* is common in both the Book of Mormon and the Bible. In Alma 1:29 and Helaman 6:12, the listing is "flocks and herds, and fatlings," which is similar to the listing of "flocks, and herds, and the camels" in Genesis 32:7. To *flocks* and *herds*, Genesis 26:14 and Genesis 24:35 add *servants*. The latter also adds *silver* and *gold*, which form part of another word group.

From its earliest pages, the Book of Mormon speaks of *gold, silver,* and *precious things* (see 1 Nephi 2:4, 11; 3:22, 24; Mosiah 19:15; 22:12; Alma 15:16; 17:14)—a list that is paralleled in several Bible passages (see 2 Kings 20:13; 2 Chronicles 21:3; Ezra 1:6; Isaiah 39:2; Daniel 11:38, 43).[5]

Some passages expand the list to include such elements as *wood, buildings, machinery, iron, copper, brass, steel,* and *ziff* (see 2 Nephi 5:15–16; Jarom 1:8; Mosiah 11:8–10). The Bible, too, adds other items to the list. In 1 Chronicles 29:2, we read of *gold, silver, brass, iron, wood, onyx stones, glistering stones,* (stones) *of divers colours, precious stones,* and *marble stones.*

Some Book of Mormon descriptions add cloth materials—*silks, scarlets, fine-twined linen*—to the basic list of *gold, silver,* and *precious things* (see 1 Nephi 13:7, 8; Alma 1:29; 4:6; 31:28; Ether 9:17; 10:23–24). This list is similar to the one found throughout the book of Revelation, which describes the same harlot or apostate church seen by Nephi in his vision (see Revelation 17:4; 18:12, 16), and in the description of the materials used by Moses to construct the tabernacle in the wilderness (see Exodus 25:4; 26:1, 31, 36; 27:16; 28:5–6, 8, 15, 33; 35:5–6, 22–23, 25, 35; 36:8, 35, 37; 38:18, 23; 39:1–3, 5, 8, 24–25, 29) and used in other Bible passages (see 2 Samuel 1:24; Proverbs 31:21–22; Ezekiel 16:10, 13; Daniel 5:7, 16, 29; Luke 16:19). *Silver, gold, raiment,* and *precious things* are noted in Genesis 24:53.

Some Book of Mormon passages seem to combine all or most of these word groups and add others. Thus Alma 1:29 and 4:6 include the *flocks/herds, gold/silver,* and *silk/linen* lists, and the former adds *grains.* Some passages combine *fields* or *grains* with some of the other lists of precious commodities already discussed (see 2 Nephi 5:11; Mosiah 7:22; Alma 3:2; 4:2; 62:29; Helaman 12:2; 3 Nephi 3:22; 6:2; Ether 9:17; 10:12).[6] Similar lists are found in the Bible (see Deuteronomy 8:13; 12:17; 14:23; 2 Chronicles 32:27–29; Jeremiah 31:12).

A passage that has come under fire from critics because it uses terms for animals not found in the New World when the Spaniards arrived is 1 Nephi 18:25: "And it came to pass that we did find upon the land of promise, as we journeyed in the wilderness, that there were beasts in the forests of every kind, both the cow and the ox, and the ass and the horse, and the goat and the wild goat, and all manner of wild animals" (compare the list in Ether 9:18–19). Several possible explanations have been proffered for this list, some of which have been discussed elsewhere. Here, I will suggest that the list may be a formulaic grouping of animal names. Such formulaic groupings are known from the Bible, where the most common combination is the *ox* and the *ass* (see Exodus 20:17; Job 6:5; 24:3; Isaiah 1:3; 32:20). But we also have the *ox* and *lamb* (see Isaiah 66:3; Jeremiah 11:19); the *cow* and *ewe* (see Leviticus 22:28); the *cow, sheep,* and *goat* (see Numbers 18:17); and the *bullock, sheep,* and *goat* (see Leviticus 22:27). One of the longer lists is the one found in Zechariah 14:15, where we have the *horse, mule, camel, ass,* and other *beasts.*

In this brief communication, I have discussed just a few word groupings that have come to my attention. I suspect that a closer examination of such groupings will reveal even more ties between the Book of Mormon and the biblical world and will show deliberate patterning of parts of the Book of Mormon text on Bible themes in subtle ways that demonstrate the extreme complexity of the Nephite record. It is that complexity that makes the Book of Mormon believable as an authentic ancient text rooted in the Near East of more than two and a half millennia ago.

Research by John A. Tvedtnes and Kevin L. Barney, originally published in the Journal of Book of Mormon Studies 6/2 *(1997): 262–68.*

NOTES

1. See Kevin L. Barney, "Poetic Diction and Parallel Word Pairs in the Book of Mormon," *Journal of Book of Mormon Studies* 4/2 (1995): 15–81. This article built on Barney's earlier study,

"Understanding Old Testament Poetry," *Ensign* (June 1990): 50–54. I had already been looking at word groups in the Nephite record, and what I found seemed to be a natural supplement to Barney's work, though I must add, as he did (see "Poetic Diction," p. 23 n. 20), that illustrations are not intended to be exhaustive and that I expect that others will continue to find new examples.

2. The translation, together with this basic overview of biblical word groups, is from William R. Watters, *Formula Criticism and the Poetry of the Old Testament*, Beiheft zur Zeitschrift für die alttestamentliche Wissenschaft, vol. 138 (Berlin: de Gruyter, 1976), 95–98. Watters refers to the phenomenon of extended word groups as "long tours." Ibid., 96. My thanks to Kevin L. Barney for bringing this study to my attention.

3. See ibid., 97–98. When the phenomenon was first observed, some scholars objected that word groups violated economies of composition, and fanciful theories were put forward to explain them. According to one such theory, word groups reflected a conscious effort by the poet to keep alive words that otherwise would have passed into oblivion from disuse. A much simpler and more likely explanation is that word groups were produced for the same reason as word pairs themselves—to create artistic poetry. Watters noted that "the point which could be made with two words in pair is made in more stunning effect with six or eight words in pair" (ibid., 109).

4. Critics will surely point out the word group *fixed, immovable, and unchangeable* in Doctrine and Covenants 88:133 as evidence that this was Joseph Smith's language. But in view of the other ties between the passages, this seems untenable. Moreover, one would expect Joseph Smith's revelations to echo earlier scriptures, such as the Bible and the Book of Mormon, since God was the source of all revelation.

5. A variant—*gold, silver, riches*—is found in Mosiah 4:19.

6. Passages in Ether, here as elsewhere in this brief study, may have been influenced by that book's Nephite editor, Moroni, rather than being part of the original Jaredite record. Note Doctrine and Covenants 136:11, which may have some dependence on the Book of Mormon passages, especially Alma 34:20–27.

50

ANOTHER NOTE ON THE
THREE DAYS OF DARKNESS

*"There was thick darkness upon all the
face of the land . . . and there was not
any light seen." (3 Nephi 8:20, 22)*

Speculation continues about the causes and consequences
of the destruction in Book of Mormon lands attending the
crucifixion of Jesus. Proposed causes have ranged from
"some mighty upheaval of the earth's crust" to floods, earth-
quakes, volcanoes, and combinations of these.[1] Assessments
of consequences have ranged from continents rising out of
the ocean to assumptions that the locality where the Book of
Mormon events took place was not unrecognizably altered at
the time of the crucifixion. The extent of the darkness has also
been discussed. What necessitates this note is some additional evidence from an ancient text, the relevance and significance of which is left to the reader.

In 1967, Claude Vandersleyen published the fragmen-
tary remains of a stele erected by the Egyptian pharaoh
Ahmose at Karnak.[2] This remarkable and unusual stele has
recently been connected with the volcanic eruption on
Thera (modern Santorini).[3] What merits attention are the
parallels to the phraseology of the Book of Mormon. The
pertinent lines of the stele inscription are as follows:

> The gods [caused] the sky to come in a tempest of
> r[ain], with darkness in the western region and the sky
> being unleashed without [cessation, louder than] the cries

of the masses, more powerful than [. . .], [while the rain raged(?)] on the mountains louder than the noise of the cataract which is at Elephantine. Every house, every quarter that they reached [. . .] floating on the water like skiffs of papyrus opposite the royal residence for a period of [. . .] days, while a torch could not be lit in the Two Lands. (lines 8–12)

THE PARALLELS

The Book of Mormon account parallels this at several points:

The Great Storm

Tempest Stele	The Book of Mormon
"The gods [caused] the sky to come in a tempest of r[ain]" (line 8).	"And it came to pass in the thirty and fourth year, in the first month, on the fourth day of the month, there arose a great storm, such an one as never had been known in all the land and there was also a great and terrible tempest" (3 Nephi 8:5–6, punctuation altered).

The preserved portion of the Tempest Stele does not actually mention rain. References to rain are all restorations. The stele inscription is restored on the basis of a literary parallel; otherwise, given the state of the stele, one might be tempted to restore something else like $\underline{d}^c n \underline{h}[ty]$ "tempest of smoke."[4] In Egypt rain rarely occurs. On the other hand, the Book of Mormon rarely mentions rain; it occurred frequently enough that only its absence merits mention.[5]

Caused by Divine Agency

Tempest Stele	Book of Mormon
"The gods [caused] the sky to come in a tempest of r[ain]" (line 8).	The Book of Mormon peoples are addressed by "a voice" (3 Nephi 9:1), later identifying itself as "Jesus Christ the Son of God" (3 Nephi 9:15), saying, among other things, "that great city of Zarahemla have I burned with fire, and the inhabitants thereof" (3 Nephi 9:3) and "that great city Moronihah have I covered with earth, and the inhabitants thereof" (3 Nephi 9:5).

In both cases the storm and its effects are directly attributed to deity. The Book of Mormon differs from the Tempest Stele in specific attribution to a particular god because Jesus Christ takes personal responsibility for it.

Loud Noises

Tempest Stele	Book of Mormon
"[louder than] the cries of the masses, more powerful than [. . .], [while the rain raged(?)] on the mountains louder than the noise of the cataract which is at Elephantine" (lines 9–10).	"and there was terrible thunder, insomuch that it did shake the whole earth as if it was about to divide asunder" (3 Nephi 8:6). When the ordeal was over, "the dreadful groanings did cease, and all the tumultuous noises did pass away" (3 Nephi 10:9).

221

The Egyptian text compares the noise of the tempest to the water plunging down the cataract at Elephantine, for the Egyptians a reference point for loud, constant noise. Modern equivalents would be to say that it was louder than the crowds at a soccer (or football) game or louder than Niagara Falls.

Inability to Light Fires

Tempest Stele	Book of Mormon
"while a torch could not be lit in the Two Lands" (line 12).	"And it came to pass that there was thick darkness upon all the face of the land, insomuch that the inhabitants thereof who had not fallen could feel the vapor of darkness; and there could be no light, because of the darkness, neither candles, neither torches; neither could there be fire kindled with their fine and exceedingly dry wood, so that there could not be any light at all; and there was not any light seen, neither fire, nor glimmer, neither the sun, nor the moon, nor the stars, for so great were the mists of darkness which were upon the face of the land" (3 Nephi 8:20–22).

The Book of Mormon has a more detailed description of the palpable darkness, but both accounts mention the inability to light a fire.[6] This could possibly be attributable to volcanic dust.[7]

Several Days of Darkness

Tempest Stele	Book of Mormon
"for a period of [. . .] days" (line 11).	"And it came to pass that it did last for the space of three days that there was no light seen" (3 Nephi 8:23).

Unfortunately, the Tempest Stele breaks off at that point so we can neither determine how close the parallel is, nor compare the magnitude of the eruptions. However, the number of days in the Temple Stele must be at least two, based on sentence construction.

Accompanied by Massive Destruction

Tempest Stele	Book of Mormon
"Then His Majesty was informed that the mortuary concessions had been entered (by water), with the tomb chambers collapsed, the funerary mansions undermined, and the pyramids fallen, having been made into that which was never made. Then His Majesty commanded to restore the temples which had fallen into ruin in this entire land: to refurbish the monuments of the gods, to erect their enclosure walls, to provide the sacred objects in the noble chamber to mask the secret	The extent of the destruction is detailed in 3 Nephi 8–9 and will not be repeated verbatim here, but it includes cities that were "burned" (3 Nephi 8:8, 14; 9:3, 9–10), "buried" (3 Nephi 8:10; 9:5–6, 8), and "sunk" (3 Nephi 8:9, 14; 9:4, 6–8), as well as the destruction of "highways" (3 Nephi 8:13) and geological deformation (see 3 Nephi 8:17–18).

places, to introduce into
their shrines the cult statues which were cast to the
ground, to set up the bra-
ziers, to erect the offering
tables, . . . to put the land
into its former state" (lines
17–21).

The translator of the Egyptian text presumes to add that
water had entered the tombs and caused water damage,
which is possible, but the text has simply *ʿq spꜣwt* "the tombs
were entered." The remainder of the damage described in the
Tempest Stele could be assigned to seismic causes. Assessing
the damage wrought in Egypt is somewhat difficult because
few if any temples survive from either the Old or Middle
Kingdom; whether this is attributable to Hyksos depreda-
tions, New Kingdom renovations, or the Thera eruption
becomes problematic. Almost all the surviving temples in
Egypt were built after the reign of Ahmose. Nevertheless, the
massive Old Kingdom pyramids at Giza, Saqqara, and elsewhere did survive substantially intact, along with their fu-
nerary temples. Furthermore, the Nile has remained in the
same general course to the present day, as evidenced by con-
tinual occupation remains at certain key sites since predy-
nastic times. Since Egypt did not change in a drastic geological fashion, we need not consider that the Book of Mormon,
when stating that "the whole face of the land was changed"
(3 Nephi 8:12), must be taken to mean that continents rose
out of the ocean; people after all did manage to find their way
to Bountiful (see 3 Nephi 11:1).

WIDER IMPLICATIONS

The prevailing winds leave Egypt directly in the path
of the volcanic debris from Thera.[8] The Thera eruption of

c. 1530 B.C. ejected an estimated twenty to thirty cubic kilometers of material thirty to thirty-five kilometers into the air, leaving rounded pumice, shells, and snails atop the destroyed palaces of the recently sacked Hyksos capital of Avaris (Tell el-Dabaʿa).[9] The resultant cataclysm caused flooding and damage throughout the whole of Egypt at least as far south as Thebes (1,400 kilometers, or 875 miles, away from Thera).

Assuming that the mechanism of destruction in the Book of Mormon was similarly a volcano, the close parallels suggest the following implications for the geography and archaeology of the Book of Mormon: Geographically, the area covered by an eruption depends on the amount of ejecta and the prevailing winds; but the Thera case shows that a similar eruption could easily black out areas 1,400 kilometers away. A Mesoamerican location for the Book of Mormon has the requisite volcanic activity and similar prevailing wind patterns for a volcano in the north to black out a southerly location and to cause "a more great and terrible destruction in the land northward" (3 Nephi 8:12), as more of the ejecta would fall closer to the eruption and collateral earthquake damage would be greater closer to the epicenter. Archaeologically, we would expect to find pumice (in varying degrees) accompanying occasional destruction layers dating to the time of the crucifixion for particular Book of Mormon sites.

Pliny's description of the destruction of Pompeii by Vesuvius in A.D. 79,[10] an account which has been used in comparison with the Book of Mormon before, differs in some important respects from the descriptions in both the Tempest Stele and the Book of Mormon. For instance, Pliny does not describe loud noises or widespread massive destruction. Pliny's description of the darkness at Vesuvius differs from that of the other two sources: "Elsewhere there was daylight by this time, but they were still in darkness, blacker and denser than any night that ever was, which they relieved by lighing torches and various kinds of lamp."[11] Both the Book of Mormon and the Tempest Stele inform us that it was impossible to light a torch. This would imply that the volcano, if such was the mechanism of destruction in the Book of Mormon, was more powerful than Vesuvius.

Obviously, several assumptions accompany these predictions, the falsity of any of which could invalidate this hypothesis. Nevertheless, it is a specifically testable hypothesis, and it is "the possibility of overthrowing it, or its falsifiability, that constitutes the possibility of testing it, and therefore the scientific character of a theory."[12] The testing of the hypothesis I leave to the appropriate specialists.

Research by John Gee, originally published in the Journal of Book of Mormon Studies *6/2 (1997): 235–44.*

NOTES

1. For references to the previous literature, see the version of this article that appeared in the *Journal of Book of Mormon Studies,* and more recently, Bart J. Kowallis, "In the Thirty and Fourth Year: A Geologist's View of the Great Destruction in 3 Nephi," *BYU Studies* 37/3 (1997–98): 136–90; and Benjamin R. Jordan, "'Many Great and Notable Cities Were Sunk': Liquefaction in the Book of Mormon," *BYU Studies* 38/3 (1999): 115–18.

2. See Claude Vandersleyen, "Une tempête sous le règne d'Amosis," *Revue d'Égyptologie* 19 (1967): 123–59.

3. See Karen P. Foster and Robert K. Ritner, "Texts, Storms, and the Thera Eruption," *Journal of Near Eastern Studies* 55/1 (1996): 1–14. The text from the stele, used in this article, is taken from this source. The restorations proposed by James P. Allen are unlikely; Malcolm H. Wiener and James P. Allen, "Separate Lives: The Ahmose Tempest Stela and the Thera Eruption," *Journal of*

Near Eastern Studies 57/1 (1998): 1–28. Wiener's conclusions are based on a misunderstanding of Foster and Ritner's thesis.

4. Normally, *dꜥ.n* is followed by what the storm is composed of, for example: *iw=f mi dꜥw t3w* "he is like a storm of wind." P. Anastasi I 18/5, in Alan H. Gardiner, *Egyptian Hieratic Texts: I* (Leipzig: Hinrichs, 1911), 30.

5. See Helaman 11:13–17; Ether 9:30–35. The other examples are in quotations with biblical parallels: 2 Nephi 14:6; 15:6 (see Isaiah 4:6; 5:6); 3 Nephi 14:25–27 (see Matthew 7:25–27); 18:13 (see Matthew 7:25–27); but see Ether 2:24.

6. Indeed, it was this detail that initially drew my attention.

7. See James L. Baer, "The Third Nephi Disaster: A Geological View," *Dialogue* 19/1 (1986): 131.

8. See John Baines and Jaromír Málek, *Atlas of Ancient Egypt* (New York: Facts on File, 1980), 68.

9. See Foster and Ritner, "Texts, Storms, and the Thera Eruption," 9–10.

10. See Pliny, *Epistulae* 6.16, in *Pliny: Letters and Panegyricus*, trans. Betty Radice (Cambridge, Mass: Harvard University Press, 1969), 433.

11. Pliny, *Epistulae* 6.16.17.

12. Karl R. Popper, *The Open Society and Its Enemies*, 5th ed. (Princeton: Princeton University Press), 2:260.

51

Two Notes on the Lord's Prayer

"Our Father who art in heaven, hallowed be thy name. Thy will be done on earth as it is in heaven. And forgive us our debts, as we forgive our debtors. And lead us not into temptation, but deliver us from evil. For thine is the kingdom, and the power, and the glory, forever. Amen." (3 Nephi 13:9–13)

Four versions of the Lord's Prayer are found in scripture, in Matthew 6, Matthew 6 JST, Luke 11, and 3 Nephi 13. Recent research enhances our appreciation of the words that Jesus chose to use.

Lead us not. An article by James H. Charlesworth argues that although the New Testament was written originally in Greek, one must consider "the Aramaic substratum of the gospels and the Semitic milieu in which earliest Christianity came to life."[1] As an example, Charlesworth explains that the Greek phraseology in the line "lead us not into temptation" (Luke 11:4) "looks suspiciously like an erroneous rendering" of the Semitic expression found in the Syriac manuscripts of this passage. That expression uses the *Aph'el* form of the Semitic verb, which may have two meanings: (1) a causative meaning, "lead us not into temptation," or (2) a permissive sense, "do not permit (or allow) us to enter into temptation."[2] Both are possible understandings of the Semitic construction, but Charlesworth favors the permissive sense (compare James 1:13).

Charlesworth's analysis is compatible with Matthew 6:14 JST: "And *suffer us not to be led* into temptation." As the footnote to Matthew 6:13 in the LDS Edition of the scriptures indeed notes, the Syriac version reads "do not let us enter into temptation."

The ambiguity that Charlesworth points out may have been welcomed by Jesus, who may have wanted his disciples to understand both senses of this verb. He may have wanted them to pray, in effect, "do not lead us into temptation, but lead us some other way," and at the same time to pray "do not permit us to enter into temptation." Thus, both English translations capture part of the richness of what the Savior may have intended.

For thine is the kingdom. On several occasions Jesus taught people how to pray. Nothing demands that he said precisely the same thing each time. In fact, his counsel against vain repetitions (see Matthew 6:7) might suggest that he did not use the same words each time he prayed or spoke about prayer, which would explain in part why the texts of the Lord's Prayer differ.[3]

The differences in audiences may shed light on these variations. For example, generally speaking, the more sacred the setting, the more profound the ending of the prayer. Prayers in the temple at Jerusalem did not end simply with "Amen" but with "Praised be the name of his glorious kingdom forever and eternally."[4] Thus, in 3 Nephi 13, when Jesus spoke at the temple in Bountiful, he concluded his prayer with more than "Amen."

On other occasions, Jesus spoke more informally. In Luke 11:1, one of the disciples asked Jesus to teach them to pray. In this intimate setting, probably in the wilderness where he often went to pray, Jesus reviewed the basic steps of prayer (see Luke 11:2–4). But he cut short that instruction to talk about two related subjects: asking God and being generous (see Luke 11:5–13). In that instructional setting he did not need to give his words on prayer a formal conclusion and simply ended with "Amen."

The longest ending for the Lord's Prayer is found in Matthew 6:15 JST: "forever *and ever*, amen." Here Jesus speaks to his apostles as he sends them into the mission field to testify of eternal truths (see Matthew 5:3–4; 6:25–27; 7:1 JST). In this priesthood setting, the ending emphasizes the everlasting nature of the kingdom of God.

Thus, variations between the four scriptural versions of the Lord's prayer are understandable. Rather than being problematic, the differences each bespeak authenticity through the authority of actual experiences.

Research by John W. Welch, originally published as a FARMS Update in Insights *(June 1996): 2.*

NOTES

1. James H. Charlesworth, "Semitisms in the New Testament and the Need to Clarify the Importance of the Syriac New Testament," in *Salvación en la Palabra* (n.p., 1986), 633.

2. Ibid., 637.

3. See John W. Welch, *Illuminating the Sermon at the Temple and Sermon on the Mount* (Provo, Utah: FARMS, 1999), 206–8.

4. Ibid., 81, 207.

52

good

WAS THERE LEPROSY
AMONG THE NEPHITES?

*"Have ye any that are lame, or blind, or halt,
or maimed, or leprous . . . ?" (3 Nephi 17:7)*

Speaking to the Nephites assembled at the temple in
Bountiful, the risen Jesus Christ said, "Have ye any that
are lame, or blind, or halt, or maimed, or *leprous* . . . ? Bring
them hither and I will heal them" (3 Nephi 17:7). Yet medical researchers do not believe that leprosy per se existed in
ancient America. How can we resolve this apparent conflict
between what the Book of Mormon describes and what
modern researchers have concluded?

Answering such a question always demands that we
first look carefully at the text. It seems safe to suppose that
behind Joseph Smith's translation of "leprous" in 3 Nephi
would have been the Hebrew word that is consistently
translated *leprosy* in the Old Testament. That Hebrew term
is *ṣāra'at*. The Jewish scholars in Alexandria who put the
Old Testament into Greek (the Septuagint) used Greek *lepra*
as the equivalent of *ṣāra'at. Lepra* is regularly referred to in
the Gospels where it is translated "leprosy."

A sizable body of scholarly writing has tried to identify
what medical condition fits the Bible's statements regarding
the nature, incidence and cure of *ṣāra'at* and *lepra*.[1] The somewhat surprising conclusion is that *ṣāra'at* "is not leprosy and

231

does not include it."[2] The Old Testament statements about the lesions and symptoms simply do not fit leprosy. In fact the known history of disease and medicine suggests that "it is doubtful if leprosy existed at all in the Ancient Near East at the time of the Old Testament,"[3] although it is possible that true leprosy had reached Judea by the time of Jesus and could have been included by New Testament writers with the diseases previously encompassed under the term ṣāraʿat.[4] Finally, the result of this research concludes simply that ṣāraʿat. denoted "several types of skin lesions which exhibit exfoliation or scaling of the skin"[5] but were not leprosy per se. Thus it appears that the English translations of the Old Testament use *leprosy* to refer to skin conditions that were not epidemiologically leprosy.

Thus it is highly unlikely that Lehi's or Mulek's parties could have brought real leprosy with them to the New World. To what disease, then, might the Savior have referred in calling for the Nephite "leprous" to be brought to him to be healed? Two candidates are *uta* (leishmaniasis) and Chagas' disease. Both attack the mucous membranes of the face and cause an appearance like leprosy.[6] Another skin disease that was present in ancient America is called *pinta;* it discolors the skin with light blotches that sound like one of the symptoms of ṣāraʿat.

Among the Aztecs, Father Sahagun reported that one of the diseases attributed to the god Tlaloc was what he translated to Spanish as "leprosy."[7] Meanwhile among those few of the dead who were deemed eligible to enter the paradisiacal land of the Tlalocs, the rain gods, were those with "certain incurable skin diseases," including what Sahagun had called "leprosy."[8]

It is reasonable, therefore, to suppose that several kinds of skin diseases existed in the American land of the Nephites which would have recalled to Book of Mormon writers the ṣāraʿat or "leprosy" of the Old Testament. When Jesus called for those suffering from those ills to come forward, the Book of Mormon term *leprous* would serve to denote their condition just as accurately as in the case of the Bible and its peoples.

We can see *leprosy* in the Book of Mormon text as one in a substantial series of terms which prudent readers will understand to demand careful explication before their actual meanings are clear.

Research by John L. Sorenson, originally published as a FARMS Update in Insights *(September 1994): 2.*

NOTES

1. See David P. Wright and Richard N. Jones, "Leprosy," in *Anchor Bible Dictionary,* ed. David N. Freedman (New York: Doubleday, 1992), 4:277–82; for further references see M. Gary Hadfield, "Neuropathology and the Scriptures," *BYU Studies* 33/2 (1993): 327, nn. 18–21.

2. Wright and Jones, "Leprosy," 278.

3. Ibid.

4. See ibid., 281.

5. Ibid., 279.

6. See Suzanne Austin Alchon, *Native Society and Disease in Colonial Ecuador* (Cambridge: Cambridge University Press, 1991), 20.

7. *Codex Florentino* 1:287.

8. J. Eric S. Thompson, *Mexico before Cortez: An Account of the Daily Life, Religion, and Ritual of the Aztecs and Kindred Peoples* (New York: Scribner's, 1933), 50.

53

good

THE DECLINE OF
THE GOD QUETZALCOATL

*"There were many churches in the land . . . which
professed to know the Christ, and yet they did
deny the more parts of his gospel." (4 Nephi 1:27)*

Some Latter-day Saints have long been struck with the
similarity between certain characteristics of the god
Quetzalcoatl, as known from native traditions in Mexico and
Guatemala, and Jesus Christ, whose visit to Lehi's descendants is described in 3 Nephi. In *An Ancient American Setting
for the Book of Mormon*,[1] the dramatic decline of the god
Quetzalcoatl in the period around A.D. 200 at the giant city of
Teotihuacan near Mexico City was discussed in comparison
with 4 Nephi. The book relied on a study by Mexican scholar Enrique Florescano.[2] A new study now presents even
clearer parallels.[3]

The face of what Mexican archaeologists term "the old
Temple of Quetzalcoatl" at Teotihuacan has been photographed by innumerable tourists. Dramatic symbolic
representations of Quetzalcoatl as a serpent dot the facade
of this impressive structure. Additional mapping, ceramic
study, and excavation have established quite surely that
this building was constructed at the same time as the huge
Pyramid of the Sun—between A.D. 150 and 200.[4] As visitors
clearly see, the original building was later covered over
with another structure bearing very different symbols.

In Book of Mormon history, this half century was the golden age following the appearance of the resurrected Jesus to the Nephites in Bountiful; however, 4 Nephi gives only two brief verses about this period (see 4 Nephi 1:19–20). (Of course we do not positively know that Teotihuacan was one of the cities of the Nephites or Lamanites, but the change in deities that Cabrera reports is so striking that we may at least speculate that worship of Jesus Christ, under the name translated by the later Aztecs as Quetzalcoatl, prevailed there.)

Cabrera's picture of the transition between the two sacred buildings is interesting: "the Plumed Serpent [representing Quetzalcoatl] . . . acquired for this [earlier] period of time a preponderant force in the political and religious aspect of Teotihuacan. This is shown by the ostentatious, sculpture-decorated structure, which to construct required enormous labor . . . making it one of the great glories of Teotihuacan." But what was the reason, the author goes on, for them to mutilate many of the enormous, plumed serpent heads and then construct a new edifice of lesser quality covering the first one? The change was not simply one of architectural style. More likely it had to do with changing political and religious power.

Cabrera continues: "The band or group of priests representing Quetzalcoatl held power at Teotihuacan from at least the time when the first structure was erected, before A.D. 200. But then other religious groups arose who were represented by the symbolism of jaguars, coyotes, birds and fishes along with other mythological beings." Priests or followers of this new religious persuasion eventually gained control of the city; the date for the change is not known precisely but is usually considered as approximately A.D. 300. Paintings and sculptures of jaguars and other symbolic animals are found widely throughout the sacred portion of the metropolis thereafter.

Fourth Nephi 1:26–41 reports the rise of new "churches" rivaling "the church of Christ," which eventually came to dominate the society. This took place about A.D. 210 to 260, a reasonable approximation to the scholars' estimate of A.D. 300.

Cabrera concludes with questions about this "period of social crisis whose causes are unknown": "Do the phenomena mentioned represent other Teotihuacan groups, or groups coming in from elsewhere, intent on establishing at Teotihuacan their own religion?" Or, "what was going on in Teotihuacan society in the area of religious and political organizations in the interval between A.D. 200 and 350?"

Those who read the Book of Mormon as authentic ancient history will feel they already have a useful explanation at least in part. But we too would like, in the author's final words, "better information, to establish more exact dates of these social events and determine their causes."

Research by John L. Sorenson, originally published as a FARMS Update in Insights *(September 1992): 2.*

NOTES

1. See John L. Sorenson, *An Ancient American Setting for the Book of Mormon* (Salt Lake City: Deseret Book and FARMS, 1985).

2. See Miguel León-Portilla, "Quetzalcóatl: espiritualismo del México antiguo," *Cuadernos Americanos* 105/4 (1959): 127–39.

3. See Rubén Cabrera Castro, "La secuencia arquitectónica del edificio de los animales mitológicos en Teotihuacan," in *Homenaje a Román Piña Chan* (Mexico: Universidad Nacional Autónoma de México, 1987), 349–71.

4. Cabrera, 364, reports a new carbon 14 date of A.D. 148.

54 *very good*

SEMITIC TEXTS WRITTEN IN EGYPTIAN CHARACTERS

"We have written this record according to our knowledge, in the characters which are called among us the reformed Egyptian." (Mormon 9:32)

The Book of Mormon indicates that it was written using Egyptian characters, called by Moroni "reformed Egyptian," though the Nephites also knew Hebrew (see Mormon 9:32–34). Nephi made "a record in the language of [his] father, which consists of the learning of the Jews and the language of the Egyptians" (1 Nephi 1:2). Evidently, the brass plates of Laban also contained Egyptian characters, for King Benjamin informed his sons that, without a knowledge of Egyptian, Lehi would not have been able to read them (see Mosiah 1:3–4).

Latter-day Saint scholars have long been divided on the issue of the language in which the Book of Mormon is written. Some have proposed that the Nephite record was simply written in Egyptian, while others have suggested that the Nephite scribes used Egyptian script ("the language of the Egyptians") to write Hebrew text ("the learning of the Jews"). While either of these is possible, this present study will elicit evidence for the latter.

Non-Latter-day Saint scholars and others have long scoffed at the idea that an Israelite group from Jerusalem should have written in Egyptian and mocked the term *reformed Egyptian* as nonsense. Since Joseph Smith's time, we have learned a great deal about Egyptian and Israelite records and realize that the Book of Mormon is correct in all respects.

The ancient Egyptians used three types of writing systems. The most well known, the hieroglyphs (Greek for "sacred symbols"), comprised nearly four hundred picture characters depicting things found in real life. A cursive script called hieratic (Greek for "sacred") was also used, principally on papyrus. Around 700 B.C., the Egyptians developed an even more cursive script that we call demotic (Greek for "popular"), which bore little resemblance to the hieroglyphs. Both hieratic and demotic were in use in Lehi's time and can properly be termed "reformed Egyptian." From the account in Mormon 9:32, it seems likely that the Nephites further reformed the characters.

Recent discoveries have provided evidence that at least some ancient Israelite scribes were, like the Nephite scribes, acquainted with both Hebrew and Egyptian. For example, a number of northwest Semitic texts are included in Egyptian magical papyri. These are mostly incantations that, instead of being translated from the original Semitic language into Egyptian, were merely transcribed in Egyptian hieratic.[1] The underlying language is a Northwest Semitic tongue, an early form of Hebrew/Canaanite.[2] The texts include the London Magical Papyrus (fourteenth century B.C.), the Harris Magical Papyrus (thirteenth century B.C.), Papyrus Anastasi I (thirteenth century B.C.), and Ostracon. The latter dates to the early eleventh century B.C., the time of Israel's judges. While a Semitic text appears on one side, the opposite side has a text that is pure Egyptian, though whether there is a connection between the two is unknown. In any event, it is clear that some Egyptian scribes were sufficiently versed in the

Northwest Semitic tongue that they were able to transliterate it using their own writing system.

Closer to Lehi's time are Israelite documents from the ninth to sixth centuries B.C., from which we learn that the Israelites adopted the Egyptian hieratic numerals and mingled them with Hebrew text.[3] More important, however, are texts in Hebrew and Aramaic—languages used by the Jews of Lehi's time—that are written in Egyptian characters. One of these is Papyrus Amherst 63, a document written in Egyptian demotic and dating to the second century B.C. The document had, like the Dead Sea Scrolls, been preserved in an earthen jar and was discovered in Thebes, Egypt, during the second half of the nineteenth century. For years, Egyptologists struggled with the text but could make no sense of it. The letters were clear, but they did not form intelligible words in Egyptian. In 1944, Raymond Bowman of the University of Chicago realized that, while the script is Egyptian, the underlying language is Aramaic.[4] Bowman managed to translate portions of the text, but it did not become the object of serious study until the 1980s. Among the writings included in the religious text is a paganized version of Psalm 20:2–6. Here, then, we have a Bible passage, in its Aramaic translation, written in late Egyptian characters.

In 1965, during excavations at the southern Judean site of Arad, a number of ostraca were found. Most of the documents were written in Hebrew and dated to c. 598–587 B.C.[5] One, however, dating "to the seventh century B.C.," was written in Egyptian hieratic. Here, then, was evidence that Egyptian writing was known in an Israelite city. This was not surprising, for Egyptian documents from an earlier time had been discovered at the Phoenician (Lebanese) city of Byblos.

More significant, however, was an ostracon uncovered at Arad in 1967.[6] Dating "toward the end of the seventh century B.C.," it reflects usage from shortly before 600 B.C., the time of Lehi. The text on the ostracon is written in a combination of Egyptian hieratic and Hebrew characters but can be read entirely as Egyptian. Of the seventeen words in the text, ten are written in hieratic and seven in Hebrew. However, all the words written in Hebrew can be read as Egyptian words, while one of them, which occurs twice, has the same meaning in both Egyptian and Hebrew.[7] Of the ten words written in hieratic script, four are numerals (one occurring in each line). One symbol, denoting a measure of capacity, occurs four times (once in each of the four lines), and the remaining Egyptian word occurs twice. Thus, while seventeen words appear on the ostracon, if one discounts the recurrence of words, only six words are written in hieratic (of which four are numerals), and six in Hebrew.

The text of the ostracon is integral, rather than a bilingual.[8] Yeivin, who translated and studied the text, wrote, "The two scripts provide supplementary information and they are intermingled. One cannot, however, be sure how the scribe who wrote the text read it, whether in Hebrew throughout, pronouncing all the apparent hieratic signs in their Hebrew equivalents, or in a mixed sort of jargon, giving the Egyptian values to the hieratic signs."[9]

Because the inscription was discovered in Israel, Yeivin never considered the possibility that all the words might have been read as Egyptian, which seems more likely in this case. One thing, however, is certain. The scribe who wrote the text knew both Hebrew and Egyptian writing systems and commingled them in a single text. Perhaps this is what Nephi meant when he said that the language of his record consisted of "the learning of the Jews and the language of the Egyptians" (1 Nephi 1:2).[10]

Additional evidence for the commingling of Hebrew and Egyptian scripts was discovered during archaeological excavations at Tell Ein-Qudeirah (biblical Kadesh-Barnea) in the Sinai Peninsula during the latter half of the 1970s. Several ostraca of the sixth and seventh centuries B.C. were uncovered. One ostracon, written mostly in hieratic characters, consists of a column of Egyptian measures and five columns of numbers. Along with the Egyptian, the Hebrew word *ʾălāphîm* ("thousands") appears twice (with the hieratic "ten" in the numeral "10,000"), while the Hebrew symbol for *shekel* (a weight measure) appears twenty-two times. Because of the order of the numerals in each column, it may be a scribal practice in writing numbers.

A second ostracon contains three vertical columns of numbers. The left-hand column has the Hebrew word *garah*, the smallest unit of Hebrew measure, after each hieratic numeral. Because the numerals are in order, Rudolph Cohen, the archaeologist who discovered the texts, concluded that "this writing is a scribal exercise." This view is supported by the discovery, at the same site, of a small ostracon with several Hebrew letters, in alphabetic order, evidently a practice text.

At both Arad and Kadesh-Barnea, there were, in addition to the "combination texts" discussed, other ostraca written entirely in either Hebrew or Egyptian hieratic. The implication is clear: Scribes or students contemporary or nearly contemporary with Lehi were being trained in both Hebrew and Egyptian writing systems. The use of Egyptian script by Lehi's descendants now becomes not only plausible, but perfectly reasonable in the light of archaeological discoveries made more than a century after Joseph Smith translated the Book of Mormon.

Research by Stephen D. Ricks, originally published as a FARMS Update in Insights *(March 1992): 2, and by John A.*

Tvedtnes and Stephen D. Ricks, originally published in the Journal of Book of Mormon Studies *5/2 (1996): 156–63.*

NOTES

1. The texts in question were written with what Albright termed the "Egyptian Syllabic Orthography," using standard Egyptian symbols in combinations designed to transliterate Semitic words. Semitic words written in the syllabic orthography are sometimes found in late Egyptian documents in the midst of Egyptian sentences; these are clearly borrowings. In the texts we list here, whole Semitic texts, rather than borrowed words, are written in Egyptian script. For a brief overview of some of the texts, see Wolfgang Helck, "Asiatische Fremdworte im Ägyptischen," in *Die Beziehungen Ägyptens zu Vorderasien im 3. und 2. Jahrtausend v. Chr.,* 2nd ed. (Wiesbaden: Harrassowitz, 1971), 528–29.

2. Hebrew is part of the Canaanite language family, usually called Northwest Semitic. This includes later forms of the Canaanite language, called Phoenician and Punic. Closely related is Ugaritic, known from thirteenth- and fourteenth-century B.C. inscriptions at the northwest Syrian city of Ugarit, and less closely related is Eblaite, known from second millennium B.C. inscriptions from nearby Ebla.

3. See R. A. Stewart MacAlister, *The Excavation of Gezer* (London: Palestine Exploration Fund, 1912), 2:276, 283, 285–87, 291; David Diringer, "On Ancient Hebrew Inscriptions Discovered at Tell Ed-Duweir (Lachish)—III," *Palestine Exploration Quarterly* (July–October 1943): 89–99; J. W. Crowfoot, G. M. Growfoot, and Kathleen M. Kenyon, *The Objects from Samaria* (London: Palestine Exploration Fund, 1957), 11–13, 16–18, 29–32; Yigael Yadin, "Ancient Judaean Weights and the Date of the Samaria Ostraca," in *Scripta Hierosolymitana* (Jerusalem: Magnes, 1961), 8:9–25; Yohanan Aharoni, "The Use of Hieratic Numerals in Hebrew Ostraca and the Shekel Weights," *Bulletin of the American Schools of Oriental Research* 184 (December 1966): 13–19; Ivan T. Kaufman, "New Evidence for Hieratic Numerals on Hebrew Weights," *Bulletin of the American Schools of*

Oriental Research 188 (December 1967): 39–41; Anson F. Rainey, "Semantic Parallels to the Samaria Ostraca," *Palestine Exploration Quarterly* (January–June 1970): 45–51.

4. See Raymond A. Bowman, "An Aramaic Religious Text in Demotic Script," *Journal of Near Eastern Studies* 3 (1944): 219–31.

5. See Yohanan Aharoni, "Hebrew Ostraca from Tel Arad," *Israel Exploration Journal* 16/1 (1966): 1–7.

6. The first Latter-day Saint notice of the significance of the Arad materials for Book of Mormon language was made by John A. Tvedtnes, "Linguistic Implications of the Tel-Arad Ostraca," *Newsletter and Proceedings of the Society for Early Historic Archaeology* 127 (October 1971): 1–5, and in abbreviated form in "The Language of My Father," *New Era* (May 1971): 19.

7. This is the preposition *m*, which means "from" in both languages. Hebrew and Egyptian are distantly related, so this word is a cognate.

8. A bilingual has a text in one language followed by a translation of the same text in another language. Many bilingual (and trilingual) inscriptions are known from the ancient Near East.

9. Shlomo Yeivin, "An Ostracon from Tel Arad Exhibiting a Combination of Two Scripts," *Journal of Egyptian Archaeology* 55 (August 1969): 98–102.

10. It remains to be determined when an Israelite or Nephite scribe would have used an Egyptian symbol instead of a Hebrew (alphabetic) letter. While some Egyptian characters are alphabetic in nature, representing a single sound, others are syllabic or ideographic and can represent whole words or syllables. This does not mean that they must be read with an Egyptian meaning, however. Akkadian scribes in Mesopotamia borrowed syllabically written words from their Sumerian predecessors but assigned them a "translation" equivalent in their own language, rather than the Sumerian pronunciation. It is possible that the Nephites, whenever possible, used Egyptian symbols that represented two or more consonants (Egyptian symbols often represent three consonants, sometimes four or five) whenever it would take less space on the plates to write the Egyptian rather than the Hebrew.

55

Two Notes on Egyptian Script

*"We have written this record according to our
knowledge, in the characters which are called
among us the reformed Egyptian." (Mormon 9:32)*

Moroni, at the end of his father's record, states, "we
have written this record according to our knowledge,
in the *characters* which are called *among us* the reformed
Egyptian" (Mormon 9:32). Since the publication of this
statement many suggestions have been made concerning
the identification of the script.[1] This note is intended to
broaden the base of possibilities thus far considered by
adding two hitherto unconsidered options.

Abnormal Hieratic

Most discussions of reformed Egyptian deal with
demotic. Yet demotic is just one of two writing styles used
in Egypt that developed from hieratic. This other style of
hieratic script, abnormal hieratic, has not received attention
and ought at least to be considered in discussions of
reformed Egyptian. Michel Malinine, who did the most
work toward deciphering and publishing abnormal hieratic
documents, did not like the term himself and preferred to
call it *cursive thébaine tardive* (late Theban cursive),[2] while
Georg Möller preferred the term *späthieratische Kursive* (late
hieratic cursive),[3] but Griffith's term, *abnormal hieratic*, is

the one that has stuck. "'Abnormal hieratic' represents the final stage of the development of cursive writing in the New Kingdom, which was elaborated and used in the southern half of Egypt and, in particular, at Thebes, and whose progressive changes can actually be followed, almost without interruption, from the end of the Eighteenth Dynasty until the penultimate reign of the Saite Dynasty."[4] An adaptation of hieratic characterized by "wild orthography," abnormal hieratic in its second phase was used in Egypt mainly for legal and administrative purposes during the Twenty-fifth and Twenty-sixth Dynasties (727–548 B.C.), after which time it was replaced by demotic.[5] Though abnormal hieratic is usually thought only to have been used in southern Egypt, it has now been dubiously argued that it was used in northern Egypt as well.[6] Be that as it may, it is yet another modified Egyptian script available in Egypt in Lehi's day.

Carved Hieratic

It is important to realize also that demotic, like hieratic (and abnormal hieratic), was usually written with a brush on papyrus until Ptolemaic times (third century B.C.), when the Greek *kalamos*, or reed pen, began to be used. Hieratic from the beginning was a script adapted for brush on papyrus; for carving, hieroglyphics were used. After the conquest of Egypt by the Libyans ushered in the Twenty-first Dynasty,[7] hieratic began to be used for carving in stone. During the Twenty-second Dynasty, hieratic stelae containing official royal decrees became common; but hieratic disappeared from official decrees with the archaizing fashion of the Saite Period (Twenty-sixth Dynasty).[8] The ductus of hieratic (and demotic) that has been engraved is altered from that found on papyrus—carving tends to be more angular, while the brush adapts itself well to rounded forms—which makes it more difficult to read if one is not used to it. When engraved, hieratic and demotic are normally engraved in stone, but there are examples of demotic engraved into metal, including a bronze palette.[9] Though, to my knowledge, no one has raised this objection before, it is worth noting that a tradition of engraving forms of cursive Egyptian is attested by Lehi's day[10] and that engraved forms of cursive do not necessarily coincide with those forms produced by brush and ink.

Research by John Gee, originally published in the Journal of Book of Mormon Studies *5/1 (1996): 162–76.*

Notes

1. A convenient summary of the suggestions is found in William J. Hamblin, "Reformed Eyptian" (FARMS, 1995).

2. See Michel Malinine, "Une affaire concernant un partage (Pap. Vienne D 12003 et D 12004)," *Revue d'Égyptologie* 25 (1973): 192.

3. See Malinine, "L'hiératique anormal," in *Textes et langages de l'Égypte pharaonique: Cent cinquante années de recherches 1822–1972: Hommage à Jean-François Champollion* (Cairo: Institut Français d'Archéologie Orientale, 1973), 1:31.

4. Malinine, *Choix des textes juridiques en hiératique anormal et en démotique* (Paris: Chamption, 1953), 1:xiv.

5. Ibid., 1:xix–xxi.

6. See Ola el-Aguizy, "About the Origins of Early Demotic in Lower Egypt," in *Life in a Multi-Cultural Society: Egypt from Cambyses to Constantine and Beyond,* ed. Janet H. Johnson (Chicago: Oriental Institute, 1992), 91–94.

7. The importance of this for Old Testament history can hardly be understated. Without the problems caused by its western and southern flanks (Libya and Nubia), Egypt would certainly have pursued its traditional course of dominating the Levantine littoral, which would not have allowed either a united

or a divided Israelite monarchy; the Israelites would have forever been fighting the Egyptians rather than the Philistines. For Egypt's foreign policy, see Donald B. Redford, *Egypt, Canaan, and Israel in Ancient Times* (Princeton: Princeton University Press, 1992), a book unfortunately marred by the author's obvious hostility toward the Bible and the religions that sprang therefrom.

8. For a recent study of the archaizing tendency of the Twenty-sixth Dynasty, see Peter Der Manuelian, *Living in the Past: Studies in Archaism of the Egyptian Twenty-sixth Dynasty* (London: Kegan Paul International, 1994). This tendency is normally noted in the art of the period; see Gay Robins, *Proportion and Style in Ancient Egyptian Art* (Austin: University of Texas Press, 1994), 256–57. Although the archaizing tendency of art is normally associated with the Twenty-sixth Dynasty, it started earlier in the Twenty-fifth Dynasty; ibid., 160; W. Stevenson Smith, *The Art and Architecture of Ancient Egypt* (New York: Penguin Books, 1958), 408.

9. See Cairo CG 30691 (Roman period), in Wilhelm Spiegelberg, *Die demotischen Denkmäler* (Leipzig: Druglin, 1904), 1:80–82 and Tafel XXVI. This document is a temple inventory; for other examples see Richard Jasnow, "The Hieratic Wooden Tablet Varille," *For His Ka: Essays Offered in Memory of Klaus Baer*, ed. David P. Silverman, The Oriental Institute of the University of Chicago Studies in Ancient Oriental Civilization, no. 55 (Chicago, Ill.: University of Chicago, 1994), 99–112, and bibliography, p. 100 n. 10.

10. See Georg Möller, *Hieratische Paläographie: Die aegyptische Buchschrift in ihrer Entwicklung von der fünften Dynastie bis zur römischen Kaiserzeit* (Leipzig: Hinrichs, 1927–36), 3:8.

56

very good

OLD WORLD PEOPLE
IN THE NEW

*"And who knoweth but the Lord will carry
us forth into a land which is choice
above all the earth?" (Ether 1:38)*

Joseph Smith is said to have "quoted [in 1842] with approval from the pulpit reports of certain Toltec [Mexican] legends which would make it appear that those people had come originally from the Near East in the time of Moses"; he did not connect the purported migration at all to the Book of Mormon.[1]

Many traditions existed in Mesoamerica that told of ancestors of the native peoples, or at least of part of them, coming from across the ocean.[2] For instance, the "Título de los Señores de Totonicapán," signed in 1554 by dignitaries of the Quiché Maya Indians of highland Guatemala, said, "the three nations of Quichés . . . came from where the sun rises, descendants of Israel."[3]

Interpreters of this document have commonly supposed that the Indians had inserted a Bible tradition about "Israel" that they had picked up from the Spaniards. (The process by which such a cultural intrusion might have taken place in the first generation after the Conquest, and why anyone would put the notion into a legally important native document, is never clear in this speculation.)

One possible source for Joseph Smith's comment can now be identified. A nineteenth-century Guatemalan historian, Domingo Juarros, published in 1809 an obscure work in Spanish that was translated into English and issued in 1823 in London as *A Statistical and Commercial History of the Kingdom of Guatemala*. Even if Joseph never saw this book, by 1842 he may have come across a newspaper piece based upon it.

Juarros said he had access to manuscripts held by families descended from Quichean royalty at the time of the Spaniards' arrival. Those were documents apart from the famous Totonicapán title or from the Popol Vuh. He reported that the manuscripts stated that their ancestors, called Toltecs, had descended "from the house of Israel." They were said to have escaped under Moses from captivity in Egypt; but being confirmed idolaters, they chose to separate from him and his brethren. At length, the story goes, they reached Mexico where they founded the famed city of Tula. The chief who commanded and conducted this multitude from one continent to the other was named Tanub. From him, it was claimed, sprang the Toltec kings of Tula. Two of the manuscripts relate that "thirteen armies" left the old continent, headed by as many principal families, all related.

Tanub's fifth successor led them from Mexico to Guatemala. There the kingdom was divided into three nations (the Quichés, Cakchiquels, and Tzutuhils), which the manuscripts said took place on "a day marked by three suns being visible at the same time," an incident that induced some Spaniards to think it was on the day of the Savior's birth, "as it is commonly asserted such a phenomenon then occurred."

When the Quiché king heard by private ambassador from his Aztec kinsman Moctezuma, then a prisoner, that white men had overcome his nation and planned to conquer the Quiché, the Quiché priests prognosticated coming disaster, based on the splitting in two of a divining stone that their forefathers had brought from Egypt and that they worshipped as a god.

How this tradition reflects real history, and how, if at all, it might relate to the Book of Mormon we do not know, but clearly certain Indian groups interpreted their own annals to mean that their ancestors were connected to the biblical history they were learning from their conquerors, even at the risk of being considered descendants of idolaters. That they simply concocted the notion of a transoceanic connection is hard to believe.

This Quiché Indian tradition of Toltec migrants from the Near East reaching Mesoamerica appears to be supported by new linguistic research reported by a senior linguist at one of this country's most prestigious universities. Dr. Mary LeCron Foster delivered two papers in 1992 at the Association of American Geographer's annual meeting in San Diego and the Language Origins Society at Cambridge University.[4] They duplicate each other considerably; the following summary is an amalgamation.

Her linguistic reconstruction shows that Afro-Asiatic languages, in particular ancient Egyptian (and related Hebrew?), are genetically close, and possibly ancestral, to geographically distant languages in both the Old and New Worlds. In the Old World they include Dravidian of southern India, Chinese, and Malayo-Polynesian, and in the New World, Quechua (the language of the Incas) and Zoquean, Mayan, Zapotec, and Mixtec in Mesoamerica. More specifically the Mixe-Zoque languages of southern Mexico, which have been hypothesized by other linguists to derive from the language spoken by the Olmec, as well as the Mayan languages of Mexico and Central America, are closely related to and probably descended from ancient Egyptian.

Another genetic relationship uncovered is between Proto-Indo-European (the ancestor of most western European tongues) and the Uto-Aztecan languages of North America, including Nahuatl (Aztec) of Mexico. She has arrived at this picture using the standard linguistic comparative method with reliance on regularity of sound changes and pattern congruence.

Quechua she says is closely related to the "Egyptoid" languages in Mesoamerica, but it also contains an admixture of Semitic vocabulary that seems to be Arabic. Various cultural parallels are correlated with the language relationships hypothesized. For instance, the Mayan origin myth in the Quiché sacred book, the Popol Vuh, tells of four great sages (Q'uq'kumatz, Tepev, Tzakol, Bitol) who arrived on the sea coast and found nothing, so they created everything. The names of these four in Mayan she finds relate to Egyptian roots in both sounds and meanings. She includes a table of twenty cognate sets of words in Egyptian, Mixe-Zoque, Mayan, and Quechua.

Some connections between Old and New World languages are so close as to throw doubt on an exclusive scenario of ancient Bering Strait crossings; hence conventional migration theories will need revision. This seems particularly true of Egyptian ties to the New World. The Olmec and the Chavin culture of Peru appeared abruptly around 1500 B.C. At this period Egypt was involved in an intense period of conquest and organized rule abroad; oceanic voyages by Egyptian ships were clearly possible then. A further example of an interesting parallel is a Zoque myth that tells of the life and death of Homshuk, the maize god, that bears much similarity to Egyptian tales of Osiris. Yet proof of these assertions lies not in a few cultural parallels but in the accuracy of the linguistic analysis, which is extensive, she says.

Research by John L. Sorenson, originally published as FARMS Updates in Insights *(April 1995): 2; (June 1995): 2.*

NOTES

1. Hugh W. Nibley, *Lehi in the Desert; The World of the Jaredites; There Were Jaredites* (Salt Lake City: Deseret Book and FARMS, 1988), 250; citing Joseph Smith, *Teachings of the Prophet Joseph Smith,* comp. Joseph Fielding Smith (Salt Lake City: Deseret Book, 1979), 267.

2. See John L. Sorenson, "Some Mesoamerican Traditions of Immigration by Sea," *El México Antiguo* 8 (1955): 425–38.

3. Adrián Recinos and Delia Goetz, trans., *The Annals of the Cakchiquels and Title of the Lords of Totonicapán* (Norman: University of Oklahoma Press, 1953), 170.

4. Although these papers remain unpublished, they are annotated in some detail in John L. Sorenson and Martin H. Raish, *Pre-Columbian Contact with the Americas across the Oceans: An Annotated Bibliography,* 2nd ed. rev. (Provo, Utah: Research Press, 1996), 1:325–26.

57

New Light on the Shining Stones of the Jaredites

"What will ye that I should prepare for
you that ye may have light?" (Ether 2:25)

The preparation of light sources for the Jaredite barges has long been an enigma to Book of Mormon readers. The Lord indicated the impracticality of using normal sources of light, saying, "Ye cannot have windows, for they will be dashed in pieces; neither shall ye take fire with you, for ye shall not go by the light of fire. . . . Therefore what will ye that I should prepare for you that ye may have light?" (Ether 2:23, 25).

In response, the brother of Jared "did molten out of a rock sixteen small stones; and they were white and clear, even as transparent glass" (Ether 3:1). Placing them before the Lord, he petitioned, "Touch these stones, O Lord, with thy finger, and prepare them that they may shine forth in darkness . . . that we may have light while we shall cross the sea" (Ether 3:4). By touching the stones, the Lord somehow changed them, causing them to emit a light bright enough to illuminate the inside of the barges.

The physical oddity of such a source of light, however, has been a cause for considerable ridicule for the Book of Mormon. Comments such as the following are typical:

> The story of Ether's stone candles overtaxes marvelousness . . . and these sixteen stone-candles gave

253

light for eight vessels while crossing the ocean to America. Who is eager to believe this story? Shall we believe it simply because we cannot disprove it? They say there is a "man on the moon," and that "the moon is made of green cheese," and we cannot disprove it—shall we therefore believe it?[1]

More recently Weldon Langfield expressed his opinion of the shining stones: "The words 'patently ridiculous' seem too kind."[2] Many critics completely dismissed the Book of Mormon because they could not believe that such a light source was physically feasible.

Sandia National Laboratories in New Mexico have recently developed radioluminescent lights that invite some interesting comparisons with the Jaredite stones. These lights are intended to "serve needs for lighting where no electricity is readily available"[3] Their life expectancy is about 20 years, and they are described as being "bright" and very "intense."

The radioluminescent lights are made from a highly porous silica matrix—*aerogel*—in which a phosphor such as zinc sulfide is dispersed. The radioactive source of the lights is tritium gas, which when incorporated into the aerogel, actually becomes chemically bonded to the aerogel matrix.[4] The radioactivity of tritium results in beta decay. The beta particles (electrons) "permeate through the open spaces of the aerogel and strike the phosphor particles, exciting them and causing them to emit light."[5] The majority of the light emitted escapes to the outside, whereas the beta radiation is contained inside the matrix. Therefore there is no appreciable external radiation.

Radioluminescent light is consistent with and supplies an intriguing parallel matching the requirements of the Jaredite stones: they are small, long-lasting, and physically harmless. It is possible that the Jaredite stones were created in a similar fashion, according to existing physical laws. Although making the molten rocks would most likely have boiled off any tritium present, it is conceivable that the Lord could have altered some other molecule in the stone to create the radioactive isotope that would produce the glowing effect. It is also possible that he could have simply infused the stones with tritium gas as the Sandia researchers have done. Interestingly, years ago Elder Spencer W. Kimball proposed that perhaps the Jaredite stones were illuminated "with radium or some other substance not yet rediscovered by our scientists."[6]

Of course we can only speculate about the process that led to the Jaredite lights, and even the Sandia researchers are quick to caution that scientific knowledge about radioluminescent lights is still in the early stages of development. Future discoveries and further developments may more closely illuminate the manner in which the molten Jaredite stones were caused to fluoresce, but for now this latest development certainly helps us appreciate that the Book of Mormon refers to realities we are only now rediscovering.

Research by Nicholas Read, Jae R. Ballif, John W. Welch, Bill Evenson, Kathleen Reynolds Gee, and Matthew Roper, originally published as a FARMS Update in Insights *(July 1992): 2.*

NOTES

1. William Sheldon, *Mormonism Examined* (Brodhead, Wis.: By the author, 1876), 139–40.

2. Weldon Langfield, *The Truth About Mormonism* (Bakersfield, Calif.: Weldon Langfield, 1991), 45.

3. Sandia National Laboratories, News Release, Albuquerque, New Mexico, September 27, 1990, p. 1.

4. See ibid., p. 3.

5. Ibid.

6. Spencer W. Kimball, untitled talk, *Conference Report* (April 1963): 64.

58

BY LAND OR BY SEA?
REVISITING THE BERING STRAITS

"They got aboard of their vessels or barges, and
set forth into the sea, commending themselves
unto the Lord their God." (Ether 6:4)

Traditionally, most anthropologists have accepted the
theory that the ancestors of all Native American cultures in the New World migrated by foot from Asia during
the Pleistocene Era when the sea level was lower and a narrow strip of land called the Bering Land Bridge connected
the two continents. But as a review in *BYU Studies* shows,[1]
Dr. E. James Dixon, in *Quest for the Origins of the First
Americans*, challenges this traditional model.[2]

Dixon is a leading authority on the archaeology of eastern Beringia, the chain of islands that once formed the
ancient land bridge connecting Asia with present-day
Alaska. Although no one doubts the existence of this land
bridge, or its potential as a conduit for human migration,
Dixon demonstrates that this could not have been the sole
mechanism for populating the Americas. He presents
impressive and compelling evidence that suggests that the
first, or at least early, inhabitants of ancient America actually arrived on ocean-worthy vessels.

The geology and paleoecology of the Beringia region
suggest that it was not until about 9500 B.C. that the
Bering Land Bridge became passable for human overland

migration. Consistent with this date, there is no documented evidence of human occupation anywhere in the Beringian corridor until about 9000 B.C. Yet there is ample evidence of early occupations along the west coasts of both North and South America that date at least two or three thousand years and in some cases many thousands of years before that. Since it appears that there was no way of crossing overland at such early dates, Dixon asserts that these settlements must have been founded by seagoing peoples.

It is well documented that the Pacific coasts of Asia were dotted anciently with numerous settlements. Dixon suggests that shortly before 12,000 B.C. the sea level rose rapidly as the climate became abruptly warmer and the sea engulfed communities around the Asian Pacific rim (something like a Pleistocene *Waterworld*). This could have triggered eastward migrations following prevailing currents into the New World. By the time the Bering Land Bridge became passable, the descendents of these early travelers had already settled over much of the western coastline of North and South America and had even moved inland in some areas.

LDS scholars have long been interested in the issue of transoceanic crossings to the ancient New World,[3] but they have found scant support among the prevailing experts. Dixon himself was at one time criticized by several of his colleagues for suggesting the possibility of transoceanic migrations and was counseled to drop the subject for fear of losing credibility within the profession.[4] Dixon believes that the idea of pre-Columbian transoceanic contacts between the New and Old Worlds is not popular because of the tendency of some individuals outside the field to go too far in explaining all similarities between the two great cultural regions indiscriminately on the basis of diffusion across the oceans.

But carefully presented research findings like Dixon's (and those from an increasing number of others) make it clear that humans anciently were capable of long-distance voyages across the oceans to visit or colonize parts of the New World. By extension, it is reasonable to conclude that small colonies of Jaredites, Lehites, and Mulekites could have made such trips as well.

Research by Allen J. Christenson, originally published as a FARMS Update in Insights *(February 1996): 2.*

NOTES

1. See Allen J. Christenson, review of *Quest for the Origins of the First Americans,* by E. James Dixon, *BYU Studies* 35/3 (1995–96): 178–80. See also Stephen C. Jett's excellent discussion of transoceanic contacts, in "Before Columbus: The Question of Early Transoceanic Interinfluences" (FARMS, 1993).

2. See E. James Dixon, *Quest for the Origins of the First Americans* (Albuquerque: University of New Mexico Press, 1993).

3. See John L. Sorenson and Martin H. Raish, *Pre-Columbian Contact with the Americas across the Oceans: An Annotated Bibliography,* 2 vols. (Provo, Utah: Research Press, 1990).

4. See Dixon, *Quest for the Origins of the First Americans,* 129.

59

VIKINGS, IRON, AND
THE BOOK OF MORMON

*"Wherefore, he came to the hill Ephraim, and he did
molten out of the hill, and made swords of steel for
those whom he had drawn away with him." (Ether 7:9)*

The question of the relationship between Mesoamerican archaeology and descriptions of the use of
iron and other metals in the Book of Mormon is a complex
one. The Jaredites, Nephites, and Mulekites came from
the ancient Near East, where metallurgy was a widespread, integral part of civilization. There is evidence
from the Book of Mormon that some elements of Near
Eastern metallurgical technology were brought to the
New World.[1]

How does this evidence relate to Mesoamerican archaeological evidence? John Sorenson provides an extensive survey of metal objects discovered in pre-Columbian
Mesoamerica, showing that various types of metals were
known and used in this region.[2] Nonetheless, it seems that
complex metallurgical knowledge and smelting techniques
were not widespread in Mesoamerica during the Book of
Mormon period. Why would Near Eastern metallurgical
knowledge not have become more widespread in Mesoamerica? Could iron working technology have been introduced in the region, yet never have been fully adopted by
the majority of the inhabitants?

A partial answer to these questions can be found by comparing the history of iron working in the Norse colonies of Greenland and Vinland (northeastern North America).[3] The Norse colonies in Greenland lasted for five centuries from c. A.D. 986–1480. During this time they made occasional exploring expeditions to modern Canada and the northeastern U.S., establishing colonies lasting at least several decades in Labrador, and quite probably elsewhere in North America.

The Vikings were familiar with all forms of medieval European metallurgy. They brought iron smelting technology to North America by about A.D. 1000, as indicated by the discovery of a smithy and iron slag at the Viking site of L'Anse aux Meadows in Labrador.[4] Yet, despite known contacts between the Vikings, Eskimos (Inuits), and Algonquian Indians,[5] iron smelting technology was never transmitted from the Vikings to the Native Americans. In other words, the Viking experience in Greenland and northeastern North America provides an example of the introduction of iron smelting technology into a new region but the failure of Native Americans to adopt that new technology.

This example is quite instructive for students of the Book of Mormon. Nephi was familiar with ancient Near Eastern metallurgical technologies, which he brought from the Near East to the New World. Metallurgy was known and utilized to a limited extent by the Nephites during certain periods. It is possible that the full range of metallurgical knowledge may have been lost at some point in time. When the Nephites migrated to new areas where ores were not readily available, knowledge of metallurgy could have been lost within a single generation. Similar pressures may have been exerted on Norse colonizers in the New World. Iron working apparently occurred under difficult circumstances in Greenland and Vinland; archaeologists have discovered an ax made from whalebone which was used in place of rare or costly iron axes.[6]

At any rate, precisely paralleling the experience of the Vikings in the New World, metal smelting technology did not spread beyond Nephite society to other peoples and regions of the New World. It apparently disappeared with the destruction of Nephite civilization, if not before, just as iron smelting disappeared in Greenland and northeastern North America with the collapse of the Viking colonies in the late fifteenth century.

Research by William J. Hamblin, originally published as a FARMS Update in Insights *(January 1993): 2.*

NOTES

1. Two important examples are found in 1 Nephi 17:9–16 and Ether 7:9. Sorenson provides a listing of all references to metals in the Book of Mormon in "Metals and Metallurgy relating to the Book of Mormon Text" (FARMS, 1992).

2. See ibid.

3. Two good sources on the Vikings in North America are Erik Wahlgren, *The Vikings and America* (New York: Thames and Hudson, 1986); and Gwyn Jones, *The Norse Atlantic Saga* (Oxford: Oxford University Press, 1986).

4. See Jones, 294–95; Wahlgren, 128.

5. See Jones, 130–35; Wahlgren, 14–16.

6. See Wahlgren, 24, figs. 21 and 22.

60

DROUGHT AND SERPENTS

"And there came forth poisonous serpents
also upon the face of the land, and did
poison many people." (Ether 9:31)

During my lengthy residence in Israel (1971–79), I had opportunity to visit the Musa Alami Farm near Jericho. The farm had been constructed after Israel's 1948 War of Independence to settle displaced Palestinian refugees. It was particularly geared toward teaching various farm skills to Palestinian boys. During the 1950s, the Church of Jesus Christ of Latter-day Saints had equipped the farm with a dairy and a starter herd and had sent dairy experts to operate that portion of the farm.

Much of the farm was in disrepair during our visit because of the 1967 Six-Day War. Orange groves had died from lack of water, and most of the fields lay fallow. During the war, all but two of the pumps bringing underground water to the surface had been destroyed, making it impossible to maintain the farm at its previous level. Most of the refugees had fled across the Jordan River to the kingdom of Jordan. The Israelis had also expropriated all the land on the western bank of the river in order to maintain security patrols along the new border.

Of particular interest to me was the effect on local wildlife. When crops were no longer being grown near the river, the mice moved westward to find grains in the few fields still under cultivation. They were, naturally, followed by serpents. From time to time, residents of the farm found vipers in and around their houses. This, they assured us, had never happened before the war.

My thoughts turned to the story in Ether 9:30–33, where we read that the Jaredites were plagued by "poisonous serpents" during a time of "great dearth" when "there was no rain upon the face of the earth." Their flocks fled southward from the serpents; some of the people also escaped in that direction, but the large number of serpents "hedge[d] up the way that the people could not pass." After the people repented, the Lord sent rain, which ended the famine, producing "fruit in the north countries" (Ether 9:35).

Several generations after the famine, "in the days of Lib the poisonous serpents were destroyed. Wherefore they did go into the land southward, to hunt food for the people of the land, for the land was covered with animals of the forest" (Ether 10:19). It was at this time that the Jaredites set aside the land southward as a game preserve (see Ether 10:21). This suggests that much of the wildlife had perished during the dearth in the land northward.

We do not know by what means—whether miraculous, natural, or by the hand of man—the serpents were eliminated. It may be that they simply dispersed throughout the region as the dearth abated, following the rodents who, in turn, were following the regenerating plant life.

A similar tale is told of the Israelites during the period of the exodus from Egypt. Soon after arriving in the wilderness, where there was "no bread, neither . . . water," they encountered poisonous serpents "and much people of Israel died." In this case, however, the serpents were not destroyed; instead, the Lord provided a miraculous means for the healing of those who had been bitten (see Numbers 21:5–9; see Deuteronomy 8:15; 2 Kings 18:4; John 3:14–5; 1 Corinthians 10:9; 1 Nephi 17:41; 2 Nephi 25:20). Nor was this an instance of occasional drought, for the desert into which the Israelites fled was perpetually barren. For this reason, rodents, accompanied by their serpent predators, would have been more common at the oases that became the Israelite campsites.

In reflecting on the time when Israel wandered "in a desert land, and in the waste howling wilderness" (Deuteronomy 32:10), Moses again connected poisonous serpents with conditions of "hunger, and . . . burning heat" (Deuteronomy 32:24). Similarly, Jeremiah prophesied a time when there would be "no grapes on the vine, nor figs on the fig tree, and the leaf shall fade," a time of war, when the people would flee into the cities for defense and the Lord would "send serpents . . . and they shall bite you" (Jeremiah 8:13–17). War often brought famine in the ancient Near East. Invading armies would consume local produce and capture foodstuffs and would often trample fields of grain during combat (compare Alma 3:2). Rodents in search of food would have migrated to the cities and been followed by the serpents.

I suspect that a similar problem would have existed among the Nephites who gathered all their animals and foodstuffs in the time of Lachoneus and Gidgiddoni, making it difficult for the invading Gadianton robber band to subsist (see 3 Nephi 4). From the Book of Mormon, we cannot know for sure if the Nephites had problems with serpents at this time, for, as Mormon wrote, "there had many things transpired which . . . cannot all be written in this book . . . but behold there are records which do contain all the proceedings of this people" (3 Nephi 5:8–9).

What is certain, however, is that the story of the poisonous serpents which plagued the Jaredites has a ring of truth about it.

Research by John A. Tvedtnes, originally published in the Journal of Book of Mormon Studies *6/1 (1997): 70–72.*

61

THE "DECAPITATION" OF SHIZ

*"And it came to pass that when Coriantumr had
leaned upon his sword, that he rested a little,
he smote off the head of Shiz." (Ether 15:30)*

Ether 15:29–32 describes the gory end of the last Jaredite battle. Exhausted, Coriantumr propped himself up with his own sword, gathered his last ounce of strength, and "smote off the head of Shiz," his archrival who had fainted beside him from the loss of blood. The smitten Shiz then "raised up on his hands and fell; and after that he had struggled for breath, he died," and Coriantumr himself collapsed.

People have long wondered how Shiz could raise himself up, fall, and gasp for breath if his head had been cut off. Dr. M. Gary Hadfield, M.D., professor of pathology (neuropathology) at the Medical College of Virginia, Virginia Commonwealth University, in Richmond, Virginia, published in *BYU Studies* in 1993[1] the following diagnosis:

> Shiz's death struggle illustrates the classic reflex posture that occurs in both humans and animals when the upper brain stem (midbrain/mesencephalon) is disconnected from the brain. The extensor muscles of the arms and legs contract, and this reflect action could cause Shiz to raise up on his hands.[2] In many patients, it is the sparing of vital respiratory and blood pressure

centers in the central (pons) and lower (medulla) brain stem that permits survival.[3]

The brain stem is located inside the base of the skull and is relatively small. It connects the brain proper, or cerebrum, with the spinal cord in the neck. Coriantumr was obviously too exhausted to do a clean job. His stroke evidently strayed a little too high. He must have cut off Shiz's head through the base of the skull, at the level of the midbrain, instead of lower through the cervical spine in the curvature of the neck. . . . Significantly, this nervous system phenomenon (decerebrate rigidity) was first reported in 1898, long after the Book of Mormon was published.[4]

Thus, the account of the staggering death of Shiz is not a figment of dramatic imagination, but the Book of Mormon account is plausibly consistent with medical science.

Moreover, linguistic analysis sustains the foregoing clinical analysis by confirming that the words *smote off* need not mean that Shiz's head was completely severed by Coriantumr. In Judges 5, an equally gruesome account is given of Sisera's death at the hands of Jael, the wife of Heber. The English translation of the relevant verses reads:

> She put her hand to the nail, and her right hand to the workmen's hammer; and with the hammer she smote Sisera, she *smote off* his head, when she had pierced and stricken through his temples. At her feet he bowed, he fell, he lay down: at her feet he bowed, he fell: where he bowed, there he fell down dead. (Judges 5:26–27; emphasis added)

This text shows that the English words *smote off* need not refer to a total decapitation, for surely Jael did not cleanly chop off Sisera's head using a hammer. Instead, the English words *smote off* here simply mean that Jael struck Sisera extremely hard. Indeed, both the Hebrew and Greek words translated as *smote off* mean "to hammer" or "to strike down with a hammer or stamp," but not generally to smite *off*, and accordingly the New English Bible reads, "with the hammer she struck Sisera, she crushed his head." No more necessarily does Joseph Smith's translation in Ether 15:30 need to mean that Shiz's head was completely cut off. Fifty or sixty percent off would easily have been enough to get the job done, leaving Shiz to reflex and die.

Research by M. Gary Hadfeld and John W. Welch, originally published as a FARMS Update in Insights *(November 1994): 2.*

NOTES

1. See M. Gary Hadfield, "Neuropathy and the Scriptures," *BYU Studies* 33/2 (1993): 312–20.

2. Hadfield, "Neuropathy and the Scriptures," 324–25; see A. B. Baker and L. H. Baker, *Clinical Neurology* (New York: Harper and Row, 1975), 1:40, 65.

3. Hadfield, "Neuropathy and the Scriptures," 328 n. 25; see J. Adams and L. W. Duchen, eds., *Greenfield's Neuropathology* (New York: Oxford University Press, 1992), 195–200.

4. Hadfield, "Neuropathy and the Scriptures," 325; see C. S. Sherrington, "Decerebrate Rigidity, and Reflex Coordination of Movements," *Journal of Physiology* 22 (1898): 319.

62

FRAGMENTS OF ORIGINAL
MANUSCRIPT DISCOVERED

"And after having received the record of the Nephites,
yea, even my servant Joseph Smith, Jun., might have
power to translate through the mercy of God, by the
power of God, the Book of Mormon." (D&C 1:29)

For more than ten years, Royal Skousen has been study-
ing the original manuscript of the Book of Mormon.
Undoubtedly one of the most significant accomplishments
in his work was the 1991 discovery, conservation, and photography of a collection of a large number of fragments
from the original manuscript.

In 1882, when Lewis Bidamon opened the cornerstone of
the Nauvoo House, he discovered that the original manuscript of the Book of Mormon, which Joseph Smith himself
had placed in the cornerstone, was mostly destroyed by water seepage. Bidamon handed out the better-preserved portions of the manuscript (between 25–30 percent of the text),
but he apparently kept for himself some smaller fragments.

In 1937, Wilford Wood of Bountiful, Utah, purchased
these fragments from Charles Bidamon of Wilmette,
Illinois. At Wood's death these fragments were passed on
to his family. In the summer of 1991, Skousen, following a
trail of published references to the fragments, was able to
view the fragments and then persuade the family to have
them conserved and photographed.

The condition of the fragments posed serious problems. They were stuck together in a 3 x 6 x 1 inch lump. Skousen enlisted the help of conservators at the BYU Library (Robert Espinosa, Cathy Bell, and Pam Barrios) to unravel and press the fragments. David Hawkinson, photographer for BYU's Museum of Art, experimented with different methods for photographing the fragments to bring out the very faint handwriting, finally succeeding with ultraviolet reflected photography.

From the resulting photos, Skousen was able to read enough to identify the six different places (covering parts of fifty-eight pages) in the original manuscript from which the fragments come: 2 Nephi 5–9, 2 Nephi 23–25, 2 Nephi 33 to Jacob 4, Jacob 5 to Enos 1, Helaman 13 to 3 Nephi 4, and Ether 3–15. Skousen has continued to work from the photographs to identify and locate the placement of all but the smallest fragments.

The main purpose of this project is to produce a critical text of the Book of Mormon—a re-creation of the original English text (as far as it can be determined) and a complete description of the substantive changes that have occurred in the text. To accomplish this, Skousen has carefully and extensively examined the original manuscript (O) and the printer's manuscript (P); created electronic versions of O, P, and twenty significant editions of the Book of Mormon; compared these by computer to discover changes; and checked all variants found by computer analysis against the actual text copies. Ultimately, FARMS hopes to publish five volumes: (1) a facsimile transcript of the existing portions of O; (2) a facsimile transcript of P; (3) a history of the text; (4) the changes the text has undergone; and (5) the critical text itself.

The result will be an invaluable tool for students of the Book of Mormon. Not only will it provide the best information on the original and printer's manuscripts, but it will also shed light on the process of translation and publication.

One of the most important findings of the project has been the identification of some previously unknown changes in the text of the Book of Mormon, most of them made when P was copied from O. Some of the other important discoveries are: (1) for seventy-two pages of P, the 1830 edition was typeset directly from O instead of P; (2) two sheets from the University of Chicago (covering Alma 3–5) are probably a forgery; (3) there is direct evidence that Joseph spelled out Book of Mormon names for his scribes on the first occurrence and apparently again later when requested; (4) a small part of O is in Joseph's own handwriting (twenty-eight words in Alma 45); and (5) the word *chapter* and the added chapter numbers were not part of the original text of the Book of Mormon but instead correspond to what Joseph Smith saw as breaks in the text.

From 1984 to 1987, FARMS published the first-ever critical text of the Book of Mormon (three volumes), which includes information on the ancient form of the text. Skousen's project focuses on recovering the English translation that Joseph Smith dictated.

Financial and other support for this continuing project has come from BYU, FARMS, the Keter Foundation, the LDS and RLDS churches (which have made possible work on O and P), and the Wilford Wood Foundation, as well as from a host of individuals.

Research by Royal Skousen, originally published as a FARMS Update in Insights *(January 1992): 2.*

63

TRANSLATION OF
THE BOOK OF MORMON

*"You had power given unto you to
translate by the means of the Urim
and Thummim." (D&C 10:1)*

Concerning the manner in which the seerstone or the "interpreters" functioned in the translation of the Book of Mormon, Joseph Smith reported only that they operated "by the gift and power of God."[1] This is particularly unfortunate, since only he was in a position to describe from personal experience how these instruments enhanced his power to translate. However, each of the Three Witnesses related, directly or indirectly, their ideas concerning the process of translation. These statements, with a few other contemporary or near-contemporary accounts, as well as some of my own reflections on translating, may provide some additional insight into the process by which Joseph translated the plates.[2]

According to Samuel W. Richards, Oliver Cowdery gave him the following description of the translation of the Book of Mormon:

> He represented Joseph as sitting at a table with the plates before him, translating them by means of the Urim and Thummim, while he (Oliver) sat beside him writing every word as Joseph spoke them to him. This was done by holding the "translators" over the hieroglyphics, the translation appearing distinctly on the

272

instrument, which had been touched by the finger of God and dedicated and consecrated for the express purpose of translating languages. Every word was distinctly visible even to every letter; and if Oliver omitted a word or failed to spell a word correctly, the translation remained on the "interpreter" until it was copied correctly.[3]

Martin Harris explained the translation to Edward Stevenson in this manner:

> By the aid of the seer stone, sentences would appear and were read by the Prophet and written by Martin, and when finished he would say, "Written," and if correctly written that sentence would disappear and another appear in its place, but if not written correctly it remained until corrected, so that the translation was just as it was engraven on the plates, precisely in the language then used.[4]

In *Address to All Believers in Christ*, David Whitmer wrote:

> I will now give you a description of the manner in which the Book of Mormon was translated. Joseph Smith would put the seer stone into a hat, and put his face in the hat, drawing it closely around his face to exclude the light; and in the darkness the spiritual light would shine. A piece of something resembling parchment would appear, and on that appeared the writing. One character at a time would appear, and under it was the interpretation in English. Brother Joseph would read off the English to Oliver Cowdery, who was his principal scribe, and when it was written down and repeated to Brother Joseph to see if it was correct, then it would disappear, and another character with the interpretation would appear. Thus the Book of Mormon was translated by the gift and power of God, and not by any power of man.[5]

The evidentiary value of these statements is, of course, lessened somewhat since (1) they derive from individuals who themselves were not actively involved in translating, (2) they were made many years after the fact, and (3) in the case of two of them (Harris and Cowdery) they come at second hand. However, they may still provide us some guidance in understanding Joseph Smith's method of translating.

What elements are common to each of these statements? At least two, both of which I think may be relied upon: (1) some instrument consecrated for the purpose of translation—a "seerstone," "translators," or "Urim and Thummim"—that was used by Joseph Smith is mentioned in each account; and (2) words or sentences in English would appear on that instrument and would then be read off to the scribe. David Whitmer, in his account, also claims that "a piece of something resembling parchment would appear, and on that appeared the writing. One character at a time would appear, and under it was the interpretation in English." This statement is somewhat problematical from a linguistic point of view. It suggests a simple one-for-one equivalency of words in the original language of the Book of Mormon and in English. This is scarcely likely in two closely related modern languages, much less in an ancient and modern language from two different language families. An examination of any page of an interlinear text (a text with a source language, such as Greek, Latin, or Hebrew, with a translation into a target language such as English below the line) will reveal a multitude of divergences from a word-for-word translation: some words are left untranslated, some are translated with more than one word, and often the order of words in the source language does not parallel (sometimes not even closely) the word order of the target language. A word-for-word rendering, as David Whitmer's statement seems to imply, would have resulted in a syntactic and semantic puree. On the other hand, the statement given on the authority of Oliver Cowdery, "this was done by holding the 'translators' over the hieroglyphics, the translation appearing distinctly on the instrument," need not imply a word-for-word rendering, but simply a close link between the words of the original and those of the translation.

The Reverend Diedrich Willers, a minister of German Reformed Church congregations in Bearytown and Fayette, New York, at the time of the Church's restoration and a celebrated opponent of the Church, wrote in 1830 to two colleagues in York, Pennsylvania, concerning the rise of the Church. In the letter he included the following account concerning the coming forth of the Book of Mormon: "The Angel indicated that . . . under these plates were hidden spectacles, without which he could not translate these plates, that by using these spectacles, he (Smith) would be in a position to read these ancient languages, which he had never studied and that the Holy Ghost would reveal to him the translation in the English language."[6] "With all its awkwardness and grammatical chaos," the translation was thus, "according to contemporary reports, a product of spiritual impressions to Joseph Smith rather than an automatic appearance of the English words. This would make Joseph Smith, despite his grammatical limitations, a translator in fact rather than a mere transcriber of the handwriting of God."[7]

If the translation took place through a process of spiritual impressions, it was still not without effort on the part of Joseph Smith, as a revelation given to Oliver Cowdery in 1829, now in the Doctrine and Covenants, suggests. In D&C 9:7–8, Oliver, who had desired the gift of translation, was told: "Behold, you have not understood; you have supposed that I would give it unto you, when you took no thought save it was to ask me. But behold, I say unto you, that you must study it out in your mind; then you must ask me if it be right, and if it is right I will cause that your bosom shall burn within you; therefore, you shall feel that it is right." Had Oliver presumed an effortless, automatic translation? These verses strongly suggest that effort was required by the translator to search for and find the appropriate expression, something which would not have been the case if the words for the English translation had automatically appeared on the seerstone or interpreters.

But what kind of effort was involved? It must have been in rendering the ideas on the plates into English. But how would Joseph Smith have known those ideas? Part of the divine process by which Joseph worked may have allowed him to think, as it were, in that language, to understand, by inspiration, the ideas of the language. The effort in translating may have taken the form of expressing the ideas on the plates in felicitous English. Such effort can sometimes be daunting. I am currently engaged in the translation of two books, one in German and one in Hebrew, the former rather longer than the Book of Mormon, the latter somewhat shorter. I have found that it is one thing to grasp in my mind the ideas of the original without translating those ideas into English but that it is quite a different matter to find the most felicitous expression for those ideas in English. There is also very considerable effort involved in continuing the process of translation hour after hour. I would consider my day an unalloyed success if I were to complete a translation of five to seven pages. This is roughly the rate at which Joseph Smith labored on the translation of the Book of Mormon.

The accounts of the Three Witnesses speak of words appearing on the seerstone or "translators." But at what point in the translation process did they appear? I believe that it was after Joseph had formulated in his mind a translation that represented with sufficient accuracy the ideas found on the original. Was there only one correct translation for the ideas found on the plates? I do not believe so. Could a "correct" translation be improved upon in word choice or in some other manner, or could these ideas have been rendered into different words? Yes. I regularly teach a graduate course in ancient Hebrew, where we read parts of the Old Testament or the Dead Sea Scrolls in Hebrew. Were I to give my students a translation examination from Hebrew into English, it is possible—indeed, likely—that I would receive from them several different renderings of the same verse in English but still consider them all essentially "correct," since each reflected with acceptable accuracy the ideas found on the original. Joseph himself seems to have felt no particular compunctions about revising the Book of Mormon, as witness the numerous changes (mostly of a grammatical nature) made by him in 1837 in the second edition of the Book of Mormon. If he had considered only one rendering acceptable, then he would certainly have refrained from making any changes in it (unless the changes resulted from errors in transcription or printing).

A reasonable scenario for the method of translating the Book of Mormon, in my estimation, would be one in which the means at Joseph's disposal (the seerstone and the interpreters) enhanced his capacity to understand (as one who knows a second language well enough to be able to think in it understands) the sense of the words and phrases on the plates as well as to grasp the relation of these words to each other. However, the actual translation was Joseph's alone and the opportunity to improve it in grammar and word choice still remained open. Thus, while it would be incorrect to minimize the divine element in the process of translation of the Book of Mormon, it would also be misleading and potentially hazardous to deny the human factor.

As explained by Elder B. H. Roberts, the Prophet grasped "every detail and shade of thought" of the original by revelation but expressed himself "in such language as he could command." On occasion that was "faulty English," which the Prophet himself and those who have succeeded him as the custodians of the word of God have had and now have a perfect right to correct.

───────────────────────────────────

Research by Stephen D. Ricks, originally published in the Journal of Book of Mormon Studies 2/2 *(1993): 201–6.*

NOTES

1. For additional analysis on this subject, see Royal Skousen, "Translating the Book of Mormon: Evidence from the Original Manuscript," in *Book of Mormon Authorship Revisited: The Evidence for Ancient Origins,* ed. Noel B. Reynolds (Provo: Utah, FARMS, 1997), 61–94; and John W. Welch, "Joseph Smith and the Translation of the Sermon at the Temple," in *Illuminating the Sermon at the Temple and Sermon on the Mount* (Provo, Utah: FARMS, 1999), 179–98.

2. *Times and Seasons* 2/9 (1 March 1842): 707; Warren Cowdery, "Manuscript History of the Church," Bk A-l, pp. 121–22. Joseph also uses the phrase "by the gift and power of God" in an 1833 letter to N. E. Seaton, in *History of the Church,* 1:315; compare his 13 November 1843 letter to James Arlington Bennett in *Times and Seasons* 4/24 (1 November 1843): 373, where he states: "By the power of God I translated the Book of Mormon from hieroglyphics."

3. Personal statement of Samuel W. Richards, 25 May 1907, cited in Richard Lloyd Anderson, "By the Gift and Power of God," *Ensign* (September 1977): 81.

4. Edward Stevenson's account of Harris's Sunday morning lecture in Salt Lake City, 4 September 1870, published in the *Deseret Evening News,* 5 September 1870, and reprinted in the

Deseret Evening News, 30 November 1881, and in the *Millennial Star* 44 (6 February 1882): 86–87. Joseph's brother William made a statement to similar effect in *William Smith on Mormonism* (Lamoni, Iowa: Herald Steam Book and Job Office, 1883), 17–18.

5. David Whitmer, *An Address to All Believers in Christ* (Richmond, Mo.: n.p., 1887), 12.

6. D. Michael Quinn, "The First Months of Mormonism: A Contemporary View by Reverend Diedrich Willers," *New York History* 54/3 (1973): 326.

7. Ibid., 321.

64

REVELATION AND THE
URIM AND THUMMIM

"You had power given unto you to
translate by the means of the Urim
and Thummim." (D&C 10:1)

In the past most biblical scholars viewed the Urim and
Thummim as a rather mechanical device used merely to
obtain a yes or no answer, similar to casting lots. This is
quite different from the function of the device described in
the Book of Mormon as "interpreters" and by the Prophet
Joseph Smith as the "Urim and Thummim." In these
descriptions of the use of the Urim and Thummim, revelation played a large role. For example, accounts of the translation of the Book of Mormon indicate that Joseph Smith
could not translate without the Spirit and that a great deal
of mental effort was necessary.[1]

However, two studies by biblical scholars on the Urim
and Thummim described in the Old Testament are more in
harmony with LDS understandings. On the basis of what
appears to be solid historical, linguistic, and textual evidence, Cornelius Van Dam rejects the mechanical view,
pointing out numerous instances in which the divine
answer is detailed and is not merely yes or no.[2] He argues
that "it seems certain that Yahweh's gift of prophetic
inspiration was involved and played a major role in the
process of giving an answer" through the Urim and

Thummim: "When revelation was requested of Yahweh, Yahweh would speak to the high priest or enlighten him and so give him the decision that was necessary. If this inspiration was not forthcoming, the high priest would know that he was in no position to make use of the UT [Urim and Thummim]."[3]

A 1990 article by C. Houtman agrees with Van Dam that the Urim and Thummim was not used merely to receive a mechanical yes or no answer. He puts forward textual evidence that suggests that for the Urim and Thummim to function, divine power had "to penetrate into the heart, the intellectual centre of the high priest, in order to enable him to 'read' the will of YHWH from the UT."[4]

It remains to be seen whether the arguments of Van Dam and Houtman will persuade biblical scholars and whether new evidence and new interpretations will support or weaken their position. But for now their arguments open the door to an understanding of the Urim and Thummim that sees a greater role for revelation, in keeping with the understanding obtained from latter-day scripture.

Other points in these two studies may also shed light on Book of Mormon passages. Van Dam argues that in many instances in the Old Testament the phrase *inquire of the Lord* indicates the use of the Urim and Thummim.[5] On at least two occasions Nephite commanders sent messengers to Alma so that he could "inquire of the Lord" as to the whereabouts of their enemies (Alma 16:6; 43:23–24). In each case Alma revealed specific directions allowing the Nephites to gain advantage over their enemies. Perhaps Alma used the Urim and Thummim to obtain this knowledge. We know he possessed the interpreters (see Mosiah 28:20; Alma 37:24), which Joseph Smith described as the Urim and Thummim, and the account in the book of Mormon fits the biblical usage described by Van Dam.

Finally, Van Dam suggests that there was a visual component to the use of the Urim and Thummim: "A special or miraculous light was somehow involved in the functioning of the UT," possibly through some kind of stone, "in order to verify that the message given by the high priest was from Yahweh."[6]

The Book of Mormon accounts of the interpreters also suggest a visual component. Ammon indicates that the king of the land of Zarahemla "has wherewith that he can look, and translate" (Mosiah 8:13), and Alma speaks of "a stone, which shall shine forth in darkness unto light" to reveal things kept secret (Alma 37:23).

Research by Matthew Roper, originally published as a FARMS Update in Insights *(December 1995): 2.*

NOTES

1. See D&C 8:1–4; 9:7–9; and Lyndon W. Cook, ed., *David Whitmer Interviews: A Restoration Witness* (Orem, Utah: Grandin, 1991), 86, 199.

2. See Cornelius Van Dam, *The Urim and Thummim* (Kampen: Uitgeverij Van Den Berg, 1986).

3. Ibid., 128.

4. C. Houtman, "The Urim and Thummim: A New Suggestion," *Vetus Testamentum* 40 (April 1990): 231.

5. See Van Dam, *Urim and Thummim*, 89–95.

6. Ibid., 130–31.

65

WAS THERE A LIBRARY IN HARMONY, PENNSYLVANIA?

*"[God] gave him power from on high, by
the means which were before prepared, to
translate the Book of Mormon." (D&C 20:8)*

In 1982, Erich Robert Paul published an article in *BYU
Studies* entitled "Joseph Smith and the Manchester (New
York) Library."[1] Essentially Paul shows that, while Joseph
Smith had potential access to a wide range of books there,
"it is likely that during the 1820s he simply was not a part
of the literary culture."[2]

Because Joseph spent little time, however, in the Man-
chester/Palmyra area from 1825 to 1829 (he moved to Harmony, Pennsylvania, in 1827 when he and Emma married),
the logical extension of Paul's study is to ask the further question, "But was there a library in Harmony, Pennsylvania?"

Even more significant than the information environment
of Palmyra was that of Harmony. If Joseph Smith had wanted
to do any kind of research while he was translating the book
of Lehi onto the 116 pages in 1828 or while he was translating
the bulk of the Book of Mormon during April and May, 1829,
he would have needed to use libraries or information sources
in or around Harmony where he was living at the time.

Harmony was a small town on the border between the
states of New York and Pennsylvania. The region was very
remote and rural. Recently we asked Erich Paul if he had

ever explored the possibility that any libraries existed around Harmony in the 1820s which Joseph Smith might have used. He responded: "In fact, I checked into this possibility only to discover that not only does Harmony and its environs hardly exist anymore, but there is no evidence of a library even existing at the time of Joseph's work."

Accordingly, those who have considered western New York as the information environment for the Book of Mormon may be 120 miles or more off target. One should think of Joseph translating in the Harmony area and, as far as that goes, in a resource vacuum.

Even if Joseph had wanted to pause to check his details against reputable sources, to scrutinize the latest theories, to learn about scholarly biblical interpretations or Jewish customs, or to verify any Book of Mormon claims against the wisdom or theologies of his day—even if he had wanted to go to a library to check such things (something he showed no inclination to do until later)—there simply was no library anywhere nearby for him to use.

While this is only a piece of circumstantial evidence for the Book of Mormon, it is still a piece. Perhaps a significant one.

Research by John W. Welch, originally published as a FARMS Update in Insights *(January 1994): 2. For a map highlighting church history sites in Western New York, see John W. Welch and J. Gregory Welch,* Charting the Book of Mormon: Visual Aids for Personal Study and Teaching *(Provo, Utah: FARMS, 1999), chart 12.*

NOTES

1. See *BYU Studies* 22/3 (1982): 333–56.
2. Robert Paul, "Joseph Smith and the Manchester (New York) Library," *BYU Studies* 22/3 (1982): 333–56.

66

CAN THE 1834 AFFIDAVITS ATTACKING THE SMITH FAMILY BE TRUSTED?

"He called me by name, and said unto me . . .
that God had a work for me to do; and that my
name . . . should be both good and evil spoken
of among all people." (JS—H 1:33)

The character and claims of Joseph Smith are fundamental to the claims of the Church he founded. Knowing this, critics of the Prophet have contended for more than a century and a half that he and his family were the kind of people from whom nobody would want to buy a used car, much less receive a plan of salvation.

The original anti-Mormon book, Eber D. Howe's 1834 *Mormonism Unvailed* [sic], featured affidavits gathered from former Smith neighbors by the excommunicated and bitter Philastus Hurlbut describing the Prophet's family as, among many other derogatory things, "lazy" and "indolent."[1] Joseph Capron, for example, declared that the Smiths' "great object appeared to be, to live without work."[2] "It was a mystery to their neighbors," said David Stafford, "how they got their living."[3]

Over the past several decades, Mormon scholars have subjected these affidavits and other such alleged "reminiscences" to sharp criticism.[4] Nevertheless, these early documents have remained an anti-Mormon treasure trove to which generations of critics have turned and returned for years.

However, in a path-breaking article just recently published, Donald L. Enders, a senior curator at the Museum of Church History and Art in Salt Lake City, presents hard evidence that deals a serious blow to the credibility of the Hurlbut-Howe affidavits.[5] Working from land and tax records, farm account books and related correspondence, soil surveys, horticultural studies, surveys of historic buildings, archaeological reports, and interviews with agricultural historians and other specialists—sources not generally used by scholars of Mormon origins—Enders concludes that, on questions of testable fact, the affidavits cannot be trusted.

The Smiths' farming techniques, it seems, were virtually a textbook illustration of the best recommendations of the day, showing them to have been, by contemporary standards, intelligent, skilled, and responsible people. And they were very hard working. To create their farm, for instance, the Smiths moved many tons of rock and cut down about six thousand trees, a large percentage of which were one hundred feet or more in height and from four to six feet in diameter. Then they fenced their property, which required cutting at least six or seven thousand ten-foot rails. They did an enormous amount of work before they were able even to begin actual daily farming.

Furthermore, in order to pay for their farm, the Smiths were obliged to hire themselves out as day laborers. Throughout the surrounding area, they dug and rocked up wells and cisterns, mowed, harvested, made cider and barrels and chairs and brooms and baskets, taught school, dug for salt, worked as carpenters and domestics, built stone walls and fireplaces, flailed grain, cut and sold cordwood, carted, washed clothes, sold garden produce, painted chairs and oil-cloth coverings, butchered, dug coal, and hauled stone. And, along the way, they produced between one thousand and seven thousand pounds of maple sugar annually. "Laziness" and "indolence" are difficult to detect in the Smith family.

What resulted from the Smiths' hard work? The 1830 tax records for Manchester Township appraise the family's holdings at the average level per acre for farms in the vicinity. Of the ten farms owned by the Staffords, Stoddards, Chases, and Caprons—residents of the neighborhood who affixed their signatures prominently to affidavits denigrating the Prophet's family—only one was assessed as more valuable per acre than the Smiths'. The others received lower appraisals—and, in some cases, *significantly* lower ones.

The conclusion to be drawn? If the Hurlbut-Howe affidavits cannot be trusted on matters that can be quantified and tested, there seems little reason to trust their judgments in the less tangible matter of character. Clearly, they reflect religious hostility and perhaps envy from their less successful neighbors. As the Prophet's brother William expressed it, "We never knew we were bad folks until Joseph told his vision. We were considered respectable till then, but at once people began to circulate falsehoods and stories in a wonderful way."[6]

Research by Daniel C. Peterson and Donald L. Enders, originally published in Insights *(September 1993): 2.*

NOTES

1. Eber D. Howe, *Mormonism Unvailed* (Painesville, Ohio: By the author, 1834), 249; see 231–69.

2. Ibid., 260.

3. Ibid., 249.

4. See, for example, Richard Lloyd Anderson, "Joseph Smith's New York Reputation Reappraised," *BYU Studies* 10 (spring 1970): 283–314.

5. See "The Joseph Smith, Sr., Family: Farmers of the Genesee," in *Joseph Smith: The Prophet, the Man,* ed. Susan Easton Black and Charles D. Tate Jr. (Provo, Utah: BYU Religious Studies Center, 1993), 213–25.

6. *Deseret Evening News,* 20 January 1894, p. 11; compare the verdict of Richard L. Bushman, *Joseph Smith and the Beginnings of Mormonism* (Urbana: University of Illinois Press, 1984), 190.

67

ROBERTS AFFIRMS BOOK OF MORMON ANTIQUITY

"These words are not of men nor of man,
but of me; wherefore, you shall testify they
are of me and not of man." (D&C 18:34)

Long unseen by LDS scholars and students, a typescript entitled *The Truth, The Way, The Life* by B. H. Roberts was recently published by BYU Studies.[1] Roberts worked on this treatise about the plan of salvation mainly in 1927 and 1928, but he was still revising it in 1930, making these pages some of his last words written for publication; he died in 1933.

Because this manuscript has long been known only for its few controversial pages on the creation, it comes as an unexpected bonus to learn that it repeatedly and unequivocally asserts the antiquity of the Book of Mormon. While such affirmative statements may seem perfectly unremarkable to casuals readers, it is precisely their routine orthodoxy that makes them so notable. Coming from one of the great intellects of the Church, whose views about the Book of Mormon supposedly became more intellectually sophisticated in his last years, these unequivocal statements will come as a disappointment to anyone who has imagined Roberts as a closet doubter or late-in-life skeptic.

These statements should especially answer the questions that some people have asked about how Roberts really felt about the Book of Mormon after he wrote his Book of

Mormon Study in 1922. That work identified several Book of Mormon problems and called urgently for further study. Some have seen that work as evidence that Roberts changed his views in the face of problematic evidence, but in light of the newly released manuscript, we now can determine that Roberts did not waver in his belief.

First, in the newly released treatise, Roberts describes the miraculous coming forth of the Book of Mormon in strong, straightforward, traditional terms: "Three years after this first revelation an angel of God named Moroni was sent to the Prophet to reveal the existence of an ancient volume of scripture known as the Book of Mormon, a book which gives an account of the hand-dealings of God with the people whom he brought to the continents of America from what we now call the 'Old World.'"[2]

He describes the Jaredites and Nephites as ancient peoples and affirms that "Joseph Smith was commanded to translate, and was given the power and means by which he could translate the unknown language of these ancient American peoples."[3]

Second, the manuscript contains several statements that necessarily assume the antiquity and literal truthfulness of this ancient American scripture. For example, in marshalling evidence for the premortal existence of Jesus, Roberts assures his readers that "the preexistent Spirit of the Christ appeared to an ancient prophet among the Jaredite people."[4] Roberts likewise speaks literally of the words that the resurrected Jesus "said to the assembled Nephites to whom he appeared on the Western Continent."[5] Indeed, Roberts believed that "no incident in the gospel history is more emphatically proven than this great truth, the resurrection of the Son of God,"[6] and he used as his key witness "the appearance of the risen Redeemer to a multitude of people in America."[7]

Third, Roberts often identifies Book of Mormon prophets by the ancient centuries in which they lived. Lehi, he says, lived "before the birth of Christ, early in the fifth [sic] century, B.C."[8] He identifies a prophecy in the book of Alma as "one written near the close of the second century B.C."[9]

Fourth, several times Roberts goes out of his way to describe Book of Mormon authors as "ancient." He calls Lehi "an ancient American prophet."[10] He buttresses another argument by citing "revelations of God to the ancient inhabitants of America."[11] He calls the book "the American volume of scripture" containing the words "of the old prophets of the ancient American race."[12]

Fifth, he treats many Book of Mormon scriptures as the unique, authoritative source of revealed knowledge on numerous important topics, especially on the nature of earth life, opposition in all things, and the atonement of Jesus Christ. He takes joy in drawing attention to doctrines "derived almost wholly from the teachings of the Book of Mormon."[13] To Roberts, the four standard works were "all of equal authority, all of them dependable sources of knowledge."[14]

Beyond seeing the Book of Mormon as ancient and authoritative, Roberts extols it as a masterful work, filled with master strokes of genius. He considers Lehi's blessing to Jacob to be a philosophical masterpiece. He becomes eloquent in describing "the words of the Christ himself to one of the ancient American prophets."[15] Rejoicing in a Book of Mormon reading, he exclaims, "How beautifully clear this principle of purity in thought is set forth."[16]

In a handwritten note on his third draft of this volume, Roberts penned the following note: "Add 'other sheep I have'—Christ mission to western continents. St. John 10 ch."[17] This note was added as Roberts went through the manuscript for the last time.

Can there be any doubt that the man who wrote such words about the Book of Mormon believed it to be what it claims to be? If he had entertained any such doubts, would he have repeatedly included such words in *The Truth, The Way, The Life,* which he hoped would be his magnum opus? It is certain that he stood by the words in this treatise, for he staunchly refused to alter its final draft. Unfortunately, these words were not around when a cloud was raised about Roberts's testimony of the Book of Mormon. Now, one would hope that this latest development will dispel any seriously lingering residue of that shadow.

Research by John W. Welch, originally published as a FARMS Update in Insights *(November 1993): 2.*

NOTES

1. See B. H. Roberts, *The Truth, The Way, The Life: An Elementary Treatise on Theology,* ed. John W. Welch (Provo, Utah: BYU Studies, 1996).
2. Ibid., 469.
3. Ibid., 470
4. Ibid., 263.
5. Ibid., 482–83.
6. Ibid., 395.
7. Ibid., 394.
8. Ibid., 401.
9. Ibid.
10. Ibid., 75.
11. Ibid., 275.
12. Ibid., 259.
13. Ibid., 444.
14. Ibid., 276.
15. Ibid., 445.
16. Ibid., 501.
17. Ibid., 179.

68

WHAT THE ORIGINAL
BOOK OF MORMON
MANUSCRIPT IS NOT

*"The Book of Mormon . . . contains a record of a fallen
people, and the fulness of the gospel of Jesus Christ . . .
which was given by inspiration, and is confirmed to
others by the ministering of angels." (D&C 20:8–10)*

For well over a decade, FARMS has sponsored extensive
research on the original manuscript of the Book of
Mormon. About twenty-five percent of the pages that
were written by Oliver Cowdery and other scribes as
Joseph Smith dictated the Book of Mormon in 1829 have
survived down to the present day.[1] While much has been
written and said about what the original manuscript is,
perhaps even more significant is a collection of facts about
what it is not.

Critics of the Book of Mormon have sought alternative
explanations to account for its existence, arguing that it is a
fraud created by Joseph Smith or by Joseph and someone
else, such as Sidney Rigdon. However, the original manuscript gives no aid or comfort to such theories nor, indeed,
to any explanations other than the account given by Joseph
Smith concerning the coming forth of the Book of Mormon.
Under careful examination, the original manuscript shows
no evidence of fraud.

The original manuscript is not a compilation of pages
worked on over a long period of time. The paper, ink,

handwriting, and everything about the collection indicates that it was created within a short time frame. It bears no trace of collaborative committee work. The work is entirely original in its origination. The manuscript is clean and straightforward.[2]

The original manuscript shows no evidence of developmental research or copying from contemporaneous books or articles. It is not the product of revision and re-thinking. It shows no evidence of rewriting to change a modern expression into an archaic-sounding phrase. It does not appear that Joseph Smith reformulated thoughts or reworked the translation to make it sound more plausible. Everything points to a uniform manner of dictation and production. It really looks like one person read and another copied, just as Joseph Smith described.[3]

What the original manuscript is not is quite impressive, especially when one begins to contemplate the number of problems that could have arisen if Joseph Smith had not been telling the truth. The original manuscript is exactly the kind of smoking gun that a prosecuting lawyer would normally love to find in trying to build a case of fraud or deception against an accused. How many mistakes, how many unavoidable problems, how many inevitable inconsistencies would not a prosecutor expect to find in such a document? The original manuscript of the Book of Mormon takes us into the workshop of the translator and his scribes; and much to the critic's chagrin, what we see is what we have been told by Joseph Smith and his companions all along.

If Joseph Smith had perpetrated a fraud and were trying to cover his tracks, this unforgiving record should have been the last thing he would have kept. Yet Joseph Smith did not dispose of the original manuscript. Despite all the hardships and atrocities the Saints experienced in their travel, the original manuscript somehow survived, until it was deposited in the cornerstone of the Nauvoo House.

In the end, in addition to all the things that the original manuscript is not, it is certainly not a problem for the historicity of the Book of Mormon.

Research by John W. Welch, originally published as a FARMS Update in Insights *(February 1998): 2.*

NOTES

1. See *Book of Mormon Critical Text: A Tool for Scholarly Reference* (Provo, Utah: FARMS, 1987), 1:xx.

2. See Royal Skousen, "Piecing Together the Original Manuscript," *BYU Today* (May 1992): 18–24; Royal Skousen, "Book of Mormon Manuscripts," in *Encyclopedia of Mormonism* (New York: Macmillan, 1992), 1:185–86; John W. Welch and Tim Rathbone, "Book of Mormon Translation by Joseph Smith," in *Encyclopedia of Mormonism,* 1:210–13.

3. See Royal Skousen, "Translating the Book of Mormon: Evidence from the Original Manuscript," in *Book of Mormon Authorship Revisited,* ed. Noel B. Reynolds (Provo, Utah: FARMS, 1997), 61–93; and Royal Skousen, "Textual Variants in the Isaiah Quotations in the Book of Mormon," in *Isaiah in the Book of Mormon,* ed. Donald W. Parry and John W. Welch (Provo, Utah: FARMS, 1998), 369–90.

69

THE SOBERING LESSON
OF THE GROLIER CODEX

"Therefore, having so great witnesses, by them shall
the world be judged. . . . those who harden their hearts
in unbelief, and reject [the Book of Mormon], it shall
turn to their own condemnation." (D&C 20:13, 15)

The story of the authenticating of the Grolier Codex twenty-five years ago still teaches some valuable lessons about the dangers of jumping to conclusions and the problems of name calling, even though the scholars involved no longer hold to their original positions. As discussed recently by John L. Sorenson, the discovery of ancient manuscripts is a touchy issue that, for some people, can be unsettling.[1]

In 1971 what seemed to be an ancient Mesoamerican codex was discovered in southern Mexico. It was claimed to stem from "unauthorized archaeology" (most archaeologists would call it looting). Mesoamerican scholars judged it a fake without giving it much, if any, scrutiny. Michael D. Coe was a principal protagonist in arguing for the authenticity of the document, eventually labeled the "Grolier Codex."[2] The famed Mayanist scholar Sir J. E. S. Thompson played the role of key antagonist.[3]

In 1992 Coe said of Thompson that he had "ignor[ed] the main argument [about the Grolier] while concentrating on some detail where he thought the chances of a quick kill were best."[4] Thompson had also criticized Yuri

Knorosov, the Soviet linguist to whom much of the credit eventually has gone for launching the successful decipherment of the Maya hieroglyphics. Thompson had considered the Knorosov position completely mistaken and labeled the Russian's work "a Marxist hoax."

The Grolier Codex is now generally acknowledged to be authentic, based on the characteristics of the document itself rather than on its unorthodox discovery. Coe believes that had the Grolier Codex had a less-prejudiced origin, "it would [have been] accepted by even the most rock-ribbed scholar as the genuine article."[5]

Those who judged the Grolier Codex a hoax made at least five mistakes, also commonly made by people critical of the Book of Mormon:

(1) They allowed the unconventional origins of the codex to prejudice the case. Just as Thompson was dogmatically dubious from the outset, many have peremptorily ruled the Book of Mormon out of scientific court.

(2) Moreover, the antagonists ruled out the Grolier Codex without giving it a close examination. Similarly, as Thomas O'Dea once reported, "the Book of Mormon has not been universally considered by its critics as one of those books that must be read in order to have an opinion of it."[6]

(3) Those who misjudged the Grolier Codex were served poorly by their closed-mindedness. They responded by reflex on the basis of opinions they had long since fixed in intellectual concrete of their own mix.

(4) When the opponents took time to examine the Grolier Codex, they chose to pick on little details that seemed easier targets than the main characteristics of that complex document. One is reminded of the pedantry of Alexander Campbell who took endless delight in pointing out minor infelicities of grammar in the first edition of the Book of Mormon.[7]

(5) Finally, if all else fails, a critic may turn to name calling. The lesson is especially poignant here, because even Coe himself once regrettably spoke of the Book of Mormon using derogatory labels.[8] That was just as unwise and irrelevant in judging the Book of Mormon as was Thompson's use of the "Marxist" brush to smear Knorosov's scholarship. Using such epithets allows the critic to avoid the drudgery of doing the serious investigation that ought to precede a judgment about the authenticity of any potentially ancient text.

The truth will some day become clearer as to the authenticity of the Book of Mormon. Until then, derogatory remarks and sloppy research do no one any good.

Research by John L. Sorenson and John W. Welch, originally published as a FARMS Update in Insights *(October 1997): 2.*

NOTES

1. See John L. Sorenson, "The Book of Mormon as a Mesoamerican Record," in *Book of Mormon Authorship Revisited: The Evidence for Ancient Origins,* ed. Noel B. Reynolds (Provo, Utah: FARMS, 1997), 484–86.

2. See Michael D. Coe, *Breaking the Maya Code* (New York: Thames and Hudson, 1992), 227–29.

3. See J. Eric S. Thompson, review of *The Maya Scribe and His World,* by Michael D. Coe, *The Book Collector* 26 (1976): 64–75.

4. Coe, *Breaking the Maya Code,* 229.

5. Ibid.

6. Thomas F. O'Dea, *The Mormons* (Chicago: University of Chicago Press, 1957), 26.

7. See Alexander Campbell, "Delusions," *Millennial Harbinger* (10 February 1831): 85–97.

8. See Michael Coe, "Mormons and Archaeology: An Outside View," *Dialogue* 8/2 (1973): 40–45.

INDEX OF PASSAGES

SUBJECT INDEX

Abinadi
  economic implications of
    curse of, 181
  on hoarding of wealth,
    185
  preserved by God until
    stewardship fulfilled, 132
  record of, placed at chias-
    tic center of book of
    Mosiah, 111
  use of simile curse on
    King Noah by, 127, 130
  use of word *state* by,
    163
abridgment
  book of Lehi as, 60–61
  of record of Helaman and
    sons by Mormon, 61, 62
  small plates as, 76
Adams, William J. Jr.
  on silver plates, 23–28
  on Vered Jericho sword,
    11–13, 15
adoption, divine, 119
aerogel, 254
agriculture
  as Nephite economic base,
    181
  as common subject of
    word groups, 212

historians as source of
  information about char-
  acter of Smith family, 286
Allred, Philip A., on Alma's
  use of word *state*, 157–63
Alma$_1$
  as attested Hebrew male
    name, 9–10
  religious coalition of, 184
  on hoarding of welath, 185
  arrival of group of, in-
    creasing diversity in
    Zarahemla, 112
Alma$_2$
  blessing God after eating,
    143–44
  curse of Korihor by,
    resembling *defixiones*, 154
  on hoarding of wealth, 185
  on nature of evidence in
    trial of Korihor, 151–52
  ordination of men to high
    priesthood by, 113
  possible use of Urim and
    Thummim by, 281, 282
  power of word of God
    emphasized by, 38
  on preservation of sacred
    records, interpreters,
    sword, 95

310

The Foundation for Ancient Research and Mormon Studies

The Foundation for Ancient Research and Mormon Studies (FARMS) encourages and supports research and publication about the Book of Mormon: Another Testament of Jesus Christ and other ancient scriptures.

FARMS is a nonprofit, tax-exempt educational foundation affiliated with Brigham Young University. Its main research interests in the scriptures include ancient history, language, literature, culture, geography, politics, religion, and law. Although research on such subjects is of secondary importance when compared with the spiritual and eternal messages of the scriptures, solid scholarly research can supply certain kinds of useful information, even if only tentatively, concerning many significant and interesting questions about the ancient backgrounds, origins, composition, and meanings of scripture.

The work of the Foundation rests on the premise that the Book of Mormon and other scriptures were written by prophets of God. Belief in this premise—in the divinity of scripture—is a matter of faith. Religious truths require divine witness to establish the faith of the believer. While scholarly research cannot replace that witness, such studies may reinforce and encourage individual testimonies by fostering understanding and appreciation of the scriptures. It is hoped that this information will help people to "come unto Christ" (Jacob 1:7) and to understand and take more seriously these ancient witnesses of the atonement of Jesus Christ, the Son of God.

The Foundation works to make interim and final reports about its research available widely, promptly, and economically, both in scholarly and in popular formats. FARMS publishes information about the Book of Mormon and other ancient scripture in the *Insights* newsletter, books and research papers, *FARMS Review of Books, Journal of Book of Mormon Studies*, reprints of published scholarly papers, and videos and audiotapes. FARMS also supports the preparation of the Collected Works of Hugh Nibley.

To facilitate the sharing of information, FARMS sponsors lectures, seminars, symposia, firesides, and radio and television broadcasts in which research findings are communicated to working scholars and to anyone interested in faithful, reliable information about the scriptures. Through Research Press, a publishing arm of the Foundation, FARMS publishes materials addressed primarily to working scholars.

For more information about the Foundation and its activities, contact the FARMS office at 1-800-327-6715 or (801) 373-5111.

FARMS Publications

Teachings of the Book of Mormon

The Geography of Book of Mormon Events: A Source Book

The Book of Mormon Text Reformatted according to
Parallelistic Patterns

Eldin Ricks's Thorough Concordance of the LDS Standard Works

A Guide to Publications on the Book of Mormon: A Selected
Annotated Bibliography

Book of Mormon Authorship Revisited: The Evidence for
Ancient Origins

Ancient Scrolls from the Dead Sea: Photographs and
Commentary on a Unique Collection of Scrolls

LDS Perspectives on the Dead Sea Scrolls

Images of Ancient America: Visualizing Book of Mormon Life

Isaiah in the Book of Mormon

King Benjamin's Speech: "That Ye May Learn Wisdom"

Mormons, Scripture, and the Ancient World: Studies in Honor
of John L. Sorenson

Latter-day Christianity: Ten Basic Issues

Illuminating the Sermon at the Temple and Sermon on the Mount

Scripture Study: Tools and Suggestions

Finding Biblical Hebrew and Other Ancient Literary Forms in
the Book of Mormon

Charting the Book of Mormon: Visual Aids for Personal Study
and Teaching

Pressing Forward with the Book of Mormon: The FARMS
Updates of the 1990s

King Benjamin's Speech Made Simple

Periodicals

Insights: A Window on the Ancient World

FARMS Review of Books

Journal of Book of Mormon Studies

Reprint Series

Book of Mormon Authorship: New Light on Ancient Origins

The Doctrine and Covenants by Themes

Offenders for a Word

Copublished with Deseret Book Company

An Ancient American Setting for the Book of Mormon
Warfare in the Book of Mormon
By Study and Also by Faith: Essays in Honor of Hugh W. Nibley
The Sermon at the Temple and the Sermon on the Mount
Rediscovering the Book of Mormon
Reexploring the Book of Mormon
Of All Things! Classic Quotations from Hugh Nibley
The Allegory of the Olive Tree
Temples of the Ancient World
Expressions of Faith: Testimonies from LDS Scholars
Feasting on the Word: The Literary Testimony of the Book of
    Mormon

The Collected Works of Hugh Nibley
Old Testament and Related Studies
Enoch the Prophet
The World and the Prophets
Mormonism and Early Christianity
Lehi in the Desert; The World of the Jaredites; There Were
    Jaredites
An Approach to the Book of Mormon
Since Cumorah
The Prophetic Book of Mormon
Approaching Zion
The Ancient State
Tinkling Cymbals and Sounding Brass
Temple and Cosmos
Brother Brigham Challenges the Saints

Published through Research Press

Pre-Columbian Contact with the Americas across the Oceans:
    An Annotated Bibliography
New World Figurine Project, vol. 1
A Comprehensive Annotated Book of Mormon Bibliography
Chiasmus in Antiquity (reprint)
Chiasmus Bibliography